Bartolomé de las Casas

Bartolomé de las Casas
Great Prophet of the Americas

PAUL S. VICKERY

Paulist Press
New York/Mahwah, N.J.

Cover design by Trudi Gershenov
Book design by Lynn Else

Library of Congress Cataloging-in-Publication Data

Vickery, Paul S.
    Bartolomé de las Casas : great prophet of the Americas / Paul S. Vickery.
      p. cm.
    Includes bibliographical references and index.
    ISBN 0-8091-4367-4 (alk. paper)
    1. Casas, Bartolomé de las, 1474-1566. 2. Explorers—America—Biography. 3. Explorers—Spain—Biography. 4. Missionaries—America—Biography. 5. Missionaries—Spain—Biography. 6. Indians, Treatment of. 7. America—Discovery and exploration—Spanish. I. Title.
    E125.C4V53 2006
    972'.02'092—dc22

2005035937

Published by Paulist Press
997 Macarthur Boulevard
Mahwah, New Jersey 07430

www.paulistpress.com

Printed and bound in the
United States of America

Contents

Contents

Introduction

Palm Sunday, 1493, was a historic day in the city of Seville, Spain. On that day Christopher Columbus, the newly appointed Admiral of the Ocean Seas, arrived, bringing with him seven strangers from a new world. They carried with them artifacts of their homeland—beautiful green parrots, masks made of fish bones and valuable stones, strips of finely wrought gold, and many other things that the Old World had never seen before. Pressing through the crowd to catch a glimpse of these "Indians," so named because of the mistaken belief that they originated in the East Indies, was a young lad nearly nine years of age. He could not have realized that his destiny and life's calling would be closely linked to the peoples represented by these unknown individuals and that he would spend his life protecting and defending them.[1]

This young boy, Bartolomé de las Casas, became one of the most influential yet controversial men of sixteenth-century Spain and the New World. Always active in his relentless pursuit of justice for the Amerindians,[2] Las Casas assumed many titles and fulfilled many roles during his long and productive life. Lewis Hanke, the well-known scholar of Las Casas, described him thus: "He was successively a reformer at the court of Spain, unsuccessful colonizer in Venezuela, friar in Hispaniola, obstructer of wars he considered unjust in Nicaragua," and, perhaps most significantly, "fighter on behalf of justice for the Indians...promoter of the plan to conquer and Christianize the Indians...by peaceful means alone...successful agitator before the court of Emperor Charles V on behalf of the New Laws, and Bishop of Chiapa."[3]

More than a cleric, political activist, or simple chronicler of the events transpiring in the New World, however, Las Casas assumed the role of being the very conscience of Catholic Spain, a nation that

1

grappled not only with the spiritual mandate to save souls but also with the human desire to acquire wealth.[4] This struggle between acquiring worldly wealth and laying up treasure in heaven would plague many colonial powers. Spain is unique in that it wrestled openly and publicly with these issues, exposing the inconsistencies of its beliefs and policies for the entire world to judge.

Bartolomé de las Casas also struggled with these same issues. Although he initially came to the New World to acquire wealth and prestige, what he saw and experienced caused him to undergo a complete change of both mind and heart. He came face to face with the fact that what he believed and preached did not coincide with his actions. Las Casas experienced a crisis of faith, and, instead of ignoring or dismissing his ethical inconsistencies, he changed his actions to conform to his beliefs. Once his spiritual eyes were opened, he consistently and tirelessly agitated, preached, wrote, and lobbied to represent the Amerindians before those who sought to exploit them for their own material benefit.[5] Above anything else, Las Casas became an active, dedicated servant of the Lord and his Church. Although not unique in his methods or message, his greatness came from the zeal with which he pursued his goals. With a single-minded determination, he committed both his body and his soul for over half a century to the cause for which God commissioned him, directing this message to those responsible for and capable of making changes.

This work examines the historical setting and specific events leading up to the spiritual awakening that transformed Las Casas's life, and interprets this experience in light of his future message. After his sudden and dramatic change of heart, Las Casas functioned as a prophet or spokesman for God and as an intermediary between the Amerindians and the monarchy. He fulfilled this role by constantly and vociferously reminding the Crown of its Christian responsibility toward its newly acquired subjects. Although his manner became more direct and confrontational as he matured, the essence of his words remained constant. Ostensibly, the justification for the Spanish presence in the Indies was the conversion of the Indians to Christianity and their subjugation to the authority of the Catholic Church. In his writings and speeches Las Casas always reminded the Crown of this duty. In the style of the Old Testament prophets, he would speak unequivocally for justice for those less powerful and against their oppression by those in power. Prophetically, Las Casas warned the Crown that the very future of Spanish well-being and favor with God rested with their ability to change their destructive practices toward the Amerindians.

On Pentecost Day, June 4, 1514, when the "darkness left his eyes," Las Casas began his work.[6] He changed both his attitude and his actions toward the enslaved and devoted his life to their protection and care. He became convinced that the only way to Christianize the native peoples, which was his overwhelming concern, was by peaceful conversion through a reasonable proclamation of the gospel and by demonstration of the love of Christ, not by coercion and Spanish steel. Because of the power of his words, this book makes copious use of Las Casas's quotes where appropriate.

This event that totally changed the focus of his life's mission, usually referred to as his first conversion, must be distinguished from his second conversion, when he made the decision to enter the Dominican Order following his failure at Cumaná. In this sense the word *conversion* does not imply the transformation from non-Christian to Christian, or the commitment to any particular church or denomination. Las Casas was a member of the Catholic Church and, as such, he was a Christian. *Conversion* refers to a life-changing decision based on new information acquired by an individual in the course of his or her life. This revelation then causes the person to alter radically his or her life's direction. While reading and meditating on Scripture, Las Casas became aware that his beliefs and actions were inconsistent. The word of God convicted and convinced him that he must change his actions to align with his beliefs. This first conversion prompted the priest to commit his talents to proclaiming the gospel and living an ethically consistent life. The second provided a platform and framework from which to proclaim his message.[7]

After his life-changing experience, Las Casas fought against the social injustice of the Spaniards and dedicated the rest of his life to alleviating the suffering of the natives. Las Casas considered himself, and acted in a manner consistent with, an Old Testament prophet in the biblical mold and as an extension and representative of the Church in the secular world. The office of prophet exists in both Hebrew and Christian traditions and is found in both the Old and New Testaments. Las Casas fit this tradition. He was constantly

3

aware of this role; in fact, he accepted it gladly as he consistently confronted the hypocrisy of the monarchy and the injustices perpetrated by those who claimed to represent it. Throughout his life, and woven into the fabric of his work, was his constant message that Spain would come under the judgment of God if it did not repent of its policies, change its actions, and make restitution for past atrocities. This is the classic message of the prophet. It was also the pattern for the life of Las Casas. Repentance and the consequent aspect of performing penance, highly emphasized in Catholicism, was a significant dimension of this experience. An examination of the writings of Las Casas reveals that his prophetic message grew ever more confrontational and judgmental as he aged and his words appeared to go unheeded. He began to emphasize that judgment would come not only for the rulers of Spain but also for the entire nation.[8]

Throughout his life Las Casas's own sense of calling and mission deepened and this assurance came across clearly in his writings. In his Last Will and Testament Las Casas wrote that "the mercy of God *has chosen me as His minister,* without any merit of my own, to represent again and again those people who live in what we call the Indies, who are the true owners of those kingdoms and territories."[9] By appealing to Scripture, the evangelistic mandate of the Church, and royal proclamations, all of which he filtered through his own personal experiences in the New World, he forced the monarchy to examine its position and the laws that were leading to the decimation of its subjects—peoples for whom, he believed, Christ had died. He prophetically warned the Crown of the impending judgment of God on Spain should these calls for change go unheeded and the nation not alter its policies. He also considered his own actions and motivations as representative of those of the entire Spanish nation. Just as he had repented and made restitution for his previous sins, so too must the monarchy. Significantly, he practiced what he preached. He acted in an ethically consistent manner from the day of his conversion at the age of thirty until his death over fifty years later.

To understand Las Casas, one must first examine the legal and moral justification for Spain's presence in the New World. From its own claims, Las Casas was justified in his condemnation of Spanish hypocrisy in dealing with the Indians. The Crown regularly acted in contradictory ways and vacillated between conversion and colonization, opting to follow a policy of acquiring wealth over converting souls. One must also analyze and describe the political and theological milieu in which Las Casas functioned. The Spanish monarchy was perhaps the leading exponent of Catholicism and its main thinkers, scholars, and jurists were steeped in the theology of the day. As both priest and reformer, Las Casas must be situated in the contemporary theological, intellectual, and political atmosphere. He was a product of his time, yet truly revolutionary in his message concerning the treatment of the Amerindians. In order to understand more fully the man and his message, we must carefully examine those crucial early days that helped form his future worldview as well as those youthful personal experiences that affected his later decisions. We will follow chronologically his life from youth to colonist to priest. Las Casas began his career in the New World as an *encomendero*. He utilized Indians by governmental donation and worked them for profit on what had formerly been their own land. Las Casas's recognition of these "abhorrent practices," repentance of them, and subsequent conversion did not happen in a vacuum. There were specific significant events that troubled his conscience, challenged his faith, and culminated in his change of heart. Events also created the stage, however, on which all of this was played out.

The collision of cultures that began on October 12, 1492, when Columbus landed on the island of Guanahaní, which he renamed San Salvador in honor of Christ, would begin a series of events that would significantly alter the knowledge of the scope, size, and nature of the known world. Quite by accident he had stumbled upon an entirely new world, the significance of which he would never realize. One of the first historians to chronicle the Spanish actions in America was the great admirer of Cortés, Francisco López de Gómara. Writing in 1552, he described Columbus's voyage as follows: "The greatest event since the creation of the world, excepting the Incarnation and death of the One who created it, is the discovery of the Indies; and because of this it is called a New World."[10] Certainly this event, and its economic, political, and theological significance to Europe, would dominate discussion during the sixteenth century. Even as Columbus sought a new trade route to open up the wealth of the East, for both Spain and himself personally, he was also motivated by spiritual and evangelistic motivations, with a growing sense of the impending millennium ushering in the age of Christ.[11] Understanding the conflict between the spirit and mammon, the motivations of conquest, and exploitation by the monarchy and *conquistadores* is fundamental to a study of Spain's role in the New World. From the beginning a mixture of motivations is obvious, and this conflict of interests would continue throughout the colonial period.

The dichotomy is evident in the life of Columbus himself. Las Casas provided an interesting perspective on Columbus and his spiritual motivation. His given name, Cristoforo, came from the Latin, "*Christum ferens,* which means bringer or bearer of Christ, and so he would sign his name at times." Las Casas also described him as being "without a doubt a very devout Catholic....Whenever gold or precious objects were brought to him he would enter his chapel, fall on his knees, asking those around him to do the same, and say, `Let us give thanks to the Lord.'"[12] Like most individuals emerging from the medieval period, he viewed material wealth, or lack of it, as a sign of the status of the spiritual condition of a person or nation. Even as Columbus pressed his claims to a share of the wealth of the New World, he was concerned for the souls of its inhabitants. Columbus truly believed he was God's messenger and the "bearer of Christianity" to the pagan world. He believed the world was soon coming to an end and it was therefore incumbent upon every Christian to bring the good news to the ends of the earth. Yet to spread the gospel and eventually succeed in the ultimate goal, to return Jerusalem to Christian rule from Muslim hands, required money. The fact that his voyage came only months after the Christian monarchs had completed the conquest of the Muslim Kingdom of Granada is significant. Both Columbus and the Catholic monarchs were obsessed with the notion of continuing the spread of Christianity, even if it required warfare to do so. The reconquest of Spain from overt and obvious Muslim enemies was one thing; the encounter with new peoples unacquainted with God's word required new strategies. Las Casas would play a significant role in the determination of Spain's theological and juridical position vis-à-vis the Amerindians.[13]

CHAPTER ONE

Las Casas and His Milieu (1484–1514)

Although Bartolomé de las Casas became one of the most revolutionary and forward-thinking individuals of his age, initially he reflected the medieval worldview from which he arose. Las Casas was born into the home of a modest Sevillian merchant. He would spend most of his life in the struggle for the human rights of a people whose existence Europeans knew nothing about until he was nine years old. Once he caught hold of the vision of his responsibility as a Christian and subsequently as an ordained priest, however, he dedicated his life to fighting for the rights of the poor and exploited. Las Casas was neither the first nor the only advocate for justice for the Native Americans. His uniqueness lay in his zealous and tireless efforts to pursue this goal. His life is an example of the influence one person can have by standing faithful to his convictions even if these views contradict contemporary thought. Through the utilization of Scripture, law, and moral influence, Las Casas had a profound role in defining and shaping Spain's colonial policies as the nation wrestled with the issues involved in moving from a narrow provincialism to a position as a world power.

His life is also a testimony that persons can change. Although originally profiting through the exploitation of others, when his eyes were opened and he realized his own guilt in participating in an unjust system, he repented. And, despite powerful opposition, he became the prophetic voice interceding on behalf of the Amerindians against the powerful who sought to continue their exploitation. In order to understand the magnitude of the changes Las Casas advocated in his desire to change official policy, it is necessary to understand the political and theological milieu in which he lived.

Spain's Legal and Moral Dilemma

During the fifteenth century, Spain and Portugal vied for supremacy on the Iberian peninsula. This conflict extended to the discovery and control of lucrative overseas trading routes to the Far East. The overland routes crossed through Muslim-controlled territories and were consequently dangerous and expensive. Portuguese voyages down the coast of Africa led to their establishing trading posts along the West African coast and seemed to give them an advantage in the race for water routes. The voyage of Columbus to the Indies, however, opened a new area of conflict between the two powers. This question of authority would have to be settled in a legal manner acceptable to the European community.[1]

In 1479, the Treaty of Alcacovas had established a precedent for the distribution of overseas properties. By the terms of this treaty, Portugal solidified its control over the Madeiras, the Azores, the Cape Verdes, and some other islands, as well as the lands of Africa. The monarchy of Castile received exclusive control over the Canary Islands. Thus, even before the voyage of Columbus, Spain and Portugal had established a legal precedent for resolving conflicts concerning overseas territories.[2]

The settlement of conflicts through treaty, however, was only one way by which international powers resolved their disputes. Another was by direct appeal to the pope, who could then act as arbiter between two Catholic countries. This brought a spiritual dimension to what might normally be considered a secular matter. The papacy itself had no desire to acquire territories, yet it felt a responsibility to bring pagans under the authority of Christ and his representative on this earth, the Church. To accomplish this, the Church granted lands to nations for the purpose of conversion. Hernando Columbus writes that as soon as his famous father returned to Palos, Spain, on March 14, 1493, he promptly requested the pontiff's approval and gift of his conquests. This papal approval would serve to confirm Spanish title to the Indies.[3]

This raises questions about the right of the papacy to influence or dictate to the Crown the secular actions it should take in discharging its legitimate nonspiritual governmental policies. The relationship between the Church and the Crown during the sixteenth century was a close one. Just as the Church on earth enjoyed a spiritual hierarchy with the pope at its apex, so was the Catholic monarchy dominant in temporal affairs; the earthly ruler reflected God's authority in the temporal universe. To discharge this responsibility most accurately and effectively, the monarch's chief weapons were not steel and arrows, but justice and truth. While the Church lent moral authority and suasion to the monarchy, it could not control or dominate it. The papacy could pressure the Crown to accept its authority by appealing to the learned through the use of theological or juridical arguments that relied on Scripture, tradition, or the church fathers. The Crown, for its part, could not ignore Rome lest it find itself out of favor with God himself, and so sought its backing whenever possible. Yet, the Catholic monarchs, the *reyes católicos,* as Ferdinand and Isabella were known, had worked diligently to extend their personal control over the Catholic Church in Spain.[4]

In 1486 the papacy had awarded the *Patronato Real,* or right of patronage, to the Catholic monarchs. This pronouncement allowed the rulers to make all church appointments within the lands of Granada and the Canaries as they reconquered these lands from the Moors. This desire to take back Muslim-controlled lands reflected the continuance of the Crusader mentality still prevalent at the time. In 1492, the Moorish Kingdom of Granada fell to Ferdinand and Isabella, thus completing the nearly eight-hundred-year war of reconquest. The year 1492 also marked the beginning of the Spanish presence in the New World, and subsequent papal bulls of 1501 and 1508 extended the *Patronato* with its privileges to the New World. Thus, the Crown had the authority to appoint or discharge clergy, raise taxes, or even effectively veto papal decrees in both the New and Old Worlds by refusing to publish them.[5] And although the *Patronato* gave the Catholic monarchs certain specified privileges within the Church, they appealed to the Spanish-born pope for a favorable ruling on their claims to the New World in an overt effort to legitimize their exploits. Consequently, Las Casas would learn to base his arguments on both theological and juridical claims and appeal not only to the Crown's sense of Christian mission, but also to its legal and practical responsibilities.

On May 4, 1493, Pope Alexander VI issued the bull *Inter Caetera.*[6] This bull awarded the temporal dominion of the newly found lands to the present rulers of Castile and Aragon and to their heirs and successors. The grant extended not only to those properties already found but also to any additional territories farther west as far as the Orient, as no Christian prince now ruled these lands. The purpose of this grant was explicit: "to the end that you might bring to the worship of our Redeemer and the profession of the Catholic faith their residents and inhabitants." This, continued the pope, was because "you have purposed with the favor of divine clemency to bring under your sway the said mainlands and islands with their residents and inhabitants and to bring them to the Catholic faith." The pontiff further emphasized the royal responsibility "as is your duty, to lead the people dwelling in those islands and countries to embrace the Christian religion." A threat accompanied the admonition.

> You should appoint to the aforesaid mainlands and islands worthy, God-fearing, learned, skilled, and experienced men, in order to instruct the aforesaid inhabitants and residents in the Catholic faith and train them in good morals. Furthermore, under penalty of excommunication *late sententie* to be incurred *ipso facto,* should anyone thus contravene, we strictly forbid all persons of whatsoever rank... to go for the purpose of trade or any other reason.[7]

To assure further the sovereignty of Spain over the newly acquired territories, the pontiff issued a second bull, *Eximiae Devotionis,* the next day. This decree confirmed what had been granted in the first bull and extended to Spain the same privileges previously granted to the king of Portugal in the East Indies. The pope further confirmed these donations in yet a third bull, *Dudum Siquidem,* issued in September 1493. In this document the pontiff threatened excommunication for anyone challenging Spanish authority in the lands already "discovered and to be discovered" and gave the Spanish Crown the right to perpetual possession of these lands and the authority to defend them against any foreign challenge.[8]

These bulls, especially *Inter Caetera,* were regarded as the juridical justification for Spanish imperialism. Both those who sought to defend Spain's colonialism in the New World and those who appealed for better treatment of its inhabitants cited these documents.[9] The effect of the papal bulls of 1493 was to make the monarchy vicars or delegates of the papacy. As Christ had passed on his authority to the apostle Peter, who then continued this delegation to the leader of the Roman Church as vicar, so, too, now did Alexander VI grant his authority to the monarchy. The responsibility, therefore, to establish, build up, and nurture the Church now fell to the *reyes católicos*.[10]

The issue of temporal authority was crucial. Based on the authority of these papal donations, the Catholic monarchy was bequeathing lands and natives to those conquering and colonizing America. Because of these sweeping papal assertions that granted temporal possessions to the Spanish Crown, other European monarchs felt justified in ignoring them. Francis I of France, for example, "in a fit of defiance, demanded to be shown the 'testament of Adam' which had bequeathed a hemisphere to the Spanish and Portuguese Crowns."[11] Even Spanish jurists questioned the right of the Church to grant temporal dominion over unbelievers. Las Casas referred to these donations many times and reminded those in authority that their legal position rested on spiritual justification. The Spanish Crown was caught between two opposing forces. On the one hand, it dared not anger God or God's representative, the pope. On the other hand, those who actually fought and invested in the New World desired to be rewarded for their efforts. As we shall see, this issue caused a great debate among the leading theologians, jurists, and moral philosophers, as the monarchy sought their advice to unravel its complexity.

The Crown, especially Queen Isabella, who seemed to have more of a concern for evangelism than did King Ferdinand, was especially interested in the nature of the relationship between the Christian world and the heathen or pagan peoples. The question of how believers should deal with unbelievers had arisen long before 1492. Indeed, many of the most influential thinkers of the time, among them the Dominican Matías de Paz and the civil jurist López de Palacios Rubios, adhered to the teaching of the thirteenth-century scholar Henry of Susa, cardinal of Ostia, also known as Ostiensis.[12] He had argued that after Christ, all legitimate power, both secular and spiritual, was granted to the pope as Christ's vicar. Thus when the pope granted the heathen lands to the Catholic monarchy through the bulls, he was exerting his rights. Because they were heathens, the Amerindians retained dominion over their lands only as long as they submitted to papal authority. Should they refuse this authority and not submit, the Church or its representatives (in this case, the Spanish monarchy) was legally justified in using whatever steps were necessary to bring them under control.[13]

In an attempt to justify legally this controversial doctrine, about 1512 the Crown issued the *Requerimiento* written by Palacios Rubios. This "requirement" was a direct response of the Crown to the protestations of Dominican priests in the New World. They had witnessed the slaughter of countless natives and challenged the monarchy to rectify the situation. Those encountering the Amerindians were to read this document aloud in an effort to cause the hearers to submit voluntarily to Spanish control. Beginning with a brief history of the world, the *Requerimiento* recounted the papal donations and how the Church was now the representative of Christ. It concluded by giving the hearers the opportunity to acknowledge the Church and the Crown as rightful authorities. Should they refuse this peaceful and reasonable invitation to give up their sovereignty, the proclaimers could, and would, take whatever action was necessary to force the hearers to submit to royal authority.

Of course, the notary read this document in Spanish, a language unknown to the hearers, and, for safety reasons, also remained out of range of native weapons and consequently beyond the range of any hearing as well. Thus, the Native Americans had no opportunity to respond even if they so desired. Because a notary was always present to attest to the fact that this formal invitation to submit had been read, the act fulfilled the legal requirement and placed the blame for any subsequent bloodshed on the shoulders of the natives. Most *conquistadores* in the field found the completion of this requirement to be a source of amusement and often mumbled it under their breath. When Las Casas heard about this pronouncement, he did not know whether to laugh or cry.[14]

Gregorio López and other scholars rejected the aspect of Henry of Susa's thought that permitted war and the seizure of property from those refusing to accept papal authority. López believed that if the Spanish reasonably presented the gospel, the natives would voluntarily submit to the pope and the Crown. If, however, the natives attacked those on peaceful missions, the Christians were justified in using punitive force. Although the Church objected on humanitarian grounds, this view tended to justify those who sought an excuse to use arms against the natives and became the accepted official position.[15]

General support for Spain's position of dominion in the New World came from an interesting if unexpected source. Writing from the University of Paris, the Scottish Dominican John Major (or Mair or Maior)—with no vested interest in the Spanish position—affirmed the armed conquest of the natives. He denied both temporal papal authority and universal dominion claimed by an emperor and emphasized that infidels held their property and governmental offices by natural law. Christian force was justified only if the pagans denied the peaceful preaching of the gospel.[16] If, after hearing the message of the gospel, the princes or leaders of the pagans did not convert, they should be deposed. If, however, the princes accepted the gospel and converted to Christianity, they demonstrated wisdom and a natural right to continue in power. Thus, it was argued, the Catholic monarchy was justified in its conquest of the Indians because of their barbarous nature and refusal to submit to the gospel. For Major, whose influential views demonstrated the continuance of medieval thought, the conquest of America was just another Crusade.[17]

Major not only wrote concerning the spiritual justification for conquest, but also, quoting Aristotle, expanded this reasoning to include a secular justification. Aristotle reasoned that, by nature, some individuals are free to determine their own fate, while others, also by nature, are born to be servants. Since this was true, Major reasoned, it was only right and proper that those born servile should willingly submit, in their own self-interest, to those possessing natural authority and command. Thus, Major became the first to apply Aristotle's views of natural servitude to a specific and entire race of people.[18]

Las Casas would severely criticize Major for his views, indicating that such views on natural slavery were like "poisons" infecting others. His main criticism centered on the fact that Major spoke of a people about whom he knew nothing. Las Casas wrote, "I am amazed John Major has so easily believed those who betray the

Indians—a docile, sincere, and clever people—by most shameful lies that they are stupid and bestial, so that these inhuman plunderers [the Spanish] might act more unrestrainedly against them." Refuting Major with his personal experience, Las Casas dismissed him: "Away then with John Major and his dreams! He knows neither the law nor the facts."[19] However, Major's views remained influential. In his famous disputation with Las Casas in 1550–51, Juan Ginés de Sepúlveda, the Italian-trained humanist and rhetorician, would cite Major as an authority in his own justification for Spanish imperialism.

Sepúlveda would become the point man for those seeking to justify Spain's treatment of the Indians. A distinguished scholar of Aristotle and master of Latin, he was also an ardent Spanish nationalist who viewed Spanish civilization as superior to all others. As such, it was Spain's duty to export this culture to the "barbarians." Espousing and expanding on Aristotle's view of natural slavery, Sepúlveda, in his dialogue of 1547, *Democrates segundo o de las justas causas de la guerra contra los indios,* argued that "it will always be just and in conformity with natural laws that such peoples [Indians] submit to the rule of the more cultured and humane princes and nations."[20] The Spaniards were justified in waging war because of the sins the Indians had committed (especially their idolatries and human sacrifices), their natural rudeness of behavior, Spain's twofold desire to protect the weaker natives from being taken advantage of by the stronger, and to spread the faith. This view followed the just war argument that Thomas Aquinas had espoused centuries before. The most significant factor, the principle that ultimately justified the war, was that it be fought with a right attitude and in a proper manner. This rationale explained the need to justify from a legal perspective the actions of the *conquistadores* and underscored the significance of the notaries who accompanied all the expeditions. These legal witnesses could then attest to the depravity of the Indians and the moral superiority of the Christians.[21]

Sepúlveda argued that the Spanish had a perfect right to rule over the Indians because "they are as inferior to the Spaniards as infants to adults and women to men." He continued his contrast of the cultures: "There is as much difference between them as there is between cruel, wild peoples and the most merciful of peoples, between the most monstrously intemperate peoples and those who are temperate and moderate in their pleasures, that is to say, between apes and men."[22] Sepúlveda's hyperbole obviously found support among those whose interests needed such justification. Influential officials, therefore, supported him in his famous Valladolid disputation with the equally hyperbolic Las Casas during 1550–51.[23]

Francisco de Vitoria and the Salamancan School

Las Casas reflected in a practical manner the theological and juridical views of the Salamancan School. Even prior to his entry into the Dominican Order and subsequent immersion in Salamancan theology, the great spiritual and intellectual influences on his life were Dominican priests connected to the University. This leading center of humanistic Dominican thought emerged from the controversies of the decade 1520–30. During this period, and as a direct result of the questions arising from the Indies, a new movement of law, theology, and logic emerged. Those from the school included the distinguished Domingo de Soto (1494–1560) and Melchor Cano (1509–60). Especially influential was the Dominican Francisco de Vitoria, whose ideas of humane treatment of the natives and peaceful colonization of America exerted a great deal of influence over Las Casas specifically, and over Spanish intellectual thought generally.[24] An understanding of his thought is essential for an appreciation of the contemporary theological-juridical milieu.

Vitoria received his training at the Dominican college in Paris under Peter Crockaert, who utilized the *Summa Theologica* of Thomas Aquinas as the foundation of his teaching. Vitoria became a leading exponent of Thomistic thought, which involved discovering and explaining the *jus naturae,* the natural law, that should govern every law of nature and any ethical dilemma that might arise. These principles are common to all people whether they are Christian or pagan. They are the laws God has implanted in all persons and are common to all regardless of place of birth.[25] Thus, his comments reflected the practicality of Thomism and involved the practice of Christianity in real-life situations rather than simple intellectual exercises. He also expanded the role of the theologian to comment on a wide variety of subjects from a theological perspective by applying theological concepts to specific political situations.[26] In 1523, Vitoria returned to Spain as a professor of theology, first at Valladolid and then at Salamanca. There he revitalized Spanish scholarship when he introduced the *Summa* as the main text of study.[27]

Because of Vitoria's reputation, the Crown sought his advice on matters relating to treatment of the natives in the New World. They were concerned by the ethical problems raised by the Dominican Antón Montesino in his famous sermon of 1511, which asked the question whether or not the Indians were really human beings. As a result, the Crown began an inquiry into the thorny yet vital problem of reconciling its Christian mission, and the ideal of a peaceful colonization and conversion of the inhabitants, with the practical dilemma of making the colonies economically profitable. In his lectures of 1538 and a subsequent treatise entitled *De Indis,* Vitoria presented his opinion on this matter, which drew upon Major and Aquinas and provided a basis for the international law that Grotius later developed.[28]

Vitoria argued that Spain had initially acted in good conscience during the conquest of the Amerindians but that the subsequent and constant reports of "so many massacres, so many plunderings of otherwise innocent men, so many princes evicted from their possessions and stripped of their rule" required an examination into Spanish policy and cast doubts over their ability to rule in an ethical manner.[29] The Indians held their land legally, and the fact that they were not Christian did not in itself disqualify them from having dominion. Although the Spanish were more intelligent and, therefore, more suited to rule, this did not justify Spain's assumption of power and confiscation of property from either private individuals or princes. This principle remained true even if the Indians could be proven to be incapable of self-government.[30]

Vitoria argued that the papal bulls that had donated the lands to the Crown were invalid. Arguing against both Matías de Paz and Palacios Rubios, he maintained that the pope's jurisdiction was strictly spiritual, not temporal. The pope's authority extended to advancing spiritual matters over the pagan world, but he had no secular authority over unbelievers. Thus, the natives were legally in possession of their property, the Spanish could not force them to accept Christianity, and, therefore, the just war theory had no validity in this case.[31] Ignorance was not a sin and, therefore, could not be a cause for war. Natural theology would reveal God to the pagans; Christians could not compel them to come to Christ. Because the pope did not have moral authority over unbelievers, unacceptable practices such as cannibalism, sodomy, and incest were likewise not legal reasons for conquest. None constituted legitimate grounds for Spain's seizing control over the Indian possessions.[32]

There existed, however, legal justification for Spanish *presence* in the New World. International law, based on natural law *(jus naturae)*, allowed one to travel and trade in a foreign country. The implicit understanding was that the visitor not mistreat the local populace. Friendship and hospitality were common to all nations and rooted in *jus naturae*. The goal was the mutual benefit of both nations. Interestingly enough, according to Vitoria, the economic benefits of such trade should accrue to the natives, as they were the host nation. Although the Spanish were justified in defending themselves against overt attack, such aggression could not lead to the taking of property because the Amerindians were waging a just war against the *conquistadores*.[33]

The teaching of Christianity was, however, the responsibility of the Church and the Spanish authorities in the New World. The newly established colonial government was therefore justified in removing all barriers to the free expression of the faith. By extension, this included the establishment of peace and political stability. It did not, however, extend to the forcing of the acceptance of Christianity. The decision to accept or reject the good news was left to the hearers. Las Casas believed so firmly in this principle that it became the theme of his book, *The Only Way*, which developed and expounded upon the biblical, and, therefore, in his view, the only acceptable method of spreading the gospel. Reason and providing the peaceful example of godly love were Las Casas's methods. Spain's power to utilize force, according to Vitoria, was limited to assuring that the conditions for preaching were available. The results were up to God.

These conditions in no way allowed the illegal seizure of property from its rightful owners.[34]

The influence of Vitoria, and those members of the Salamancan School who succeeded him, was significant. Learned men such as Melchor Cano, who assumed Vitoria's chair at Salamanca upon his death in 1546, and Diego de Covarrubias, a member of the royal commission established to study the "Indian problem," forced the Crown to confront the issue of Spain's legal and theological justification for its presence and activities in the New World. These individuals also challenged the previous school of thought, espoused by Matías de Paz, Palacios Rubios, and Sepúlveda, that had extended papal authority to the secular as well as the spiritual realm.[35]

Although there is disagreement over the exact relationship between the Salamancan School and Las Casas, he was certainly aware of and influenced by their thought.[36] Las Casas's primary motivation for both action and writing, however, always remained his Christian belief and his burning desire to see the conversion of the Native Americans to the Catholic faith. Although he utilized juridical arguments, this was for the purpose of advancing the spiritual. Through evangelization of the Indians, Spain was fulfilling both its legal and spiritual obligations. Because the Crown was acting as a good steward of God's word and command, God would spare the nation and its leadership from divine wrath. Thus, Las Casas fulfilled his role not only as priest, but also as a prophet. The latter he emphasized when he warned of the consequences to Spain if its rulers neglected their evangelizing responsibilities. As one example of this dual role, Las Casas wrote in his prologue to the *Historia,* "What really moved me to write this book was the great and desperate need of all Spain to have truth and enlightenment on all things concerning the world of the Indian." His priestly concern for the natives and prophetic words to his native land caused him to continue: "What damage, calamities, disruptions, decimations of kingdoms, how many souls lost, how many unforgivable sins committed, how much blindness and deadness of conscience," as a result of these failings by Spain, "what harms and evils have occurred and still each day happen to the kingdoms of Castile, *I am very sure we will never know, nor be even able to estimate, until that great and final day of terrible judgment and divine justice.*" The priest and legal scholar continued by expressing his concern that the Catholic faith and Christian tradition and customs had suffered irreparable harm in the New World because of "the ignorance of the principal end for which divine Providence intended the discovery of these lands and peoples, which is only, because we are mortal, *the conversion and salvation of these souls, therefore all temporal matters must be subordinate to this end.*"[37] The legal justification, while important and necessary, was subordinate to and dependent on theological and ethical considerations. Indeed, the political and juridical rationale used the theological as its basis. Without the reliance on, and understanding of, theology, the juridical argument was irrational.

The legal justification for the Spanish control over the Indies was thus grounded in a responsibility to convert the natives and to take charge of their "spiritual well-being." According to the papal bulls, which comprised the basic authority for Spain's presence in the Indies, the accomplishment of these goals was Spain's primary purpose in America. This authority did not extend to the seizure of persons and property. In fact, the bulls specifically prohibited this action. Las Casas, in the course of his more than half century of advocacy on behalf of the natives, would continually remind the Crown of both its authority and its concurrent responsibility, basing his arguments on his theological presuppositions derived from the Catholic faith.

The Monarchy Responds

The fact that the monarchy recognized and accepted this responsibility and rationale from the beginning is further indicated by a lengthy statement Ferdinand and Isabella gave to Columbus on May 29, 1493, prior to his second voyage. Among other instructions, the monarchs specifically charged Columbus to work diligently for the conversion of the inhabitants of both the islands and mainland to the Catholic faith. To accomplish this task, Fray Buyl accompanied the expedition and led the first group of priests to the New World. The instructions also contained the provision that Columbus was to punish severely any person who mistreated the Indians.[38] In issuing

Franz Kollarz, *Christopher Columbus before King Ferdinand and Queen Isabella.* Foto Marburg/Art Resource.

these commands, the monarchs reiterated and affirmed the meaning of the bull promulgated by the pope only weeks before.

Upon his return to Hispaniola, however, Columbus encountered a situation that he felt justified the enslavement of certain Taino Indians. The natives had burned his original settlement and killed its inhabitants. According to the natives' account of these actions, this attack was initiated as retaliation for Spanish mistreatment. Columbus, however, felt obligated to wage a punitive campaign and acquired slaves in this "just war." The Spanish also waged war against and captured Caribs, who practiced cannibalism and lived on neighboring islands, enslaving them ostensibly for the purpose of converting them to Christianity and thereby changing their appetites. Traditionally slavery had been the accepted form of punishment for captured prisoners of war. Columbus may even have intended to emulate the profitable African slave trade of the Portuguese. Queen Isabella, however, acting consistently with her previous directives and mindful of her responsibility, ordered an end to this slave trade and subsequently mandated the release of those already in captivity.[39] This action greatly frustrated the colonists.

The Crown now faced a dilemma that would plague it for the remainder of the colonial era. On the one hand, Spain's legal and moral justification for being in the Indies was the conversion of the Amerindians and their protection as vassals and members of the Church. On the other hand, the *conquistadores,* who had risked their lives and in some cases their fortunes to extend the domain of the monarchs, expected to achieve material wealth in the form of land, natives, or valuable goods. Their goal in coming to the New World was not primarily to extend God's kingdom. They sought to improve their social and economic lot. Bernal Díaz del Castillo, the soldier-historian who accompanied Cortés on his conquest of Mexico, curtly explained this duality: "We came here to serve God, and also to get rich."[40]

When the Crown supported those such as the priests who labored on behalf of the Indians and sought to end their exploitation, the colonists protested. Yet, when the monarchy allowed the settlers to utilize the native labor and expropriate their possessions, the Church rightly reminded them of their responsibility to protect this group of their vassals. This classic dichotomy would constantly bedevil the monarchy during the conquest and colonization of the Indies. As Lesley Byrd Simpson so clearly writes, "There could be but one workable solution: as long as the issue was so sharply drawn, it will be found that in no case did the Crown sacrifice its material interests, which were identical to those of the colonists, to any otherworldly concept of spiritual duty."[41] In an effort to meet both obligations, in 1503, the Spanish instituted a system that would become the focal point of Las Casas and his message—the *encomienda*. The results of this exploitative and hypocritical policy were disastrous for the indigenous populations.

"An Amazing Piece of Sophistry"

Based on the moribund feudal system of Europe, the idea of the *encomienda* was fairly simple and solved the two problems faced by the Spaniards in the New World. On the one hand, the natives were to be entrusted, or commended, to the Spanish for protection, care, and, most important, instruction in the Catholic faith. On the other hand, they were to provide labor for the enterprises of gold extraction and agricultural production. Since their arrival, the Spanish had utilized native labor. As we shall soon see, this system of labor was ultimately legalized in 1503. Unfortunately, the practice of this system, unchecked by any semblance of order and under the control of unscrupulous individuals, gave rise to the excesses and near extermination of those to be cared for and taught.[42] The system allowed for the exploitation of the weaker by the stronger. This was perhaps an inevitable outcome when we consider how this system came about.

From the arrival of Columbus and the establishment of his first colony in 1492 until 1502, when Nicolás de Ovando the royal governor arrived, conditions on the island of Española were chaotic. With no formal governmental system and extremely primitive conditions, each colonist became a law unto himself. Part of the problem was the type of colonist who came to the New World. Far from being interested in establishing new farms or businesses, these individuals included penniless noblemen, convicts, criminals, ex-soldiers, adventurers, and assorted castoffs from society.[43] In an effort to encourage settlement, the Crown even offered to let those who would work keep up to one-third of the gold they mined. On all other income sources they needed to pay only the required royal fifth. At the request of Columbus, who was having trouble recruiting colonists for an expedition, the Catholic monarchs issued an edict in 1497 that commuted the sentences of criminals if they would agree to go to the Indies. Those who deserved the death penalty had to serve two years; those who had committed some other capital offense, only one year; and those who were to be banished from Spain could likewise serve this banishment in the New World.[44]

Thus, the men who populated the Antilles during the first crucial years of the Spanish occupation were described by Columbus as being unworthy of receiving "water from God or man." They viewed the Indians as inferior beings who existed only to make their life easier. What the colonists lacked was a theology or philosophy that would justify their exploitation in such a manner as to make it acceptable to the monarchy and the Church. They were not there to work with their hands, but to get rich, become *hidalgos* (or gentlemen-nobles), and return to Spain. Without royal authority present, there was no one to control them.[45]

Also, for most Spaniards, the Indians were inferior persons given to profane and idolatrous practices. They went about naked and had no agricultural system comparable to that of Europe. They therefore warranted instruction in both theology and agriculture, and, because of their inferior nature, needed to be forced to do so. The development of the *encomienda* system was thus based on a theological rationalization that would morally justify these actions. Both of these principles were developed in an atmosphere of anarchy by the human refuse of Spain.

Columbus began the system of Indian tribute to be paid to the monarchs. This tax consisted of a certain amount of gold or an *arroba* of cotton. Soon, however, necessity forced Columbus to allow the utilization of the Indians for labor to cultivate food to keep the Spanish from starving. In a request to the monarchy, he asked that he be allowed to utilize their labor for a few years until the Spanish could get settled and grow strong as a colony.[46] In his evaluation of Columbus, whom he admired greatly, Las Casas concluded that he had overstepped his authority and instigated and then perpetuated the idea that the natives were docile and existed to serve the monarchy. According to Las Casas, these ideas, and the system that arose from them, later became the foundation for all the evil that the Indies had to suffer.[47]

During the years 1496–98, Columbus was in Spain and left Hispaniola under the authority of his brother Bartholomew. Frustrated with his leadership, Francisco Roldán revolted, gaining the support of many of the colonists. Christopher Columbus, upon his return to the island, gave Roldán and his followers a number of Indians to do their work for them in an effort to maintain their loyalty. Other Spaniards, however, continued to rebel against the authority of the Columbus brothers. Upset at the apparent anarchy and angered that Columbus had given away "her subjects," Isabella dispatched Francisco de Bobadilla to investigate. Upon his arrival, he discovered that the brothers were trying to bring order to the island by hunting down and lynching Spanish rebels. Bobadilla responded by immediately sending the Columbus brothers back to Spain in chains.[48]

Bobadilla also increased the workload of the Indians by forcing them to work in the mines. They were required to pay a one peso tribute for every eleven they extracted. But charges of mismanagement and abuse and the fear that a new feudalism was emerging in the Indies prompted the monarchy to send a new governor, the Extremaduran Nicolás de Ovando, with a contingent of 2500 men, to the Indies. It was as a member of this fleet that the young Bartolomé de las Casas arrived in the New World in April 1502.

Ovando came to the New World with instructions concerning the treatment of the Native Americans. In a series of orders that the monarchy gave to Ovando dated September 16, 1501, he was reminded that his chief duty was to see that the Indians were taught the Catholic faith. As mentioned, this admonition was at the heart of the Spanish presence in the New World, and the monarchy continued to emphasize the evangelistic nature of their venture in all legislation that dealt with the Native Americans. Because of these instructions, Las Casas and the other reformers had firm and extensive legal ground on which to base their message and prophetic warnings. The colonists were to treat the Indians well, not rob them, and return any women who had been taken involuntarily. Concerning the tribute to be paid to the Crown by all her subjects, the queen ordered they be compelled to work, but be paid a fair wage. These instructions became the basis for the system of forced labor, known as the *mita,* or *repartimiento,* which endured even into the postcolonial period.[49]

Ovando received further instructions on March 20 and 29, 1503, indicating that the Indians should live in *reducciónes,* or local communities, where they could better receive instruction and care from a priest. These priests were to teach them to pay their tithes to the Church and the Crown and the official in charge was to see that the Indians carried out their necessary service to the community. Ovando was to report on the best way of paying the natives for their work.[50]

Apparently the Indians were not inclined to live under the tutelage of the colonists and generally avoided contact with them. The natives utilized this form of passive resistance because they realized that open armed rebellion was ineffective. Because the colonists needed the natives to produce food as well as wealth, Ovando asked for further clarification of the system from Isabella. His goal was to implement the medieval feudal system with which he was familiar in Spain. In December 1503 he received a royal *cédula,* or official document, from Isabella, which legalized and formally established the *encomienda* system in the New World.[51]

This document, called "an amazing piece of sophistry" by Lesley Byrd Simpson, made legal the system of forced labor and became the foundation for all future Indian labor legislation.[52] A careful reading of this *cédula* will show that while it confirmed the freedom of the Amerindians, it tied conversion to Christianity and forced labor:

> Whereas, the King my Lord and I agreed...that the Indian inhabitants of the island of Española *are free and not subject to forced service*...and whereas we are now told that because of the excessive liberty enjoyed by the said Indians *they avoid contact and community with the Spanish* to such an extent that they will not even work for wages, but wander about idle and cannot be had by the

Christians to convert to our Holy Catholic Faith; and in order that the Christians may not lack people to work their holdings for their maintenance and extract the gold that exists on the island…and whereas we desire that the said Indians be converted to our Holy Catholic Faith and taught in its doctrines; and whereas this can better be done by having the Indians live in community with the Christians of the island and go among them and associate with them, by which means they will help each other…[Because of the above], I have commanded…you will *compel and force the said Indians to associate with the Christians* of the island and to work on their buildings, and to gather and mine the gold and other metals, and to till the fields and produce food for the Christian inhabitants…and you are to pay on the day he works the wages and maintenance you think he should have…and you are to order each cacique to take charge of a certain number of the said Indians, so that you may make them work wherever necessary, and so that on feast days and other such days as you think proper, they may be gathered together to hear and be taught in the things of the Faith…This the Indians shall perform *as free people, which they are and not slaves.* And see to it they are well treated, *those who become Christians better than the others,* and do not consent or allow that any person do them harm or oppress them.[53]

The rationale for forced contact with the Spanish was designated as primarily for evangelizing. In fact, those who converted to Christianity were to receive special care and privileges. Traditionally, scholars have evaluated the system based on the necessity and role of forced labor that developed and that then resulted in a subsequent loss of life. Yet, the issue of forced contact for the purpose of evangelizing and religious instruction is overlooked. At the heart of this system was an idea based on false assumptions that forced contact with Christians could lead to conversion. By stressing the fact that even though he himself and his partner Pedro de Rentería treated the Indians well, they were still guilty of self-righteous and paternalistic behavior, Las Casas emphasized that the system was corrupt and no amount of forced contact for evangelizing could change this. The system bred the type of abuse that led to a total degradation of the Indian. It took an epiphany for Las Casas to realize this. Once this event happened, he recognized that forced contact for the purpose of evangelism was invalid and there had to be another way to bring the gospel to those who had not yet heard.

Based on the principles outlined in the *cédula*, the Indians were free subjects of the Crown with all the rights and privileges granted to others. Nevertheless, the physical abuses that arose from the application of this system are legend. Problems inherent in this system included an effective lack of royal oversight and the fact that each *encomendero* treated his workers as he desired. Although technically and legally free, the Indians were enslaved and utilized for the good of the Spanish through the strength of arms, not free choice. The Spaniards forced them to live in their midst so that they could be evangelized and receive religious instruction. The Crown apparently acted hypocritically and used religion as a mask to cover its real intent—which was the use of the labor of the Indian.

Las Casas, however, saw through the hypocrisy and emphasized the other aspect of this relationship, the need for evangelization for the Amerindians and salvation through repentance for the Spaniard. The priest called the monarchy to task, both arguing the juridical case, even using the words of the very legislation mandated from the Crown, and emphasizing the underlying theological basis of these directives and pointing up the need for enforcement. After having lived and worked in the New World for a number of years, Las Casas recognized that forced conversion was ineffective. In his work *The Only Way*, he argued from St. Thomas and the church fathers as well as from Scripture that the only biblical and valid method for evangelization of infidels was by peaceful means and through an appeal to their reason based on a living example. Coercion had no place in this and would be counterproductive. Las Casas wrote the initial draft of *The Only Way* in 1534. At that point he was a Dominican and was fresh from a victory in dealing with the Indian rebel Enriquillo. Coupling this experience with what he had previously experienced, he wrote, "It is now clear that the way Christ wanted for preaching the Gospel, and willed for His apostles and their successors, was to win the mind with reasons and win the will with motives, gently, graciously."[54]

It had become clear to him at the time that the queen, even if her motivation was correct, by forcing close contact between the two peoples, was attempting to bring the Indians into the Church in the wrong way. Las Casas not only fought against the *encomienda* system because of its coerced labor but also because of its faulty method of evangelization. Forced contact between the Spaniards and Indians yielded no results. "What is clear is that Christ gave His apostles permission and power to preach the Gospel to those willing to hear it, and that only! Not power to punish the unwilling by any force, pressure, or harshness."[55] As Christ passed this authority, responsibility, and method on to the apostles, they in turn passed it on to those coming after. The modus had not changed, but, unfortunately for the Indians, the application had. As mentioned, it would take the priest nearly thirty years to come to this conclusion.

That the primary intent, as well as justification, of the queen was evangelization is evidenced through the words of her Last Will and Testament. Prior to her death on November 26, 1504, Isabella named her husband, Ferdinand, as regent of the Indies, and expressed her wish for the type of government she desired:

> Whereas, when the islands and mainland of the Ocean Sea were conceded to us by the Holy Apostolic See, our principal intention...was to procure, induce, bring, and convert their peoples to our Holy Catholic Faith, and to send to the said islands and mainland bishops, religious, clerics, and other learned and God fearing persons, to instruct the inhabitants and dwellers therein in the Catholic Faith, and to instruct them in, and to bestow upon them, good customs, exercising all proper diligence in this [therefore], I beg the King my Lord very affectionately, and I charge and command my said daughter and the said prince her husband [Juana "la loca" and Philip I] to carry this out, and that it be their principal purpose, and that they put into it much diligence; and they are not to consent, or give permission, that the Indian inhabitants and dwellers in the said islands or mainland...receive any damage in their

persons or goods, but are to order that they be well and
justly treated; and if they have received any damage it is to
be remedied; and it is to be provided that everything
enjoined and commanded us in the said concession be
strictly observed.[56]

The final words of Queen Isabella confirmed not only the papal
donation of the Indies to Spain, but also that the prime responsibility of the Spanish colonization was conversion through peaceful
means.

This became the basic message of Las Casas, and he was not
alone in his belief in peaceful conversion. During the conquest of
Mexico (1519–21), the zealous Cortés tried to force Christianity on
the native peoples he encountered. He destroyed pagan idols and
altars and erected crosses. The Mercedarian priest, Fray Bartolomé
de Olmedo, the first apostle of New Spain, urged caution and a
process of instruction in the faith prior to destroying idols and forcing the faith upon the Tlaxcalans. He argued that a violent and complete disregard for the native practices would prove both
inflammatory and counterproductive. It was also not the way of
Christ. Thus, the priest urged reason, education, and persuasion as
the appropriate methods of sharing the faith.[57]

Yet, the controversy over the treatment of the Native
Americans raged during the entire sixteenth century. The specific
method of evangelization that the individual Spaniard chose roughly
corresponded to his view of the nature of the Indian and the benefits
the native received by his subjugation. Meanwhile, the impact of the
conquest and the system of forced labor on the native cultures was
swift, total, and destructive. During the first fifty years of Spanish
domination, the Europeans completely changed the governmental,
social, and religious superstructures of the Indians. Although the
indigenous cultures were already familiar with conquest by other
native peoples, the new form of destruction was more violent and
from a completely alien culture. This conquest totally modified the
existing norms of civilization and invariably placed the native culture
in a subordinate relationship to the Spanish.[58] Much to the chagrin of
Las Casas, violence and death marked even the advent of
Christianity, more obviously in the conquest of the natives by the

conquistadores, slightly less so through the effects of unknown diseases. Moreover, priests who followed or accompanied the *conquistadores* destroyed idols and punished those who refused to convert or to modify their traditions. Outright native resistance, however, was limited and within a generation the survivors had outwardly accepted the new religion. Despite Gómara's assertion that all Indians had converted to Christianity, in practice it was syncretism, for example, the acceptance of some aspects of Christianity, which merged with local custom and tradition, that became the norm.[59]

Through disease, to which the Amerindians had no immunity, or maltreatment or outright slaughter, the native populations of the West Indies were virtually extinct by about 1550. Along the Caribbean coastline and in central Mexico, most recent estimates indicate about 90 percent depopulation by the end of the sixteenth century. Certainly those societies with the closest and most prolonged exposure to the Europeans suffered the greatest decline. Along with the virtual extinction of the population and the subsequent seizure of now vacant lands by the conquerors, the social structure of the remaining Indians was disrupted as the new administration forced the survivors together into artificially constructed villages.[60] Alarmed by the destruction of possible converts as well as the reduction of their labor supply, the monarchy sought to stop this slaughter and protect its interests.

Las Casas was a product of and participant in this ongoing intellectual, juridical, and spiritual struggle. His contribution became one of focusing attention on the hypocrisy of these destructive practices. He also attempted to remind the Crown of its authority and the attendant responsibility that was theirs by virtue of the papal donations. After his life-changing experience, during which he realized both the guilt of the Crown as well as his own complicity in the *encomienda* system, Las Casas utilized both legal and spiritual weapons in defense of the Amerindians. Through his writings, Las Casas created vivid images of the slaughter of the Amerindians and brought their plight to the attention of the rest of the world.[61]

In order to understand and appreciate the magnitude of the change in the life of Las Casas after his first conversion in 1514, it is crucial to study in some detail the first years of his life and his initial experiences in the New World. Although there are few details about his personal life in his works, for he did not set out to write either a diary or an autobiography, we do get a glimpse into the events that shaped his thought and began to work on his conscience. These experiences would culminate in his decision to dedicate his life to the preservation of those whom he too had exploited along with his countrymen. Primarily through his *Apologética historia sumaria, Brevísima relación,* and *Historia general,* Las Casas provides not only a picture of the relationships between Spanish and Indian but also insights into how he viewed himself and his initial role in America.

By examining specific examples that he remembered and chronicled years later, we can discover events that he considered important, relevant, and moving. These are the memories he culled from so many experiences and considered significant enough to record. Las Casas then contrasted these events with his future role as one who has repented of his actions and prophetically acts as an intermediary between the Amerindians and the Crown, representing the former against the latter. His role became one of recalling and publicizing his own painful remembrances in an effort to warn the Crown of impending judgment. His goal was to force the Spaniards, who were guilty of the same type of exploitation as he, to recognize their culpability, experience remorse, and subsequently make amends for their actions as he himself sought to do.

CHAPTER TWO

The Early Years of Las Casas

Bartolomé de las Casas was born in Seville, Spain, in 1484.[1] Little is known of his ancestry or early years. He apparently came from a family of "Old Christians," because all four of his grandparents had been baptized. Yet, he was also descended from *conversos* on his father's side. His father, Pedro de Las Casas, was from Tarifa and may have had two sisters. His mother apparently died while he was still very young because little is known about her.[2]

In 1493, Pedro, along with his brothers, Francisco, Diego, and Gabriel de Peñalosa, accompanied Columbus on his second voyage to the New World. There, Pedro spent five years as a merchant before returning to Spain in 1498. While he was away, the young Bartolomé studied Latin and other subjects with another possible relative, Luis de Peñalosa, prebendary of the Cathedral of Seville.[3]

When Pedro de Las Casas returned in 1498, he brought with him a young Taino Indian slave. This lad was one of the three hundred that Columbus awarded the men who had accompanied him on the voyage of 1493. Pedro gave this Indian, named Juanico, to his son, who was favorably impressed by his demeanor and activity. He became a manservant/companion to Bartolomé and accompanied him as he began his studies for the priesthood at Salamanca in 1498. When Queen Isabella learned that Columbus had obtained and distributed these slaves, she angrily declared, "What right does the Admiral have to give anyone my vassals?" In late June 1500, she ordered the natives, including the one belonging to Las Casas, returned to the Indies with the new governor and *visitador* Francisco de Bobadilla. Although disappointed at the loss of his companion, Las Casas returned to his studies and Juanico returned to the Indies. Las Casas must have been favorably impressed with the abilities of Juanico, because the two agreed to meet later in the New World.[4]

32

Because of complaints against Columbus and his lack of ability to keep peace in the colonies, the monarchy decided to replace him as governor. According to the *Historia* of Las Casas, in 1502, the knight commander of the Order of Alcántara, Nicolas de Ovando, arrived in Hispaniola. This expedition consisted of 2500 men, mostly knights and nobles. It also included the first twelve Franciscan friars in the New World under the guidance of the pious Alonso de Espinal. Las Casas remembered Ovando as a good man, capable of governing the Spanish but with no empathy for Indians. He had an air of authority about him, loved justice, and was honest in both word and deed. He was an enemy of both greed and avarice. Yet, during his tenure in office, the Indians suffered greatly despite specific royal instructions. These directives specified that the Crown considered the Amerindians to be vassals in the same sense as those from Castile and ordered them to be instructed in the faith as though they were fellow Christians.[5]

> Bartolomé de Las Casas also arrived on Hispaniola with the Ovando expedition. Although information concerning this period of Las Casas's life is sketchy, it appears he had come to assist his father in the family business. This business involved provisioning the colonists and was going poorly. By 1502, Las Casas had completed his canonical studies, but was unable to afford the fee traditionally presented to the faculty to actually receive his final degree. Due to his canonical studies and knowledge of Latin, the young man could aspire to become a teacher of Catholicism, or *doctrinero,* receive a decent salary, and instruct the Indians in their new faith. Thus did the young businessman, trained as a canonical jurist, arrive in the place where his destiny called.[6]

The colonists on the island received the new arrivals with much joy because they brought both news and, perhaps more important, food from home. Upon disembarking with the colonists, Las Casas heard, "with his own ears," two bits of information that were causing quite a commotion on Hispaniola. An Indian slave girl had found a unique gold nugget; it weighed thirty-five pounds and was worth

36,000 gold pesos. She belonged to a team of slaves (between fifteen and forty males and females) whom Governor Bobadilla had assigned to work for a pair of Spaniards. The finding of gold was always an exciting event among the colonists, and this was especially so when the piece was large enough "to roast a whole pig on it." (Las Casas dryly remarked that he bet that the girl who had found the nugget did not get even a bite of the pig!) The second piece of information was related to the first. Indians in a certain province had revolted against Spanish abuse. The news caused great joy among the settlers because now they had sufficient justification to attack and take captive the natives, and then sell those captured as slaves.[7] The announcement concerning the finding of gold and the enslavement of Indians greatly pleased the colonists; both events meant wealth to the recipients.

Far from being disappointed with the news that greeted him upon his arrival in Santo Domingo, Las Casas was equally excited about the prospect of wealth. He, too, had come to get rich and rejoiced with the others at the good news and fortune it could bring.[8] But he also recorded a further remembrance about his arrival in the New World and the attitude of the natives. He noted how peaceful and free they were and that they received the Spanish as if they were all their brothers. When he had disembarked in 1502, the Indians were happy to greet them and brought them food.[9]

The specific early activities of Las Casas on Hispaniola are difficult to ascertain since he provides us with few details. It appears, however, that he both performed his duties as *doctrinero* and needed to earn a living. Thus, he was engaged in the family business. It is likely that funding for priests was sporadic at best, and they, therefore, either lived in poverty or participated in some secular activity to earn a living. Las Casas does, however, indicate that upon arrival the expedition of which he was a part immediately went to the gold fields in search of wealth. This search was a disaster. With a biting sarcasm that is evident throughout his *Historia,* he writes, "After arriving at the mines, because gold unlike fruit lies underground and does not grow on trees and therefore is not easily picked, they had to dig for it…and they had never dug for anything in their lives." Because of this unexpected hard work, "they rested often and ate too much."[10] Soon more than one thousand of the original 2500 had died, and 500 of those remaining were sick. They died at such a rate that the priests could not bury them fast enough. Because this account of the expedition appears to contain the details of an eyewitness, it seems likely that Las Casas was one of those personally engaged in the mining process.[11]

Las Casas also participated in some way, possibly as either chaplain or provisioner, with the military campaigns against the rebellious natives. Apparently he did not take part in the first campaign in the province of Higuey. This was the original revolt that had provoked such joy upon the arrival of the Ovando expedition. What provoked this revolt, according to Las Casas, was that a Spanish ship arrived off the island of Saona, in Higuey province, to receive provision from the natives. Spanish ships often did this. For sport, one of the Spaniards, who had a dog trained to attack and kill humans, set his dog on the local chief, who was walking about in an agitated manner waving a cane and urging his subjects to load the food quickly. Las Casas chronicles the event: "The dog sprang on the *cacique* and with powerful jaws tore at his stomach pulling out the intestines as the chief staggered away."[12] Although the Indians tried to save him, he quickly died. The Spaniards then sailed away with their "good dog." Soon after this attack, in retaliation the natives killed eight sailors who visited the island in search of provisions. In an attempt to justify the actions of the natives, Las Casas invoked a principle from the just war argument. He contended that a nation at war with another is not obligated to discern guilt or innocence of the belligerents. The natives, therefore, legally executed judgment on the eight Spaniards since the actions of the previous group constituted war. This was true, according to Las Casas, "since at that time there was not a single Spaniard on the island who did not offend or harm the Indians."[13] Las Casas provides further insight into the nature of the Spanish and their treatment of the natives with another narrative: "It was a general rule for the Spaniards to be cruel, not just cruel, but extraordinarily cruel. This was so that this harsh and bitter treatment would keep the Indians from daring to think of themselves as human beings—or even to have a moment to think period." To maintain this fear and, according to Las Casas, demonstrate their cruelty, the Spaniards "would cut the hands of an Indian, leaving them only dangling by a piece of skin and then send him on his way saying, 'Go spread the news to your chiefs.'"[14]

Because this narrative is in the style of a first-person account, it is evident that Las Casas took part in the second Higuey campaign. He constantly referred to events that he personally witnessed. "All that I have said is true, because I saw it, and told what I had seen."[15] On another occasion he wrote, "All this I have seen with my own physical mortal eyes."[16] This emphasis on the eyewitness account was important for Las Casas, and he often criticized those who wrote only about what they had heard and not seen. His experiences as witness to events would separate him from the theologians and jurists who argued theoretically about the New World from the comfort of Spain. His personal experiences, coupled with the sixteenth-century intellectual formation of a priest and canonical scholar, made him an authority (as he constantly reminds the reader). Therefore, when he spoke or wrote, it was from an authoritative perspective. Consequently, according to Las Casas, what he wrote about was true. Thus, his goal was to assure his readers that his explanation of events and descriptions of America were the most accurate and legitimate.[17]

Juan de Esquivel led the second campaign in Higuey. The expedition included about four hundred Spaniards. Indian allies also accompanied these expeditions, which were sent to pacify the rebellious areas. The warfare itself was more like a slaughter or sporting event than an actual military contest. As described by Las Casas, "In reality their wars are like child's play, they have only naked bellies to protect them from the mighty steel weapons of the Spanish."[18] During this campaign, the Spanish slaughtered between six and seven hundred Indians and took many others as prisoners. Thus, they avenged the killing of the eight Spaniards.

During another expedition to Xaraguá Las Casas received his second slave. Apparently the Indians in this village, under a female chief, Anacaona, had somehow angered *comendedor* Lares. He subsequently arrived at the village with his troops. The Spaniards enjoyed a feast and were treated "like royal guests." Lares responded to this act of kindness by forcing all the Indian chiefs into a dwelling and then setting fire to the house, burning all who were in it. As a mark of honor, the Spanish hanged Queen Anacaona and presented

Las Casas with a slave from those remaining. He apparently accepted this slave as his due without moral reservation.[19]

Las Casas does not tell us why or how, but at some point in 1506, he traveled to Seville, where he was ordained deacon. Following this event, he and Bartholomew Columbus made the trip to Rome, the center of Christendom. Coming from what was in those days the more pious Spain, Las Casas was shocked by the participants' rowdy and licentious behavior during the "Festival of the Flutes" prior to Lent. It was in Rome, however, that on March 3, 1507, at the age of twenty-three, the former *doctrinero* was formally ordained a priest. Subsequently, he returned to Salamanca and received the bachelor of canon law degree and probably continued with graduate studies in this field.[20]

Sometime prior to 1510, the newly ordained priest, along with Diego Columbus, the recently appointed governor of the Antilles, his new bride, María de Toledo, and Bartholomew Columbus, returned to Hispaniola. With an obvious amount of pride, yet trying to sound humble, Las Casas chronicled these events nearly four decades later. He wrote that on that island in 1510, "a new priest, named Bartolomé de Las Casas, from Seville, one of the pioneers on this island, was the first one to sing new mass in all of the Indies." Helen Rand Parish believes this was a first Mass sung by Las Casas in his home church, not necessarily the first Mass sung by anyone in the Indies. The new governor, his wife, and many of the settlers on the island were present for this event, which coincided with the smelting of the gold collected during that year.[21]

Noble Indians, or Dirty Dogs?

Since the beginning of the Spanish presence in the New World, the colonists had disagreed over the nature of the Indians. Could they receive the Christian faith and live as the Spaniards did, or were they some other type of inferior humanity and therefore rationally incapable of understanding Christianity? There were basically two schools of thought concerning the nature of the Amerindians. The colonists viewed the natives as either "noble savages" or "dirty dogs."

These interpretations of the inherent abilities of the Indians became evident both in the secular and theological realms. In the worldly realm, those who relied on the Indians as their source of wealth, and therefore needed to exploit them for their own gain, tended to view them as inferior by nature. Those, like the priests who ministered to them and actually became acquainted with them in an effort at evangelization and with a desire to reform the system on their behalf, tended to idealize their traits. Thus, the true nature of the Indian, like the European a human being with feelings, fears, and traditions, became obscured as the two extremes continually clashed.[22]

Perhaps the most prolific and popular individual subscribing to the "dirty dog" opinion was the royal officer and official historian Gonzalo Fernández de Oviedo. This historian, whom Las Casas called "a deadly enemy of the Indians," had been in the New World since 1514.[23] He arrived in America as a government bureaucrat when he accompanied Pedro Arias de Ávila (Pedrarias) to the northern coast of South America. His first official responsibility in the New World was to read the newly authorized *Requerimiento* to the natives. Another of his official duties was to regulate the iron that branded Indian slaves on the forehead as a mark of their slavery. Oviedo, therefore, charged a fee for each branded Indian. Thus he profited from and had a stake in the continuation of this system. Interestingly, he failed to note this fact in his supposedly unbiased history.[24]

Because of his official position and experience in the New World, the Council of the Indies sought Oviedo's opinion on questions concerning the nature of the Indians. For those desiring to justify the natural inferiority of the Amerindian, he became one of the most eloquent spokesmen. He considered the Indians to be "naturally lazy and vicious, melancholic, cowardly, and in general a lying, shiftless people. Their marriages are not a sacrament but a sacrilege. They are idolatrous, libidinous, and commit sodomy." As far as their activities were concerned, "Their chief desire is to eat, drink, worship heathen idols, and commit bestial obscenities."[25] Another of his often quoted passages concerns the physical attributes of the natives.

> I also happened to think of something I have observed many times with regard to these Indians. Their skulls are four times thicker than those of the Christians. And so

> when one wages war with them and comes to hand to
> hand fighting, one must be very careful not to hit them on
> the head with the sword, because I have seen many
> swords broken in this fashion. In addition to being thick,
> their skulls are very strong.[26]

In general, Oviedo viewed the Indians as being incapable of understanding the Catholic faith and therefore of becoming Christians.

The ability and desire of the Indians to receive salvation is at the heart of the dispute concerning the nature of the natives. In his *Historia general,* Oviedo argued that Columbus and the Spanish had now been decades in the New World. Also, there was no lack of dedicated preachers to evangelize. Therefore, if the Indians were rational beings, they should have been able to understand something as crucial as the salvation of their souls by this time. In an effort to explain this failure on their part, he contended they were not only unwilling but also incapable of understanding the message of the Catholic faith.[27] The leap between the apparent inability of the Indians to receive salvation and God's seeming desire that they therefore be enslaved by the righteous Spanish was a short one.

Because the Amerindian was "beastlike in his understanding (*entendimiento bestial*) and inclined toward evil (*mal inclinado*)," the Christian was justified in enslaving and maltreating him. In Oviedo's view, God actually desired them to come to a speedy end because of their abominable practices.[28] Although their repentance and subsequent conversion was theoretically possible, Oviedo believed they were incapable of making such a choice. By converting sinful practices into ultimate, unpardonable sins, Oviedo and his followers thereby passed judgment on an entire race of people. Las Casas, however, believed no one was outside the reach of God and reminded Oviedo that there were other people, including his own ancestors, who committed just as grave sins. God spared them, however, because of their repentance. In fact, God would judge the actions of the Christians more harshly. The Spaniards, by their robbing, killing, and plundering, had actually been the impediment to the conversion of the natives. This was the greater sin.[29]

Nevertheless, Oviedo, the historian turned theologian, passed judgment on the Indians and condemned them to eternal damnation because of their characteristics and practices.[30] The significance of the ideas of Oviedo cannot be underestimated. He was a government official, had considerable experience in the New World, and was the official historian for Spain. Those seeking justification for their deeds or beliefs could look to him as a source. His ideas became the foundation of the arguments of Sepúlveda in his later dispute with Las Casas.[31] This angered the latter greatly, as he had no love for the official historian. After his famous debate of 1550–51 with Sepúlveda over the nature of the Amerindian, Las Casas both summarized his own views and attacked those of the royal chronicler. An examination of Las Casas's writings reveals that although he disagreed with Oviedo's conclusions, he identified with his position.

Concerning the views of Oviedo, Las Casas, who obviously represented the "noble savage" school of thought, wrote, "Oviedo is not ashamed to write these lies, scattered in various passages of history, from which he stupidly promises himself immortality."[32] The Defender of the Indians also answered the charges leveled by Oviedo against the nature of the Indian: "Although these slanderous lies, falsely written against a sincere and decent people,…a people who from the very beginning were worthy of high praise for their docility, their character, and their very well established state…Oviedo nonetheless has his judge."[33] Concerning the charges of sodomy brought by Oviedo, he wrote, "Now Oviedo fabricated his history—or better his trifles—from stories told to him by…a certain sailor named Fernando Pérez, who…had never landed on Española."[34] Thus did Las Casas dispense not only with Oviedo's views of the natives but also with his veracity and claims to give an eyewitness account in writing his history.

Despite his dislike for Oviedo, a feeling that began with their first meeting in 1519, and his disagreement with his assessment of the nature of the natives and the use to which this work had been put, Las Casas ended his thought concerning the official historian by demonstrating a forgiving, pastoral attitude. Probably identifying with Oviedo prior to his own conversion, he wrote, "It is not surprising that Oviedo reviles the Indians with so many slanderous lies;…he was one of those looters who went to the mainland in 1513 at the time of Pedrarias."[35] Las Casas then recounted Oviedo's own words from his history. In this passage Oviedo brags at being a part of the pacification of the Indians, to which the priest responds, undoubt-edly remembering his own role in the pacification of Cuba, "by 'paci-fication' this sycophant means killing God's rational creatures with Turkish savagery for little or no cause, and with astounding infamy to the name Christian, to sacrifice souls to hell who might have come to know Christ."[36] Remembering again his past and how through the reading of God's word he had come to repent of his past actions, Las Casas wrote, "But may Christ be kind to me and grant them the spirit of penance for his glory, for if these sins are true, they are light and humane in comparison with those about which I must remain silent in view of the multitude, immensity, and seriousness of the cruelties they perpetrated."[37] Like Las Casas, the unrepentant *clérigo* of forty years prior, Oviedo and those he represented justified their abuse of the Indians by regarding them as incapable of receiving the gospel through reason and persuasion. Because of this inability, *encomenderos* were therefore justified in placing them "under the care of" the Spanish. According to Oviedo and those who used his argument, the natives were to blame for their own destruction because of their actions and apparent refusal to change and embrace Christianity. At the same time the Spaniards justified their own actions toward them because of their intransigence.

Another theme germane to the conversion of Las Casas is his characterization of those who exploited the natives as being blind and unable to distinguish their true abilities and inclinations. Specifically concerning Oviedo, he wrote, "Because of these brutal crimes, God has blinded his eyes, along with those of the other plunderers who were infamous for their pride, greed, brutality, lust for power, and ambition."[38] Remember it was the *clérigo* who wrote that he himself was known as a greedy man, prospering at the expense of his Indians, proud in his treatment of them, and cer-tainly filled with ambition to get ahead. It was this man who had "the darkness lifted from his eyes" and thereafter lived to defend those he had previously exploited.[39] One can almost sense the emo-tion in his writing as he continued remembering from years before his own transgressions, "in order that he [Oviedo] should not be allowed by God to know that those naked people were mild, sim-ple, and meek...or how ready and willing they were to accept the Christian religion."[40]

Finally, Las Casas confronted him with being a part of the system, profiting by it, and not being honest enough to admit it as he himself had done. He punctuated this section of rebuttal to the history of Oviedo by identifying with him, but as one who needed to repent of his beliefs. He also, however, wrote prophetically concerning Oviedo's future if he failed to repent. "Oviedo nonetheless has his judge. Christ lives, and holds a whip in his hand. Oviedo will give an account to him...But I know that I must pardon an ignorant man."[41] Here the priest was content to leave judgment in the hands of God. Las Casas recognized that he himself, before his awakening, was just as blind as Oviedo.

Before a close examination of the actual conversion of Las Casas, it is necessary to discuss the antecedents of his message in America. Las Casas may have been the most vocal and persistent advocate of justice for the oppressed, but he was neither the only nor the first. The seeds that were sown by a sermon, in what Hanke called "the first cry on behalf of human liberty in the New World," took nearly four years to bear fruit.[42]

"A Greater Sin Than the Killing of Insects"

As previously mentioned, the first four Dominicans probably arrived in the New World in September 1510. According to Las Casas, they came "to light the darkness which was then present, and which since has grown even thicker."[43] Under the leadership of Fray Pedro de Córdoba, who at twenty-eight years old was the youngest of the priests, the Dominicans settled in a straw hut on the property of a "good Christian," Pedro de Lumbreras. Significantly, Las Casas provides us with the detail that the vicar had taken the habit at Saint Stephens, in Salamanca, while still very young.[44] Apparently, Las Casas considered Córdoba a saint, and, despite the similarity of their ages, looked to him for his spiritual formation and direction. Certainly every description of Córdoba by Las Casas is favorable. After establishing their quarters, the priests began living a very simple, yet exemplary, lifestyle of piety, which contrasted with the general spiritual climate on Hispaniola.[45]

Instead of merely preaching against the corruption of the faith, which was evident to all, the Dominicans provided an example to follow. This principle would not be lost on Las Casas, who recognized example as important as proclamation. He wrote, "Every Christian on that island [Hispaniola] had perverted the Christian practices, especially in regards to fasting and practicing abstinence as required by the Church." In contrast to the typical impiety of the colonists, the Dominicans set the example: "The friars by means of their preaching, and even more through their severe penance and abstinence, brought the Spaniards to an awareness of their behavior."[46] Regarding their preaching, Córdoba was the first one to preach to the Indians the gospel message since the arrival of the Spanish. Las Casas heard Córdoba in the nearby village of Concepción de la Vega and was impressed by his message. He also expressed amazement that the majority of the Indians died without ever hearing the message of the gospel. Soon after this event, Fray Domingo de Mendoza, accompanied by other "stalwart, sturdy and dedicated religious," arrived in Santo Domingo. Those who came with him also imbibed the simple, spiritual life of the order. Both Spaniards and natives profited by their preaching and example.[47]

In this atmosphere, the Dominicans contemplated the condition of the Indian. They questioned the nature of the relationship between the Christian Spaniard and the pagan Indian. Among the first attitudes they noticed was the seeming unconcern for the Indian except as a piece of capital. Treated as animals, the natives were being exterminated by those who used them. The Dominicans also questioned why there were so few Indians yet alive after only fifteen or sixteen years of Spanish rule when initially there had been so many of them.[48]

According to Las Casas, there were two types of Spaniards. There existed those who were very cruel, "without mercy or pity, whose only desire was to get rich on the blood of the Indian." Others were not so cruel and "felt sorry for the Indians." Yet both of these "placed their own natural physical interests above the health and salvation of the exploited."[49] Only one man, Pedro de Rentería, the partner of Las Casas, was merciful toward the natives. Although Las

Casas placed himself in the category of the "not so cruel," it is note-worthy that he praised only the positive attitude of Rentería and wrote nothing about himself or his actions at the time.

Perhaps as an example of the power of repentance, Las Casas provided us with the example of Juan Garcés. This murderer had fled into the mountains after knifing his wife, who was from a prominent native family of Concepción. He lived there in exile several years until he heard of the arrival of the Dominicans. Because of their example of living a holy life, he went to them, repented of his past deeds, asked for forgiveness, and expressed a desire to serve God the rest of his life. "They accepted him with kindness after seeing signs of his conversion and hatred of his past life and desire to do penance."[50] Like Las Casas, he also had taken part in the "execrable cruelties" committed against the natives and was ashamed of his actions. The fact that the Dominicans, as God's representatives, could give absolution to one such as Garcés was not lost upon the future Dominican. Atonement could be made for past actions through repentance and penance.

The priests soon decided to do something about what they saw. They decided to use their most effective weapon, moral and spiritual arguments, to stop the destruction of the Amerindians. The Dominicans began to pray, keep vigils, and seek guidance as to the best way to fight this injustice. They had to speak for those who had no other defense. They also realized the difficulty of their task. Those who lived off the labor of another would not easily be changed. After prayer and reflection they decided to preach that those who oppressed the Indians were guilty of mortal sin, and their reward would be "going to hell."[51] The question now became who would preach such a condemnatory sermon.

After much discussion among the Dominicans, they all agreed on the content of the sermon and chose their best preacher, Antón Montesino, to deliver it. Las Casas described him: "[Montesino] had the gift of preaching, he was sharp in rebuking sin, and above all, very choleric in his words and sermons, which was very efficient and thought to reap great results."[52] The novelty of his message, which was the first of its type in the New World, was that the killing of the natives was more sinful and would receive greater condemnation from God than the "killing of insects." This message reflected the moral outrage of the Dominicans and was the culmination of nearly two years of observation, praying, and effort to stop the persecution and destruction of the natives. Montesino was to deliver this message on the fourth week of Advent, 1511, coinciding with the event in St. John's Gospel in which John the Baptist answers the question of the Pharisees with the expression, "I am the voice crying out in the wilderness."[53] Las Casas provides us with the only text of this sermon. Although he does not appear to have been present at its preaching, he certainly would have had access to written copies of the message even before he wrote his *Historia* in the Dominican monastery.[54] The enormous impact of this sermon not only on Las Casas but on the entire theological-juridical discussion is obvious by its far-reaching effects. Las Casas recorded it as follows:

> You are all in mortal sin! You live in it and you die in it! Why? Because of the cruelty and tyranny you use with these innocent people. Tell me, with what right, with what justice, do you hold these Indians in such cruel and horrible servitude? On what authority have you waged such detestable wars on these people, in their mild, peaceful lands, in which you have consumed such infinitudes of them, wreaking upon them this death and unheard-of havoc? How is it that you hold them so crushed and exhausted, giving them nothing to eat, nor any treatment for their diseases, which you cause them to be infected with through the surfeit of their toils, so that they "die on you" [as you say]—you mean, you kill them—mining gold for you day after day? And what care do you take that anyone catechize them, so that they may come to know their God and Creator, be baptized, hear Mass, observe Sundays and Holy Days? Are they not human beings? Have they no rational souls? Are you not obligated to love them as you love yourselves? Do you not understand this? Do you not grasp this? How is it that you sleep so soundly, so lethargically? Know for a certainty that in the state in which you are you can no more be saved than Moors or Turks who have not, nor wish to have, the faith of Jesus Christ.[55]

Montesino preached this sermon to the most important people on all Hispaniola, including Governor Diego Columbus. After confronting the Spanish with their sins and challenging them to rethink their Christian responsibilities, the preacher left the meeting amid a hum of controversy and returned to his straw hut to eat his thin cabbage soup. The offended met at the home of the governor to enjoy a more substantial repast.[56]

The significance of this message cannot be overestimated. This "first cry on behalf of human liberty," in the form of a sermon, drew the battle lines and framed the basic issues for the upcoming struggle into which Las Casas placed himself.[57] Carro believed that "the voice of P. Montesino, in 1511, was not an isolated voice, the product of overactive zeal, without a theological-juridical base, and critical of his country." Through his questions, which thundered out at the hearers, "we see reflected the total Thomistic theological-juridical tradition, we view the origin of human rights, and the origin of international law, we see the first antecedents of the New Laws of the Indies, which became fleshed out through the teaching of the theologians."[58] The initial results of the message were not as impressive, however. Las Casas reports that the reaction among the hearers was mixed, "some with astonishment, some quite out of their senses, some hardened in their attitudes, and some feeling sorry"; yet, significantly, he concluded, "no one, as I understand it, was converted."[59]

Meeting with the governor, the Christians did not debate the significance of the sermon, the questions raised, or even the manner of delivery, but rather they viewed Montesino as preaching treason. They challenged his authority to question what they personally did with the "property" the Crown had placed at their disposal. According to the colonists, many of whom were in the employ of the Crown, Montesino preached against the lordship of the king in the Indies. They did not, or would not, recognize that Montesino did not challenge the Spanish usufruct of the New World or the monarchy's right to exact tribute from the Indians, but merely criticized the brutal treatment of the natives.[60]

The major thrust of Montesino's sermon, however, was evangelism and the need for the colonists to demonstrate the gospel by their actions to the natives. The result of the mistreatment of the natives was their consequent death, both physically and spiritually. This death was the result of greed, avarice, and lack of love on the part of the colonists, and one that occurred without the Indians having had the opportunity to hear and witness the gospel. The Christians (including, presumably, the Franciscans who had been on the island since 1502) were providing no opportunity for training in spiritual matters, thereby neglecting this responsibility. In fact, they were negative examples because of their mistreatment of the indigenous peoples. Evangelism was the rationale for their presence (Alexander's donation), and it became the focus of the Dominicans. The fact that they announced that the colonists were in mortal sin because of their lack of concern for the natives attested to the theological foundation of their protest. The priests were, therefore, not only concerned with the treatment and use of the Indians but also with their mortal souls. Physical death of the natives was the result and not the cause of the Spanish failure in evangelism and Christian concern. Without emphasizing the theological nature of the Dominicans' message, the priests would be simply political reformers, traitors to the Crown as charged by the offended officials, and, perhaps worst of all, guilty of hypocrisy to their order and to their faith. Above all, the Dominicans' desire was to include the Indian in the Church. At the same time, through their example and works, the Spaniards themselves should demonstrate they were a part of the Church. Evangelization, not political justification, provided the basis for the Dominicans' message.[61]

After discussion among themselves, the offended Christians decided to go to the Dominican vicar, Pedro de Córdoba, and register their protest. Upon arriving at the convent and being met by Córdoba, the governor and his group angrily demanded to speak with Montesino. After tempers cooled, Montesino spoke with them. They demanded to know how he could preach against the fact that the king awarded them the Indians and that they had been won by much fighting. If he did not retract his words, they would go to his superiors. Montesino replied that the reason he had preached this "new doctrine," as they called it, was for their own benefit. This message was the product of the collective thought and feeling of all four of the Dominicans. He added, "They had decided to preach the truth of the Gospel because *it was necessary for the salvation of all the Spaniards as well as the Indians of this island.* They had seen so many perish without any more care than if they were beasts of the field."[62] Without the preaching and living out of the gospel message both Spaniards and natives were perishing without salvation—the Indians because they had not heard the message, the Spaniards because they did not live it. His admonition to repent, however, fell on deaf ears. If they were to obey the message of the preaching they would have had to give up the native labor by which they acquired their gold. This they apparently were incapable of doing. The colonists left when the Dominicans agreed to reconsider the message.

The next Sunday the church was again full as the offended colonists believed they would hear a retraction by a repentant priest. They heard no such thing. Montesino repeated what he had preached the previous Sunday. He emphasized that a Spaniard could not save his soul while oppressing another. Furthermore, the priests would no longer hear their confessions as long as they continued to exploit the natives. Needless to say, these words did not impress or convert the colonists, who again left grumbling and determined to do something about these Dominicans.[63]

Years later, in a reflective moment when remembering and chronicling this event, Las Casas identified himself and his attitude at the time not with the Dominicans, but with the colonists who were blinded by their own greed and ambition. "It is a dangerous thing, and worthy of many tears, when persons are caught up in sin. This is especially so when they have improved themselves at the expense of defrauding others." The penitent priest had at one time advanced on the back of others. Recalling his own epiphany, which would soon occur, and the change that was worked in his life at that moment, he added, "it is difficult for them to change by human actions alone. God must do a great miracle."[64] At the center of his thoughts and words was always the one moment in which he received his sight and changed the course of his life.

As previously mentioned, it is unclear if Las Casas heard the message as it was preached. Certainly, however, he soon learned of it. One of the friars who heard his confession shortly after this event denied him absolution from his sins because Las Casas was an *encomendero*. Despite this rebuff, however, Las Casas was not yet convinced or convicted of the justice of the priestly claims. These events continued to trouble his conscience, however, as they mounted up and as he witnessed the Christians commit more atrocities in the name of the God they served.

News of Montesino's message spread quickly to Spain and to his superior in the order, Antonio de Loaysa, the Dominican provincial. Bowing to political pressure, he wrote at least two letters to the friars on Hispaniola ordering them to refrain from preaching on this matter.[65] Recognizing the challenge to his authority and treasury, King Ferdinand also wrote to Governor Diego Columbus instructing him to send back to Spain any priest who preached such doctrines.[66]

It is obvious by this directive that Ferdinand chose to align with the colonists in this dispute with the religious reformers. Unlike the more pious Isabella, he seemed to have been more influenced by the acquisition of wealth than the saving of souls. Although Spain had been in the Indies only twenty years, neither the colonies nor their inhabitants were of particular interest to the monarch as long as things went smoothly and the revenue continued. In comparison to the rest of his kingdom, the New World possessions were of such minor importance that two key individuals, Bishop Juan de Fonseca, the king's main advisor to the Indies, and Lope de Conchillos, Ferdinand's secretary, handled all the affairs for this region, and economic benefit outweighed spiritual and humanitarian considerations.[67] Perhaps it is not surprising that in the distribution of Indians, these individuals received the largest share. The king received 1430, Fonseca 244, and Lope de Conchillos 264. Other colonists who were close advisors to the king also received an equally large *repartimiento.* The call to eliminate the system that divided the land and natives among the Spaniards and make subsequent restitution to the natives therefore met with strong opposition among powerful forces.[68]

In his *Historia,* Las Casas initially explained the actions of the monarch in his typical fashion by blaming the apparent disinterest and lack of support for the reformist cause, not on greed or lack of concern, but on bad counsel. We shall notice how, in the course of his life and writings, Las Casas became ever more confrontational and direct in his challenge to the reigning monarch. After the letters that rebuked Montesino and demonstrated the lack of support for the Dominicans in the Indies, Las Casas attributed this royal response to poor advice. "You see how easy it is to deceive Kings, how destructive to the kingdom to listen to poor advice, and how oppression rules where truth is silent." Las Casas also gave a further rationale for the ruler's behavior: "He was old and tired."[69] The actions of another group, however, were not as easily explained.

The behavior of the Franciscans in this early controversy puzzled many, including Las Casas. As mentioned, they arrived in the New World with Ovando in 1502. Initially, they established convents and were somewhat successful at evangelization. Resistance by the colonists caused them to change their focus, however, and now the order emphasized the education of the sons of the local nobility.[70] Their attitude seemed to be—and there is very little evidence concerning their activities—that the destruction of the Indians was some sort of divine retribution for idolatry.[71]

Las Casas characterizes their leader, Espinal, as being somewhat limited in knowledge, though well-meaning. The colonists chose him to represent their cause in Spain, and he went apparently unaware of the motivations of those he represented. According to the former *encomendero,* the Franciscan was also unaware that the colonists were guilty of mortal sin and under compulsion to make amends for their activity. Apparently the friar did not know exactly what was happening, since Indians were allotted to those who provided materially for the Franciscans and did not work directly for the order. Therefore, the Franciscans were not directly involved in their exploitation. Las Casas, who knew Espinal well, attributed his actions to ignorance and not malice.[72]

The Laws of Burgos

The king decided to call for a meeting to resolve the issues now boiling in the Indies. The colonists, sparing no expense, sent the Franciscan friar Espinal to Spain to represent their interests. The Dominicans sent their best preacher, Montesino. The actual meeting itself is described by Las Casas in some detail and with characteristic sarcasm (for example, he describes the entry of Espinal into the court: "and the king received him as if he were the angel Saint Michael just sent from God").[73] The result of these meetings was the enactment of the Laws of Burgos, promulgated December 27, 1512.[74]

These laws were explicitly intended to define the responsibilities of the *encomenderos,* yet in reality they articulated the condition of the Indies as they actually existed. Most important, they provided no method of enforcement for the violation of the mandates. In other words, these directives were another case of royal direction without any real teeth to assure their enforcement. Compliance with the provisions of these laws was left in the hands of the very ones they were designed to limit. Thus, in practice they did nothing to ameliorate conditions.[75]

Fray Bartolomé, writing over forty years after the passage of these laws, criticized them severely. At this point he recognized they had the effect of legally justifying the destruction of the natives. "These laws, some thirty in number, some, actually the majority, were wicked, cruel, tyrannical, and contrary to natural law, and which no reason, argument, or fiction may in any manner excuse. Others were impossible [to observe], irrational, and worse than barbaric." Continuing his theme of excusing the monarchy for these poor decisions, he added, "These were not the laws of the King."[76]

This condemnation of the system was not new, however. This same theme recurs in the writings of Las Casas from the beginning. One of the most significant aspects of the life of Las Casas is that his message did not change over the years. In his first written denouncement of the system in 1516, Bartolomé wrote: "There are twelve causes for this destruction [of the Indian] which have occurred since the beginning, [these twelve] can be reduced to two:...too much work due to the greed of the Spanish, and poor treatment."[77] In another *memorial* of the same year, he wrote, "The reason the Indians died and continue to die is mainly because of the system of giving them to individuals."[78] This principal reason then leads to the other ways in which they are killed, especially forcing them to live apart from their home in villages created by the Spanish. From the beginning, Las Casas condemned the idea of placing the natives in close proximity to the Spaniards, either for conversion or for service. He saw the problem inherent in this situation from the beginning.

According to the Crown, the main problem for the effective spreading of the gospel to the natives was their lack of proximity to the colonists. The Christians again used evangelism as the pretext for placing the natives in *reducciónes*. Las Casas constantly rejected this idea, not only as poor evangelism, as already noted, but also as poor economics. The moving of the Indians, even for short distances, resulted in their death. Thus, the bringing of Indians to live in close proximity to the Spanish caused their destruction and eventually would destroy the labor supply. The practical Las Casas used not only spiritual but also economic reasons in his arguments.[79]

The Laws of Burgos served to further strengthen the legal claim of the *encomenderos* to the use of their "property" and frustrated the Dominicans, who sought real reform in the system. Although the laws contained some provisions for the better treatment of the Indians, such as that the Spanish should no longer physically or verbally insult the natives or call them "dogs," and should provide hammocks for them to sleep in, they failed to stop the destruction of the Amerindian. Basically, living conditions and treatment remained the same.[80]

Slowly the events of his life began to influence the priest. Las Casas reflected on what he had seen and heard. The sermons of the Dominicans rang in his ears, and the injustices he saw convinced him of the veracity of their condemnation. The supposed "reforms" had accomplished nothing. The reality of what he saw, as well as his own actions, failed to coincide with the Christianity he professed.

At the beginning of 1513, about the same time as the Laws of Burgos went into effect, Padre Las Casas received the commission as chaplain to accompany Pánfilo de Narváez's expedition to pacify the Indians on Cuba. This island was under the authority of Governor Diego Velázquez, whom Diego Columbus had recently appointed. Some of the young priest's most memorable and life-changing events occurred in Cuba. Las Casas believed the Cuban experience to be among the defining moments of his life. It led directly to the point of his complete change of life. He would refer to events in Cuba many times in the coming years, and they would guide him to his first conversion and prophetic call. During these campaigns, Las Casas came face to face with the full impact of the Spanish slaughter of the natives and began to empathize with their plight. In his writings Las

Theodore de Bry, *Columbus in Spain with Bartolomé de las Casas.*
Private collection. Snark/Art Resource.

Casas identifies specific personal experiences and describes specific individuals in an attempt to involve the reader in the action. His goal is to personalize the slaughter. When possible, he names the Indians to make them appear as "people of flesh and blood" and not mere statistics.[81] The dehumanizing slaughter of the "pacification" campaigns always led to death in such numbers that the actual suffering of the individual could be easily overlooked since mind-numbing statistics tend to desensitize suffering on a personal level. The priest's writings do not allow this luxury but, rather, lead the reader to experience the personal pain of the individual.

One specific individual that Las Casas introduces on a personal basis is Hatuey, a refugee from Hispaniola. Hatuey was a leading *cacique,* or local chief, who had fled to Cuba with some of his people to escape the Spaniards. Upon hearing that they were now coming to that island, he gathered his people together to warn them and to let them know what to expect. In an attempt to prevent the Spaniards from coming to the island, he spoke to his village, as recorded by Las Casas: "'They [the Spanish] have a god whom they worship and adore, and it is in order to get that god from us so that they can worship him that they conquer and kill us.'" Hatuey then pointed to a basket full of gold trinkets and jewelry and continued, "'Here is the god of the Christians.'" The natives then danced until they were exhausted in an effort to pay homage to this god and to make him keep the Spanish away from their home.[82] Unfortunately, this exercise was futile. Eventually, the Spaniards captured the *cacique* and most of his people. Before the chief's execution for rebellion, a Franciscan friar explained Christianity to him and asked if he desired to spend eternity in heaven or hell. One can almost sense Las Casas weeping as he related what happened next. "The lord Hatuey thought for a short time and asked the friar if Christians went to heaven." After the priest replied that only the good ones make this trip, "he retorted, without need for further reflection, that, if that was the case, he chose to go to hell to ensure that he would never again have to clap eyes on those cruel brutes."[83] Sarcastically, Las Casas commented that this was the reputation earned for the Christian faith as a consequence of the actions of the so-called Christians in the New World. He concluded his section on the "reduction" of Cuba by recounting that many of the Indians not only committed suicide by hanging themselves, but also hung their children, or aborted them, in order to keep them out of the hands of the Spaniards.[84]

Other incidents that lodged in the memory of Las Casas occurred amid the slaughter of thousands of peaceful natives. As Narváez and his troops approached the village of Caonao, they came upon two thousand unarmed Indians seated on the grass awaiting their arrival. Nearby was a *bohío,* or large straw house, containing an additional five hundred. Las Casas himself was in another part of the town. Suddenly mounted troops attacked and began a merciless slaughter of these innocents. The *clérigo* rushed up to Narváez, who sat stoically on his horse, and yelled at him to stop the carnage. Although Narváez could easily have ordered his troops to cease the killing, he did nothing. The priest then tried to protect the five hundred in the *bohío,* but the Spanish arrived and began to kill them also. Full of both anger and grief, Las Casas baptized a young man who fell into his arms to die. This man, disemboweled with a sword and holding his intestines in his hands, received the sacrament and died.

With palpable emotion, Las Casas recounted the story of another individual whose right shoulder was cut off by a Spanish sword. He lay there in pain and misery for about a week until the Spanish and the priest left the village. Remembering forty years later, he wrote, "The cleric kept within himself much regret for not treating the man with a kind of turtle-oil paste, which he used to treat so many others. This ointment could have sealed the wound which may then have healed in about a week." This man's face must have haunted Las Casas because he continued: "Maybe if he [Las Casas] had replaced the bone in its socket, sewing up his entire right side with a mending needle, he would have gotten better." Regretfully he concluded, "Finally, nothing else was known of him. He could not possibly have survived."[85] Amid the slaughter of so many, the names and faces of individuals stood out after all these years. Their faces and deaths continued to haunt the priest until the end of his life. Although shaken by these events, Las Casas was able to busy himself with the pursuits of wealth.

Soon after the end of the campaign that brought Cuba fully under Spanish control, Governor Velázquez awarded land, and Indians to work it, to Las Casas and his friend, Pedro de Rentería.

Rentería was not only pious and devout, but also a good business-man. Las Casas then devoted himself to agriculture, cattle raising, and mining enterprises. Thus, Las Casas became an *encomendero* and began to live off of the labor of his Indians. Although he treated well the Indians he held in *encomienda,* he neglected their religious training and was more concerned with the profit he could obtain from their labor.[86] In this attitude he was representative of those *encomenderos* whose goal was to maximize profits through the acquisition of gold, regardless of the human cost.

According to Las Casas, greed was the motivating factor behind the Spaniards' abuse of the Indians. This greed almost cost the Spaniards their own lives as they nearly starved to death. Use of the Indians to mine gold instead of to produce food soon had disastrous results: "Greed made it so that the Spaniards did not cultivate the land while they did harvest the gold which they had done nothing to produce."[87] Thus, even the Spaniards were hungry. Of course, the natives received the least food and were responsible for the most work; thus, they died the quickest. They were required not only to mine the gold, but also, on their own time, to grow their own food. The weak, elderly, and infirm were left in the villages. With no one to care for them, they died by the thousands. As Las Casas traveled on his priestly rounds throughout Cuba, he constantly heard the natives cry, *"hambre, hambre"* (hungry, hungry) wherever he walked.[88] These specific events troubled the mind of the young cleric and would be important stepping stones leading to the repentance, conversion experience, and prophetic call that would take place on Pentecost Sunday, 1514.

CHAPTER THREE

The Darkness Turns to Light (1514–16)

The conversion of a soul is the miracle of a moment.
The manufacture of a saint is the work of a lifetime.[1]

It is within the context of the events just described that the turning point in the life of Bartolomé de las Casas took place. This event occurred just before Pentecost Sunday, 1514, while he was on the island of Cuba. All his previous life experiences were prologue and all significant future events pointed back to this one. To this moment he constantly referred in both his writing and preaching. At this moment in his life he recognized and accepted the call on his life. This chapter examines the specific events surrounding this experience and its immediate results. After this epiphany, Las Casas repented of his former way of life and began to attack the system of which he had been a part. This is sometimes referred to as his first conversion, to distinguish it from his decision to enter the Dominican Order in 1522, his second conversion.

Psychologists have defined conversion as a reorientation of self. In most general terms, one's self, or identity, is replaced by another.[2] There can be religious conversions as well as those that have nothing to do with religion. Those who study this process agree on four major criteria in a definition of conversion: "First, conversion is a profound change in self. Second, this change is not simply a matter of maturation, but most typically is identified with a decision, sudden or gradual, to accept another perspective within which the new self is to be identified. Third, this change in itself constitutes a change in the entire mode of one's life—a new centering of concern, interest, and

57

action. Fourth, and finally this new change is seen as 'higher' or as an emancipation from a previous dilemma or less valuable life."[3]

The experience of Las Casas certainly fit this definition. He changed his entire self for another and committed himself to this new way of life. This change was most definitely a sudden conversion, though events did precede and assist in bringing it about.

There are basically two types of conversion. The sudden conversion occurs when the person feels himself or herself in the grip of forces beyond his or her control. Often this experience presents itself in a moment of crisis to which the person surrenders the self, and tends to accompany feelings of guilt or unworthiness. Gradual conversion is more subtle. This type of experience is generally the product of an actual search for answers. The process is also more cognitive and includes a gradual acceptance of the new life over the old, with no clearly defined moment of change.[4] Las Casas most closely fits into the former category, although this does not seem to account for the myriad of events that led to the moment of decision.

The experiences in the life of Las Casas before his first conversion, especially those narrated in the first chapter, had a definite effect on his mind and being. Otherwise, he would not have recalled them forty years later in writing about his life. Despite this time of "incubation or preparation," however, there was also a definite moment of conversion. At this moment he received a commission or calling, or what Henry James might call a "twice born" experience. James explains that some "melancholy temperaments" are literally compelled by a crisis situation to accept or to realize a faith in an instant.[5]

Las Casas did face a crisis; what he saw and experienced did not coincide with his faith. Either his faith must not be valid or he had to align his practice with its tenets. Thus, the crisis was brought on by the reading of Scripture and consequent confrontation between the clearly directive nature of the word of God and the actions of one who claimed to believe, practice, and even teach this faith. In response to this crisis, Las Casas reaffirmed his faith and acted in accord with its tenets. He repented and changed his way of life to conform to his beliefs.

At this time, the future Dominican was not only an *encomendero,* as we have discussed, but also a priest. As such, he was responsible for the celebration of Mass on the upcoming Pentecost

Sunday. While studying a text and some previous sermons in preparation for this service, he began to reflect on those events in his life that contradicted the message in the sermon he was about to preach. Those experiences began to weigh on his conscience. Through reflection, prayer, and meditation, he realized what he personally had done, the evils of the system in which he was involved, and what he must now do. His firsthand account of these events written many years later explain his thoughts. He appeared to be brutally honest in both his self-praise and condemnation. As usual, he wrote about himself in the third person.

> Diego Velázquez and the group of Spaniards with him left the port of Xagua to go and found a settlement of Spaniards in the province, where they established the town called Sancti Espiritus. Apart from Bartolomé de Las Casas, there was not a single cleric or friar on the whole island, except for one in the town of Baracoa. The feast of Pentecost was coming up. So he agreed to leave his home on the Arimaó River a league from Xagua where his holdings were and go and say mass for them and preach to them on that feast. Las Casas looked over the previous sermons he had preached on that feast and his other sermons for that season. He began to meditate on some passages of Sacred Scripture. If my memory serves me, the first and most important was from Ecclesiasticus 34:18 ff.:
>
> Unclean is the offering sacrificed by an oppressor. [Such] mockeries of the unjust are not pleasing [to God]. The Lord is pleased only by those who keep to the way of truth and justice. The Most High does not accept the gifts of unjust people, He does not look well upon their offerings. Their sins will not be expiated by repeat-sacrifices. The one whose sacrifice comes from the goods of the poor is like one who kills his neighbor. The one who sheds blood and the one who defrauds the laborer are kin and kind.
>
> He began to reflect on the misery, the forced labor the Indians had to undergo. He was helped in this by what he had heard and experienced on the island of Hispaniola, by what the Dominicans preached continually—no one

could, in good conscience, hold the Indians in *encomienda*, and those friars would not confess and absolve any who so held them—a preaching Las Casas had refused to accept...

He spent some days thinking about the situation, each day getting surer and surer from what he read concerning what was legal and what was actual, measuring the one by the other, until he came to the same truth by himself. Everything in these Indies that was done to the Indians was tyrannical and unjust. Everything he read to firm up his judgment he found favorable, and he used to say strongly that from the very moment he began to dispel the darkness of that ignorance, he never read a book in Latin or Spanish—a countless number over the span of forty-two years—where he did not find some argument or authority to prove or support the justice of those Indian peoples, and to condemn the injustices done to them.[6]

A thoughtful reading of this passage indicates that Las Casas's conversion resulted from his belief that one can be touched or reached by God while reading Scripture. Meditation was the catalyst that caused him to reflect on his life and actions. He now recognized his need for change in order for him to be acceptable to God. He then filtered the attitudes and actions of his life up to that point through the prism of these biblical passages. Bartolomé wrote that after "meditating upon some passages of Sacred Scripture," especially the deuterocanonical book of Ecclesiasticus, he began to apply the word of God to the situations he experienced. He applied his theology to the practical and saw a paradox. There existed an inconsistency in the direction he received from the Scripture, and therefore in what he must preach as a priest and in his daily practices. He must then harmonize his actions with his preaching. Las Casas saw the ethical dichotomy and inconsistency between his beliefs and his actions and could no longer live in two worlds—the world of the *encomendero*, who made his living from the backs of the poor, and the world of the *clérigo*, whose offering he now viewed as unacceptable to God because of its uncleanness. He was no longer among the "just," but now must, according to the definition given in Ecclesiasticus, place himself among the "unjust," or those not pleasing to God. Not only was his life not pleasing to God, but also there could be no expiation, no sacrifice, no way to make this sin all right with God if he continued in it. The Dominican who refused him absolution and therefore declared him to be in mortal sin was right. It was as if the Scripture held a mirror to his face and showed him how he looked to God. The picture was not pretty. God equated this *encomendero,* despite the fact he was a benevolent one, with "one who kills his neighbor." Murder was a mortal sin, and the one who practiced it could not expect to live in the presence of God forever more. This was his fate, according to the Scripture he encountered, if he did not repent and change his life.

This realization applied not only to himself but also to all those engaged in this practice. If he, being a good *encomendero,* could not achieve salvation by continuing in this practice, how much more difficult must it be for those who were really evil? He realized that the system itself bred the conditions that led to death for all those engaged in it. The Indian was condemned to eternal separation from God, because he would not hear the message from the Spaniard who treated him so brutally. The Spaniard (Christian) likewise was condemned because of his refusal to repent from the mortal sin in which he was engaged. Death, both physical and, most important, spiritual, was the natural result of this injustice.[7] Once armed with the truth in his own life, the priest, and increasingly the mouthpiece of God, or prophet, then became concerned for the others who were likewise damned. All of the experiences over the past twelve years returned to his memory, and he knew he had to make a change in his manner of life. Injustice in one's own life must first be eliminated before preaching and attempting to bring justice to others. Las Casas knew that his ministry would be ineffective if he preached the gospel but did not evidence it through his own life.

It is necessary here to make a brief theological distinction between conversion of those who are unbelievers, an action that leads to salvation of the eternal soul and membership in the Church, and the conversion of Christians, such as Las Casas, which also implies salvation. Las Casas continually sought to evangelize, to bring the good news, the gospel, the message of Christ, to the Indian. Indeed, he reminds us continually, this is the primary justification for the Spanish presence in the New World. At the heart of this theology is Las Casas's conviction, based on a sound biblical foundation, that God has chosen persons from every nation to come to a knowledge of Christ. This is the conversion of the unbeliever. He wrote:

> It was due to the will and work of Christ, the head of the Church, that God's chosen should be called, should be culled from every race, every tribe, every language, every corner of the world. Thus, no race, no nation on this entire globe would be left totally untouched by the free gift of divine grace. Some among them, be they few or many, are to be taken into eternal life. We must hold this to be true also of our Indian nations.[8]

Of course, if they were chosen to receive the gospel, that presupposes that they were rational beings, made in the image and likeness of God, and therefore capable of accepting the sacrifice of Christ. This is not trying to impose twenty-first-century Protestant theology on Las Casas. His goal was not just to "get them saved" but baptized and into the Catholic Church. The view of the Church in the sixteenth century followed that of Cyprian: "outside the Church there is no salvation." This position was refined by Aquinas, who asserted that to be saved, one needed to believe in the incarnation, the redemption, and the Trinity.[9] Las Casas, and the Salamancan School, recognized the uniqueness of the Indies, the discovery of which certainly upset the scheme of their previously nicely configured world. Their beliefs as to whether the Indians were saved or not before they heard the gospel need not concern us here. Las Casas, specifically stating his views concerning predestination, wrote in the prologue to his *Historia* that God had chosen some from all nations for salvation. Although all are called, Christ's atonement was unlimited and God alone knows those whom he has chosen. No person or theology can exclude them from God's kingdom. The responsibility of the Church is to bring the message; the results are in God's hands.[10] But what of the Christian Spaniards?

Las Casas was also very much concerned with what Gutiérrez calls "the salvation of the faithful,"[11] or what Anton Peter labels a "double conversion."[12] Both agree that the main thrust of Las Casas's message was evangelism, but he also demanded that justice accompany Christian teaching. Those who professed Christianity but did not evidence its demands on their lives were in as much mortal danger as the pagan. In a letter to the then-confessor to Emperor Charles V, Father Bartolomé de Carranza, Las Casas wrote that it was deceitful to think that the *encomiendas* and *repartimientos* were established for the teaching of doctrine to the Indians. By this point in his life he had come to this realization. He was sure that the "worldly laymen who came in those days were vicious idiots," and they needed salvation as much as the Indians who had never heard of idols or other vices that might prevent them from receiving the gospel. They certainly were incapable of teaching the natives anything about Christianity.[13] In a letter to the bishop of Charcas, Las Casas wrote that those individuals who die in a state of not having been absolved of their sins (as he was before his conversion) and not repenting and making restitution were damned. He wrote that "[the *encomenderos*] will go to hell along with their confessors, and the bishops who appointed them."[14] Thus, not only the ignorant infidel but also the Christian who was not living according to the standards of the gospel were unable to receive salvation. We may, therefore, interpret Las Casas's conversion from the perspective of his being a member of the Church, a Christian, but not living according to the tenets of the gospel. Therefore, he was living a life indistinguishable from that of an unbeliever. What he then was converted to was a penitent person who received absolution and was now at peace with God. To maintain this relationship with God and assure his ultimate salvation, Las Casas must now demonstrate his faith by his works, and work for justice for the oppressed. Thus, though nominally a Christian, he had been living a lie. He was like those mentioned in St. Matthew's Gospel who cried out "Lord, Lord," but were not permitted into the kingdom because they failed to do the will of the Father (Matt 7:21).[15] Difficulties arise, however, when the doctrine of social conversion, which is the second half of Peter's double conversion, is emphasized at the expense of orthodox Christianity.

After discussing the two types of conversion, personal and social, Peter then makes the transition from Las Casas to the liberation theology of today. He believes that Las Casas and his social conversion are applicable to the present theology and practice. Reflecting the theological ideas of Gutiérrez, he asks, "How can we announce the God of love in the midst of the reality of Latin America? How do you make the poor and oppressed, whose human dignity and self worth is systematically destroyed, understand that God loves them?" His answer—and here he compares this theology with that of Las Casas—is that the Church must identify itself physically and spiritually with the poor. The Church, like Las Casas, must become a visible sign of the unconditional love of Christ. There must be a "hermeneutical conversion," that is, the Scripture must be viewed from the perspective of the poor. This interpretation will result in an "epistemological rupture" in which the evolution of daily practice out of doctrine is converted to the justification of practice through scriptural support.[16] Therefore, it turns the previous manner of "doing theology" around, placing practice above dogma.

Peter and his mentor Gutiérrez view the gospel from the eyes of the poor. Indeed, Gutiérrez makes the statement that the "poor are preferred by God."[17] The concern of both Peter and Gutiérrez, like that of Las Casas, is to bring the gospel to the poor of the world. They work in that context and reflect that perspective. Peter emphasizes that the poor are the location in which Christ meets the individual and this, therefore, is a privileged position to be in.[18] Although it is not the intent of this work to criticize the doctrines of liberation theology, which reflect a specific theology relatively new to Christian tradition, orthodox teaching emphasizes that Christ does not favor one class of persons over the other. The wealthy can also be moved to compassion and to encounter Christ. What Las Casas and traditional orthodox Christianity emphasize is the fact that justice is more valuable than gold to rich and poor alike. Too often the pursuit of wealth becomes a stumbling block for those who should be searching after justice. It is the love of money, not money itself, which is the root of all sorts of evil (1 Tim 6:10). The desire for wealth, not the wealth itself, was what fundamentally destroyed the Indians. As Bartolomé wrote, "Christ did not come into the world to die for gold, but to suffer for persons, so that they may be saved."[19] Scripture does make it clear that it is easier for the poor to come to know God, but their poverty does not somehow make them more privileged. They may have fewer distractions and more readily recognize their spiritual need as a result of their material need. The responsibility of the rich is to care for the poor. Therefore, they have a greater responsibility. Peter is accurate in his assessment that good deeds must follow salvation. Justice must accompany the gospel. These are the two faces of Christianity: salvation by means of the gospel, and then reforming or transforming society through deeds of justice and ending oppression. Yet, this does not somehow place the poor in a privileged or preferred position relative to the gospel.

After reading and meditating on Scripture, Las Casas knew he needed to change. Although it only took a moment for Las Casas to realize his sinful state, the outworking of this realization took the rest of his life as experience and scriptural revelation illuminated not only his own life and practice but also the injustice in the society around him. This illumination caused him to continue to read and study and to recognize that all that had been done to the Indians was unjust. What Las Casas now understood was that he was part of a corrupt system. The blindness to this fact is what left him. Henceforth he would be alert not only to the sins of commission, or his own reprehensible actions, but also to the sins of omission. The latter involve not doing what one ought to do, either by feigning ignorance or by looking the other way.[20] He now recognized his responsibility to act and not passively enjoy a system that brought him benefits at the expense of others. The text was the catalyst for the crisis that brought these thoughts into focus, but the preceding events leading up to this specific moment were also part of the process.

The Process of Conversion Begins

Las Casas began to divest himself of his material possessions in an orderly and consistent manner in response to his enlightenment. As he explained his encounter with God's word, "He [Las Casas] then made the decision to preach his conclusion, but since his holding Indians meant holding a contradiction of his own preaching he determined to give them up so as to be free to condemn allotments."[21] He determined to give the Indians he held in *encomienda* back to Governor Velázquez, although he knew they would probably die, as Velázquez would just give them to someone else who would not treat them as well.[22] If his transformation had not been sudden and dramatic, and Las Casas had not been concerned with immediately matching his beliefs with his actions, he most probably would have made more profitable arrangements before announcing his intention to the governor. Also, due to his paternalistic nature, he might have made specific arrangements for another Spaniard to care for his Indians instead of just turning them over to Velázquez. This was the logical attempt by a man to live according to his convictions and discharge his responsibilities in an exemplary manner as he became aware of them.

Las Casas owned this allotment in partnership with an honest, pious man, Pedro de Rentería. He was away at the time on an expedition to buy pigs and corn to make their farm more profitable. Had the priest known beforehand about his conversion and planned this to happen, he never would have let his partner go on such an expedition. He did go to the governor, however. "He stated that no one in that situation [as an *encomendero*] *could be saved,* and he stated he intended to preach this *to escape the danger,* and to do what his priesthood required."[23] Las Casas then gave the Indians back to the governor but asked for the business to be confidential until Rentería returned.

As expected, this revelation shocked the governor, who did what he could to change the padre's mind. What stunned Velázquez as much as anything was the fact that at this time the friar was not a member of the mendicant Order of Dominicans. Therefore, he was allowed to have wealth and property. Las Casas also had a growing reputation for being prosperous and even greedy. What happened that he should now suddenly give up the source of this growing wealth? How did this miraculous, sudden, and unexpected change occur? He said he would give Las Casas two weeks to think his decision over. The response of the newly enlightened priest was, "if I ever repent of the decision I broached to you, if I ever want to hold Indians again...if you accept my plea to have them, even if I wept blood, may God be the one to punish you severely, may God never forgive this sin."[24] The effect of this decision and subsequent example caused respect for Las Casas to grow on the island, and treatment toward some of the Indians improved.

As Las Casas concluded this section, "Such an action [giving up his Indians] was considered then and always the consummate proof

that could demonstrate sanctity."[25] Las Casas knew that actions spoke
for beliefs. He consistently berated those who said one thing but did
another. He believed that setting free his Indians demonstrated the
reality of his faith. This action was what made the conversion a reality and what ultimately saved his soul. According to Las Casas, good
works are an essential part of the Christian life. One cannot call one-
self a Christian and, at the same time, oppress those weaker and less
fortunate. Christian actions must proceed from Christian beliefs or it
makes a mockery of the belief system and what Christ represented.
The priest would preach against the ethical inconsistency of
hypocrisy the rest of his life. Repentance for previous action implies
a change both of attitude and of action. Both changes were evident
in the life of the priest from Seville.[26] Las Casas did not minimize the
importance of a profession of faith or the sacraments, but he indicated that faith without works is useless (James 2:20). There
remained only for Las Casas to make his decision public to the rest
of the Spaniards in an effort to have them emulate his behavior. In
the *Historia* he wrote:

> The padre made the secret public the following way. He
> was preaching on the feast day of the Assumption of Our
> Lady[27] in that place where he was [the town of Sancti
> Espiritus] mentioned earlier. *He was explaining the con-*
> *templative and the active life, the theme of the gospel*
> *reading of the day, talking about the spiritual and tem-*
> *poral works of mercy.* He had to make clear to his hear-
> ers their obligation to perform these works toward the
> native peoples they made use of so cruelly; he had to
> blame the merciless, negligent, mindless ways they lived
> off the natives. For which it struck him as the right
> moment to reveal the secret agreement he had set up
> with the governor. And he said, "My Lord, I give you
> freedom to reveal to everyone concerning what we agree
> on in secret—I take that freedom myself in order to
> reveal it to those here present." This said, he began to
> expose to them their own blindness, the injustices, the
> tyrannies, the cruelties they committed against such
> innocent, such gentle people. *They could not save their*

souls, neither those who held Indians by allotment, nor the ones who handed them out. They were bound by obligation to make restitution. He himself, once he knew the danger of damnation in which he lived, had given up his Indians, had given up many other things connected with the holding of Indians. The congregation was stupefied, even fearful of what he said to them. Some felt compunction, others thought it a bad dream, hearing bizarre statements such as: No one could hold Indians in servitude without sinning. As if to say they could not make use of the beasts of the field! Unbelievable.[28]

Thus did the newly repentant Las Casas make public his decision and at the same time challenge his hearers to do the same. This specific action was the initial salvo in his attack on the *encomienda* system and those involved in it. He made public the inward spiritual decision resulting from the epiphany. He chose to put into practice the dictates of his conscience and faith. The preaching of this sermon demonstrated his change of conscience and confirmed his complete repentance of the former way of life. This change, then, is the conversion of the Christian believer. It is the recognition that practice must comply with belief, that one must demonstrate by outward actions what one holds as inner convictions. It involves a change both in one's attitude and in one's actions about a matter of conscience.[29]

Thus concluded one of the most significant events in the life of Bartolomé de las Casas. At the same time the next phase of it began. This repentance from his former life as *encomendero* and dedication to his new one as a spokesman for God began as a direct result of his encounter with God through the reading of Ecclesiasticus. Throughout the rest of his life, and in all of his major works, he referred to this moment and its significance. His desire was that each *peninsular,* or Spaniard, as well as the nation of Spain itself, would have a similar encounter, repent of previous actions, and make restitution to the Indians. With this epiphany he received both his call and message from God and dedicated himself to the fulfillment of this ministry, the ministry of a prophet in the biblical tradition.

Chapter Three

The Prophetic Period Begins

After this experience, Las Casas was convinced of the injustices that he, along with all the Spaniards, had perpetrated through their exploitation and imperialism. He could no longer justify or rationalize away these injustices and knew that he must dedicate his life to bringing justice to those being exploited. Therefore, after he gave up his Indians, consolidated his holdings with his partner Rentería, sold them, and took the profits to live on for the next three years of his life, he left for Spain.[30] For, using all the worldly wisdom that he had accumulated over the past twelve years in the New World, he knew that in order to change the system he would need to go to the seat of power and apply not only spiritual pressure, as he had witnessed the Dominicans attempt, but also political pressure on the system. The marshaling of both spiritual and secular arguments in his apologetic would become the trademark of this single-minded cleric who believed that he was on a mission from God. To accomplish this task, he turned for advice and counsel to the Dominicans.

In order to leave Cuba safely, Las Casas, now known as a proponent of Indian rights and, therefore, no friend of the colonists, drew up a document that detailed his activities on behalf of the Crown over the last three and a half years. He then let it be known that he was returning to Paris to continue his studies.[31] On his way back to Europe, he stopped at Hispaniola to consult with Pedro de Córdoba. The Dominican leader had previously sent Montesino back to Spain to lobby King Ferdinand on behalf of the natives. Although the monarch recognized the need for some type of reform, the desire for wealth overrode that for reform.[32] Córdoba told Las Casas: "You will not labor in vain because God will oversee the projects, but be certain of this, we will never achieve our objectives while the King lives." Although disappointed at hearing these words, Las Casas responded that God was giving him the zeal and desire to carry out the works with which he had charged him. Because of this, "I hope that the Lord helps me, yet if I am not successful, I will have done my duty as a Christian."[33] Unfortunately for the Indians, the king and his first reform council at Burgos had, in effect, already legalized the *encomienda* by issuing the Laws of Burgos.

As previously mentioned, these laws were more a description of the actual state of affairs in the Indies than a royal directive concerning a more humane treatment of the natives. They also reflect an attitude about the Indians with which the reformers would have to contend. The preamble to these laws states, "Whereas, it has become evident through long experience that nothing has sufficed to bring the said chiefs and Indians to a knowledge of our faith (by which our Lord is disserved), since by nature they are inclined to idleness and vice, and have no manner of virtue or doctrine." As it was the duty of the council to seek a remedy for this situation, they decreed that the Indians would have to live near to the Spaniards and be entrusted to their care. Although there were some concessions to the natives—they were not to serve as carriers, the Spanish were forbidden to whip them or call them "dogs," and the sons of chiefs were to receive education—the net result changed little. In 1514, Rodrigo de Albuquerque arrived in Hispaniola to allot the natives to the *encomenderos*. He also gave each one a paper requiring them to instruct those in their charge in the Catholic faith. No mechanism, however, was established to enforce these laws.[34]

Most of those involved in making policy for the Indies were also involved in some way with the *encomienda* system. King Ferdinand was the largest holder of Indians. Two other powerful individuals with whom Las Casas would have to deal, and who were also *encomenderos,* were Secretary Lope de Conchillos and Juan Rodríguez de Fonseca, bishop of Burgos. Fonseca achieved the status of chief authority over matters dealing with the Indies.[35] Thus the situation confronting the reformers appeared bleak.

Although disappointed at his own previous efforts to reform the situation, Fray Pedro appointed Montesino to travel with Las Casas and assist him in any way possible. This he did when they arrived in Seville, as Montesino introduced him to the friend of Columbus, the archbishop Fray Diego de Deza. Deza was the Dominican head of all the priests in the New World and gave Las Casas letters of introduction to the king and his court. On Christmas Eve, 1515, Las Casas met with an ailing Ferdinand at Plascencia.[36]

After a long meeting with the king, and with the promise to meet again, Las Casas met first with Secretary Conchillos. He received Las Casas well, spoke kindly with him, and finally asked what he wanted. Conchillos promised to give him whatever he desired in the Indies. In response, Las Casas, sensing the intent to silence his defense of the Amerindians, declared that he was now free from materialism. The Lord had also removed greed when lifting the darkness from him. He explained how God had elected him to speak out against the moral outrages he had seen. Certainly the material advantages that Conchillos could offer him could not compare with the purposes and plans that God had planned for him. The quest for personal gain, so evident in his earlier life as *encomendero*, no longer motivated the cleric. Although he certainly agreed that the Crown should receive the usufruct of the New World—indeed, that was the basis on which he makes most of his appeals to the monarchy—he personally desired the conversion of the natives and not material gain.[37]

Las Casas then met with Bishop Fonseca and apprised him of the conditions in the Indies. The bishop's response stunned Las Casas and confirmed his suspicions of the attitudes he was up against. To Las Casas's disclosure that while in Cuba he was present for the death of seven thousand Indian children in three months, Fonseca responded, "What does that have to do with me, or the King?"[38] It was because of this behavior from the king's principal advisors that Las Casas initially blamed them for the destructive policies of the Crown. As he and his message matured, however, he became increasingly confrontational with the Crown and direct in his warnings to the reigning sovereign. Initially, however, his method was to blame the monarch's advisors. Perhaps Las Casas did this so that he would have someone to whom he could appeal their decisions. He never met Ferdinand again because the aging king died on January 25, 1516.[39]

Las Casas's appeal to the material interests of the monarchy should not be viewed as a double-minded stance on his part. On the one hand, he interpreted the claim of the Spanish over the New World to be valid and in accordance with the papal donations. This interpretation was consistent with the medieval worldview and the consequent imperialism for both material benefits and spiritual evangelism. On the other hand, he was being "as wise as a serpent" in his efforts to spare the slaughter of the inhabitants and new subjects. Las Casas was single-minded; his desire was to spare the Indians from destruction and convert them to Christianity, which he viewed as having eternal consequences and therefore more important than the temporal exploitation. In order to accomplish this task, he used methods that sometimes brought criticism. For him, there was no dichotomy. Thus in his works there are constant references to the potential wealth available to the Crown. This wealth proved ever more necessary as the lavish lifestyle and foreign involvements of the new King Charles V (Charles I in Spain) necessitated an ever-increasing need for revenue to repay his creditors.[40] Las Casas's appeal to the pragmatic was for the purpose of relieving the suffering of his beloved Indians. Yet he realized that those who had never seen the suffering or did not feel the spiritual burden that he felt or simply had their own interests at heart needed economic motivation. Otherwise there would be no practical reason to change their destructive policies. For example, the priest wrote: "[Las Casas] says that the population of more than fifty of the Lucayo islands is lost, these were sites where churches could be built, so that both God and your Royal Highness would be served." Then, to bring the practical side to bear, Las Casas continued, "your income would also be increased because of the richness and fruitfulness of the land. If adequately treated from the beginning, Your Highness would now have incalculable wealth from it."[41] The priest attempted to demonstrate how sparing the lives of the natives would also materially benefit the monarch.

After the death of Ferdinand, Las Casas met with the two regents of Spain for the young Prince Charles. These were Adrian of Utrecht, a Flemish ambassador and representative of the prince, and Cardinal Ximénez de Cisneros. The priest immediately presented them with a report he had prepared for the king. This denunciation of Spanish atrocities in the Antilles was his first written public document on this subject. The report itself focused on the lack of responsibility demonstrated by the colonists for the care of the natives. He included many of the themes he later developed and expanded in his book, *A Brief Account of the Destruction of the Indies.* These issues included the lack of gratitude the Spaniards had shown to the original inhabitants who had greeted them so warmly, the abuse of the Indians in the mines and subsequent starvation because they could not grow food, and the lack of respect for the directives of the

Crown. Perhaps most significant, Las Casas emphasized the theme that the natives wanted nothing to do with the Christian religion after their experiences with the Spanish. Apparently in reference to the Hatuey incident, Las Casas, in an obvious attempt to shock the king as well as to indicate his own grief and shame, expressed that the natives said that they would rather go to hell where they would no longer have any dealings with the Christians than go to heaven and see them again. This would be a painful and recurring theme in his writings.[42]

Also in 1516, Las Casas wrote his first significant tract, a list of remedies for the Indians of Cuba. Prepared as a complement to the grievances and presented to Cisneros, this tract was intended to give specific suggestions for reforming colonial policy. In addition, he appended a detailed suggested policy for the implementation of these proposals on other islands and territories in the Indies.[43] This *memorial* impressed upon Cisneros the need to make changes in the Indies. In an attempt to prevent friction between the Dominicans and the Franciscans, he appointed a committee of three Jeronymites, or priests from the Order of St. Jerome, to implement changes and to conduct an investigation for future recommendations.

Cisneros asked Las Casas for his recommendations as to the qualifications these individuals should possess. He did not take the priest's suggestion, however, of appointing a single administrator over Indian affairs.[44] Cisneros did appoint the Segovian lawyer Alonso de Suazo, who had earned the respect of all because of his judicial abilities and reputation for fairness, to accompany the mission. As the *juez visitador,* Suazo was also to act as representative for the Indians who had no other official advocate and who were incapable of representing themselves in their claim for justice. As a result of pressure from Las Casas, this event marked the first time the Crown appointed an official to investigate charges made on behalf of the Indians.[45] Finally, Cisneros appointed Las Casas as the advisor to the friars and, with an annual salary of one hundred gold pesos per year, the *"procurador o protector de todos los indios de las Indias."*[46]

This appointment began the intense new work of the newly converted friar, who was now at home both in the halls of the king's court and in the Church. His writings had had the intended effect of focusing royal attention on the plight of the rapidly diminishing native populations. He had received an official title, and his mission began. This mission would not prove as fruitful as Las Casas hoped. In fact, because of the influence of the colonists on the Jeronymites even before their departure, the mission was doomed from the start. Yet, the responsibility of the prophet is to present the message. This Las Casas did. He consistently proclaimed not only the problem but also specific *remedios,* or solutions, to these problems. In order to understand what changed the focus of his life and mission, and to appreciate the challenge Las Casas faced in bringing about his vision, we must examine in more detail both the conversion itself and the system out of which it came.

CHAPTER FOUR

The Ministry Begins (1514–22)

Although Las Casas had now repented of his former life, received his "prophetic call,"[1] identified himself with the reformers, and traveled to Spain to confront the monarchy and its representatives with the truth of what was happening in the Indies, the style of his message was still evolving. Initially, from the time of his change of heart in 1514 until his decision to join the Dominican Order in 1522, the priest knew that he dare not appeal only to the spiritual interests of the colonists but must emphasize the practical and profitable to make his plans acceptable. He knew that he must be, in biblical language, "as wise as a serpent, but as harmless as a dove." His views were so radical and would involve such a change of heart on the part of the hearers, that he knew he had to make these ideas palatable to the practical-minded and profit-oriented. Undeniably, during these years his message was as equally concerned with colonization as with evangelization, but this would change as he matured and became more outspoken and direct in his views and solutions. The seeds of this mature message were, however, always present.

From the beginning, evangelization was uppermost in his heart and goals for America. Concurrent with this was an end to the *encomienda* system that was causing the physical death of the natives. These themes were repeated many times throughout his life. They were also accompanied by a call to repent lest the judgment of God fall on Spain and its leadership. This burden of evangelizing the natives and changing the heart of the Spanish Christians, shouldered at the same time as his enlightenment took place, began to consume the newly inspired priest. Yet, the prophet did have to mature and become more refined in his methods, even as he increasingly confronted the motives and spelled out the consequences of those opposing him. His technique would become more sophisticated and his message more mature and theologically astute, but the motivation for this and the basic tenets of it would not change. Using the worldly wisdom he had already acquired, therefore, he designed his initial proposals to appeal to the self-interest of those who could help him.

Undoubtedly, Las Casas had a very definite sense of being God's choice to bring repentance to Spain and return it to its primary responsibility in the New World—the evangelization of the natives. With his change of outlook came also the responsibility to speak on behalf of God and against the deadly system of slavery as well as the *encomienda*. This burden was not only for the evangelism of the Amerindians, but it also matured to include justice for all the oppressed, including the Africans. Las Casas felt a strong responsibility to warn the Spanish nation of the destruction and judgment that would befall it if it did not repent of its unchristian attitudes and deeds in America and to provide specific remedies for change. Sure of both his calling and his message, Las Casas, in an ethically consistent manner, influenced the policies and actions of Spain in the New World. Despite failures, learning experiences, and setbacks, his message did not change, even if perhaps his methods did.

In his initial proposals, "A Memorial of Grievances Done to the Indians" (1516) and the supplement to this, "Memorial of Remedies for the Indians" (1516), both of which he presented to Cardinal Cisneros, he articulated much of what would become his major themes and demonstrated that from the beginning the former successful businessman would emphasize the practical nature of his reforms while keeping the ultimate, most significant goals in view. Within the first few years of his reformist ministry, Las Casas discovered the method of appealing to the material well-being of the ruling powers. After he refocused his life for the acquisition of spiritual riches, however, he utilized his talents in the performance of his duties as a spokesman for God.

Las Casas soon realized that the conversion of the Indians in and of itself would not be sufficient motivation for the Crown to assist him in the achievement of his ultimate goals. In dealing with the bishop of Burgos, Juan Rodríguez de Fonseca, concerning colonizing Tierra Firme with farmers, he wrote, "The cleric was astounded to find out that the Bishop failed to consider conversion as profitable in itself." With a sense of much grief the cleric continued, "He thought about appealing to the Bishop's lack of sensitivity by questioning his sacrilegious zeal to increase the King's treasury, by reminding him of his spiritual duty to care for so many souls."[2] He knew from his previous dealings with Fonseca, however, how much he disliked him and his plans and always rejected them both. Because of this attitude, he needed to invent a plan that would appeal to Fonseca's material interests. Despite the fact that the bishop represented the Catholic Church, his main motivation was apparently the acquisition of wealth and not concern for souls. Therefore, the former businessman appealed primarily to the profit motives of the bishop, the representative of the Church, in order that he might fulfill his spiritual duties. Even though Bartolomé appealed to the business interests of the Crown, he was aware of what he was doing and knowingly took this action. He recognized that to get the support of those motivated by money he must demonstrate why the evangelization of the labor force was to the advantage of the managers. As he looked back on his activities during the early years of his ministry, the mature Las Casas wrote, "The *clérigo*'s maxim was that unless the solution to the problem worked as much on behalf of the Spanish as the Indians, the latter would never be saved." Thus in order to make his remedies acceptable to the colonists and the Crown, "he based the freedom and conversion of the Indians on purely materialistic interests of those who could help him achieve his goals."[3] The worldly wisdom of the man was not lost in the process that converted him from *encomendero* to spokesman for God. In order to achieve a higher purpose, he utilized the methods with which he was most familiar. Later, of course, as he saw these methods were having little effect, he dropped all pretenses at economic motivation; but, initially, he pursued this ostensible goal. Before examining these first writings of Las Casas, it is necessary to look at him in light of the prophetic tradition.

The Prophetic Style: Challenge and Remedios

It becomes evident through the study of the writings of Las Casas that he believed God had chosen him to bring a specific message to the Spanish, and this sense of divine call is what motivated the man and defined the message. Using both Scripture and the church fathers, filtering these through his own experience and refining them by his Dominican theological training, he developed a theme that he repeated and refined over the years.

This theme involved the repentance of Spain, the cessation of ongoing destructive practices, and restitution for past atrocities, lest God bring the entire nation to judgment. Thus, the pattern that Las Casas followed in his own personal awakening also became the blueprint for the entire nation. Repentance was the key element in the prophetic call and acceptance of this call. It was the repentance of Las Casas, whereby he changed both his way of thinking and his actions; repentance that allowed the blindness to leave his eyes and by which he saw the corruption in the system itself and not just in the individual *encomendero*; and repentance that caused him to desire to make restitution for his past actions and participation. Repentance also played a significant role, after his failure at Cumaná, in his decision to join the Dominican Order, an event that further changed his life's direction. From that moment in which his eyes opened to the injustice in the Spanish system, his life became an act of penance. It was a life dedicated to making up for past sins so that God would not reject him and refuse him absolution as the Dominican priest had once done. There were times when he questioned God's forgiveness in his life. Yet, in his Last Will and Testament, as we shall see in the final chapter, he seemed to accept that his penance was sufficient, though that of Spain was still lacking. Before examining this message, which so many have called prophetic,[4] let us examine the simple definition of the word *prophet* from both a classical and a biblical perspective.

Las Casas does fit the definition of the term *prophet* from both a secular and a theological perspective. The Greek word *prophetes* literally means "one who proclaims or speaks for another."[5] In classical Greece this meant one who interpreted the will of the gods to the general populace, one whom individuals consulted about the specific intent of the gods in a given situation. Their methods could involve listening to oracles, divining dreams, or making sense out of chicken entrails. Prophets were also able to state or present issues in a clear way. They had the ability to articulate and clarify concerns of the day in such a way that all could comprehend them. The hearer then decided whether to heed the message or reject the prophet.[6]

The gift of prophecy in the New Testament is one way in which the Church is built up or strengthened (Ephesians 5). This office has been present since the founding of the Church. This word also carried the connotation of one who spoke on behalf of God and thereby interpreted the word of God to a specific people at a given time in history. In other words, prophets made Scripture relevant and understandable to those listening to it. During the first centuries of the development of the Christian Church, false and true prophets were judged by the Church according to their consistency with the written word of God. Prophets have held a respected office in the Church since the time of the Chief Prophet, Christ himself.[7]

The Hebrew word for prophet, *nabi,* means "one who is called," and also carries the connotation of an authorized spokesperson. The word contains the meaning not only of forthtelling, or speaking on behalf of someone else, such as God, but also foretelling, or predicting future events. A true prophet could only be a person who had a clearly defined directive to share. This message needed to conform to the already revealed truths about God or be consistent with God's character and morality. The prophet was always aware that God had chosen him; he was certain about this choice and about his task of conveying a specific message to a particular people at a particular place or in a determined circumstance. The common denominator of all prophets is the clear sense of being chosen.[8]

The call of a prophet, according to both biblical and secular accounts, could come in a number of ways—through prayer and meditation, after reflective study, in conjunction with specific occurrences, or suddenly. Just as the occupations and backgrounds of the prophets varied, so too did the way they received and understood their charge. Although the basic message came from outside the prophet, for example, from God, the interpretation and presentation of that message reflected the individual personality of the prophet. The prophet's own language, mannerisms, customs, and tradition would then be used to transmit the message.[9]

Certainly in the previous chapter we saw that Las Casas had a definite sense of a divine encounter. What psychologists call a "crisis" arose in his life. As he encountered God through the pages of Scripture, he realized the inconsistency of his words and deeds. He knew that God had enlightened him, and that the "darkness left his eyes." From that day on, all he read or saw confirmed this sense and consequently he changed his attitude and actions. His own sense of purpose and mission grew as his message developed and matured through the years. Like the biblical prophets, Las Casas utilized his own style and experiences to interpret the word of God to his generation.

On January 23, 1516, King Ferdinand died. Wasting no time, Las Casas met with the regent Cardinal Cisneros and presented him with his first written proposal for the salvation of his beloved natives. This tract, a *Memorial de remedios,* is the first indication we have of the budding prophet and his message. His desire and goal was to bring liberty to the Indians and to prevent their slaughter, while evangelizing them in the Catholic faith. His message needed time to develop, evolve, and be refined. The prophet had been called and the basics of the message received. Yet, the specific manner and emphasis of these goals was to take a lifetime to develop.

From the beginning of his message to the Crown, Las Casas emphasized the evangelical nature of the Spanish presence in the Indies. One theme that dominated his writings was given in this first tract. "The principal end for which all has been ordained, or could be ordained, and the prime goal for which we must strive, is the salvation of the Indians, which must be effected through the Christian doctrine as His Highness commands."[10] Although in this document he did not specifically refer to the Alexandrine bull of donation, the allusion to it was obvious. The "principal end," as the priest called it, was training in Christian doctrine. This was the theory behind the *encomienda* and the stated purpose of commending the natives to the Christians. The Spanish were responsible for teaching Catholic doctrine to the Amerindians and demonstrating the faith to them by caring for them in a Christian manner.

The rationale behind the system was that by placing the Indians in close proximity to the Spanish, they would be able to both receive instruction and see the Christian faith modeled. Indeed, in the second remedy in this document, Las Casas recommended that no Indian be commended to individual Spaniards, but that the natives be placed together in a communal section of each Spanish town. Although this was only a minor variation in the first article of the Laws of Burgos, he recognized the benefit that should proceed from this arrangement. Las Casas insisted that, in accordance with Christ's command, the faith must be proclaimed in message and witness. In this there were great problems: "The Spanish, to whom the Indians were commended, do not know what to teach, and if some do know, because of the little charitable love they have, do not demonstrate it, but are more concerned with getting rich than saving souls."[11] The consistency of both word and deed was crucial not only to the message of Las Casas but also to his own life.

Significantly Las Casas closed the tract with the same admonition concerning the role of the Spanish. We might also notice the beginnings of the sarcasm that will creep into his works.

> I beseech your most reverend lordship, that you consider, as without a doubt I know you will consider, that the first and last aim that must motivate us in the remedy for those sad souls must be God, and how to attract them to heaven; because God did not redeem them nor discover them so that they might be cast into hell, [with the Spanish] having no thought for them but to acquire wealth. This does not seem unreasonable, let alone a great burden.[12]

Thus God and the necessity for bringing salvation to the natives motivated the prophet and, according to Las Casas, must motivate the Christian in all that he or she does. The ultimate motivation for one's actions must be faith in God. This faith will strengthen an individual's sense of purpose and provide courage when success appears doubtful.

In the first specific remedy, Las Casas proposed an immediate cessation of all Indian labor in the islands until the monarchy could have a chance to investigate the situation fully. This was to put a stop to the rapid population decrease. The Indians were dying at such at rate that soon there would be no more of them. During this idle time, when the natives could rest, they could put on some weight and regain their strength. Next, Las Casas demonstrated his business sense by appealing to the practical side of the monarchy. He explained that the Indians should be allowed to rest, so that they could work better when they did return to work in the future. Thus, he tied together the health and physical salvation of the native with the profit motivation of the oppressor.[13]

Furthermore, in order to find out exactly what was happening in the Indies, to prevent the further slaughter of the "almost innumerable natives that have perished," and to emphasize the work of spiritual salvation, the Crown should send a religious, of good moral character, not greedy, and not part of the enterprise of the Indies. He could be accompanied on each island by a priest who lived on that island, knew the situation, and would therefore reveal the truth to the monarchy and not seek his own personal gain. In this manner the authorities could make good decisions based on objective facts. This would then appeal to all concerned as it regarded the protection of the Indian and the interests of the Christians.[14]

The second remedy, as mentioned above, suggested that the Indians not be placed with individuals, but in a common area in each village or town. This also made provision for the Spanish leader of each village to provide food for the workers and care for their needs. They could then also most effectively provide them with Christian training. Again emphasizing the practical alongside the spiritual, Las Casas suggested:

> This community, made under the suggested conditions, will prevent the accidental death of the Indians, like has happened, and they will live. There will then be a place for them to be instructed in the faith unto salvation, and not destruction. Your Majesty will then have a guaranteed income and your lands populated and filled with vassals; and because the people in this land multiply so rapidly, their usefulness will also increase to the great benefit and permanence of the kingdom. Moreover, [the Spanish] will

not commit such grave and abominable sins, because there will not be the opportunity for the greedy to stuff themselves, diminishing and killing Your Majesty's vassals, having no regard except for their own interests.[15]

Thus, Las Casas made the proposal to the monarchy by tying together the spiritual and physical needs of the Amerindians, and appealing to the practical necessity of the Spanish. We can also see his use of guilt on the monarchy by appealing to the sense of sin attributed to the Christian Spanish. This too will be a recurring theme as he sought to prick the conscience of those responsible.

In the third *remedio* Las Casas developed one of his favorite concepts. This was the settlement of the New World by peasants and farmers from the Old. He would have the opportunity to implement this grand experiment on Tierra Firme in just a few years. Each farmer would have five Indians and their families assigned to him. The farmer could then instruct the natives in effective agricultural techniques and thereby increase the productivity of the land. Las Casas hoped miscegenation would also occur and the colonists would then have an interest both in the economy of the land and in increasing the population. Also, the farmer would be a model for Christian behavior and teach his "disciples" in the way of the faith. Again, because of this, the monarchy would be served and prosper. Las Casas's goal was for members of the religious orders to enter the land eventually, live in proximity to the natives, and by reason and persuasion bring them to the faith. This experiment would culminate in his venture in Verapaz.[16]

The other *remedios* covered a wide range of areas, with the emphasis being the care and salvation of the Indians. One proposal recommended that those who violated the proposed laws would be punished by the Crown. A pious religious would enforce these laws and attempt to change the attitude of merely paying lip service to the official directives, known as *"obedezco pero no cumplo"* (I obey, but do not comply), which characterized the attitude of the Spanish toward royal legislation. The Indians would receive the same type of punishment as the Spanish. This would effectively end the double standard whereby Indians received harsh treatment for minor offenses and peninsulars received no penalty for their deadly behavior. Las Casas also asked for the establishment of the Inquisition in the New World to stem any heretical activities. A further provision suggested that the natives receive the new legislation in their own language. This was recommended so they might better comprehend that the old way of doing things had changed.

Las Casas and Slavery

Undoubtedly the *remedio* that caused the most controversy was the eleventh, which called for the replacement of Indian workers with African slaves. Las Casas wrote: "In place of the Indians that are in these communities, Your Majesty could substitute twenty blacks, or other slaves, in the mines...they will collect more gold than twice as many Indians."[17] Exactly what he meant by the "other slaves" is clarified a few pages later. In the context of explaining how rich the land is, Las Casas wrote that slaves, "both black and white," could be brought from Castile to raise sugar and collect gold.[18] At the time in Spain there were slaves from all ethnic backgrounds. Significantly, Las Casas does not condemn the institution of slavery so prevalent in the world at the time. This change in thinking would evolve later, as he expanded his area of concern from the Amerindians only to all under oppression. Because of the controversial nature of this proposal and because it encompassed an issue that showed a real maturation in the message of Las Casas, we shall examine his position concerning slavery in some detail. For although the priest initially called for the importation of blacks as slaves, by the end of his life the blindness would again leave him and he would equate the treatment of the Indians with that of the Africans, calling the enslavement of both "unjust and tyrannical."[19]

The institution of slavery is as old as the human race. Most ancient civilizations, such as Egypt, Greece, and Rome, practiced slavery. Philosophers such as Plato and Aristotle endorsed slavery, and even the great religions like Christianity and Islam utilized it. The basis for this slavery was varied, involving such reasons as capture in war, conviction for a crime, or even the sale of self or children to avoid starvation or to pay debts. Thus, in the world from which Las

Casas came, slavery was a common sight. Slavery in the New World, however, took on a new form.[20]

By the middle of the fifteenth century, the Portuguese had begun exploring and then making raids on the west coast of Africa for the purpose of bringing slaves back to Europe. Because Africa was primarily Muslim, and therefore an ancient foe of Christendom, the Portuguese felt justified enslaving Africans as a continuation of the Crusades. These wars then were just wars, and as such slavery was legal and the taking of Africans as slaves was legitimate. Also, because slavery was practiced among Africans, if they themselves did not capture individuals by raiding, the Christians were merely buying slaves from others who had enslaved them. This was a totally different issue from that faced in the New World. The question of enslaving the Amerindians, as discussed previously, revolved around the legality of their basic human nature and the type of warfare in which they were captured. According to Las Casas, they had been enslaved and deprived of liberty unjustly, and therefore they were not to be enslaved. The legality of African slaves was not an issue at the time, and almost all theologians and jurists accepted slavery if based on traditionally legal titles.[21]

Prior to the involvement of Las Casas in the issue of African slavery through his eleventh *remedio* hundreds of black slaves had arrived in the New World. His petition to send Africans, who had the reputation for being able to work in the heat longer than either Europeans or Indians, was not the first. In his book *Bartolomé de Las Casas: Contra Los Negros?* Isacio Pérez gave an exhaustive list of the chronology of those seeking to bring African slaves to the New World. Among those making this request were the Jeronymites, who asked that Cisneros allow slaves to be imported directly from Guinea, the comptroller of Hispaniola, Gil González Dávila, and others.[22] Even the Dominicans, in a letter signed by Pedro de Córdoba, asked the Crown to allow the importation of slaves as a temporary compensation for those Spaniards who had to give up their Indians. Those who had none should be allowed to purchase some on credit.[23] Thus the issue of African slavery was not one of legality, and Las Casas did not originate the practice. Africans living in Spain, along with whites who were also enslaved in a "just manner," were requested and sent to the New World. Las Casas does not deal with the legitimacy of the institution of slavery. He argued neither for nor against the practice. As a man of his times he merely accepted the situation as it was. This position changed, however, as he became better acquainted with the facts of the system.

In addition to the request for slaves in his eleventh *remedio,* Las Casas, in future years and writings, made two additional requests for slaves in the New World. In his 1531 "Carta al Consejo de Indias," he recommended that the Crown loan "five or six hundred" blacks to each of the islands to replace the Indians no longer alive.[24] After three years, the population would increase, the rents would be paid to the monarchy, and they could then recoup the cost of the slaves. Also, in the construction of new outposts and towns, Christians could bring with them "Negro slaves, Moors, or those of other standing, to serve them, live by their own hands, or in any other way not damaging to the Indians."[25] He made the same type of request for the loan of black slaves in the 1542 "Memorial de Remedios."[26] Again, the attraction was the increase in revenue that would result from the larger population. The priest continued to show concern for those Indians dying in droves by appealing to the practical nature of the Crown. Yet, something about the African trade troubled the cleric.

Las Casas made his final request for slaves in 1543, after he was ordained bishop and while he prepared to go to his diocese. He requested that Emperor Charles V grant him license to "bring [to Chiapa] two dozen black slaves, void of all rights both in Seville as in the Indies…for the maintenance of the religious."[27] These are the written requests by Las Casas for African slaves to be utilized in the New World. As mentioned by Pérez, he was not responsible for enslaving the Africans or for mistreating them, either during the trip to the Indies or after their arrival. He merely utilized an established system, until the darkness once again left his eyes.[28]

About the year 1547, the now bishop of Chiapa stopped in Lisbon to find out exactly what was happening in Africa concerning the slave trade. At the time Portugal monopolized the Guinea slave trade. Probably during this visit he learned of works by Portuguese historians concerning the beginning of the trade on that continent and discovered how the raiders actually acquired these persons.[29] This was the beginning of the events that led to Las Casas's awaken-

Theodore de Bry, *Mutilation of Native Americans by the Spanish Conquistadores*. An illustration in *Historia de las Indias* by Bartolomé de las Casas. Bibliotheque Nationale, Paris. Snark/Art Resource.

ing to the evils of the slave trade. With the information he received at the time and on reflection, by 1554 he added chapters 17 to 27 to the first books of his *Historia*.[30]

These chapters, which detail how Portugal arrived in Africa and under what circumstances the Portuguese obtained the slaves, would also reveal the process by which Las Casas became enlightened about the evils and injustice of the system of black slavery as it was then practiced. Recounting the story from the Portuguese chroniclers, the bishop again decried the capture, enslavement, and slaughter of innocents by Christians. Worse, from the bishop's perspective, they practiced these acts in God's name and credited God with making the trade so profitable. This was the exact opposite of what the evangelistic purpose of the Church should be in pagan lands. As happened in the Indies, "they killed and sent to hell so many unbelievers that they left the entire land in shock and hatred of the name Christian, and filled them with grief and bitterness."[31] Thus did Las Casas come to grips with the fact that the slaves were not taken by just means and that the servitude inflicted on them was just as evil and unjustified as that committed on the Indians. In fact, the infidels in Africa, like the Amerindians, could have waged the just war against the Christians who had so maliciously attacked them.[32] The prophet, interpreting the word of God in a specific time and place to a specific situation and made aware of injustice through the enlightenment of knowledge, now continued to deepen and expand his message to include all those who were suffering as well as the institution responsible for their enslavement.

Significantly, Las Casas remembered and reflected a second time on the passage of Scripture that had caused his first conversion. This happened after he read the account of the Portuguese raiders. After capturing a number of slaves, they chose the best one to give to the church in Lagos. Their desire was to give God a tithe, or a portion of the booty. This infuriated the priest, who wrote: "As if God were some wicked and violent tyrant whom they could please, and He might therefore approve of the tyrannies of those who made the offering."[33] He then paraphrased the verse from Ecclesiasticus that had meant so much to him in the past: "God does not approve those who harm their neighbors sinfully, then offer God a sacrifice from their ill-gotten goods. Such a sacrifice is instead like honoring and serving a father by hacking his son to pieces as he looks on."[34] The fact that they gave a part of their goods to God cannot excuse the fact they are guilty of mortal sin. God cannot be bought off by gifts, however great or small. Las Casas now emerged from the fog that had surrounded him concerning this issue. Through experience and reflecting on the word of God, once again he was faithful to and consistent with the message received from God *as he became aware of it*. He subsequently defended the rights of the black slaves in the same manner as he had fought for those of the Indians.

In later chapters of his *Historia* Las Casas continued to explain his position, making it ever more clear and detailed.[35] He recounted his initial involvement in the matter in that those who had Indian slaves offered to give them up if he could help get them a license for the importation of Africans. At the time, he pointed out, he did not know how the Africans had come to be slaves. They were already in Spain, and he supposed they became slaves through the process of a just war. When he discovered how unjustly they were taken, "he would not have suggested it for all the world, because the blacks were enslaved unjustly, tyrannically, from the beginning, as had been the Indians."[36] He now directly equated the unjust treatment of the Indians and the Africans, both of whom the Europeans exploited for their own good and profit. For the priest simply to explain away his actions, however, was not sufficient. He realized that repentance, and consequent action to validate this attitude, must also be involved.

Las Casas described in another chapter how, after explaining again the manner in which he proposed the importation of blacks and obtained permission from the Crown to import some blacks from Castile, he now considered these actions immoral and judged himself. For him this was an act of penance. This time, instead of self-righteously excusing his own sins of ignorance or even emphasizing that this was a way in which the natives could be set free, he took total responsibility for his lack of action. He frankly and sadly wrote, "Many years later, the cleric regretted the counsel he gave the King regarding this matter. He judged himself culpable, through inadvertence, as he would later see and ascertain that it was just as unjust to enslave the blacks as the Indians." Even though he had no knowledge concerning this matter at the time, "he was uncertain that his ignorance and good intentions would excuse him from the judgment of God."[37] This despite the fact that he assumed they were justly captured at the time. Sins of omission are just as heinous as those of commission. Las Casas now viewed the entire enterprise as being abominable to God and regretted his part in it.

Perhaps the saddest part for the repentant cleric was the fact that the number of sugar mills and the number of African slaves continued to increase. In the year he wrote this, about 1560, he stated that there were thirty thousand blacks on Hispaniola and probably 100,000 in the Indies as a whole.[38] Furthermore, the Indians he had hoped to see set free by the colonists were also not helped. Their numbers continued to dwindle through death. As a conclusion to this section, Las Casas placed the blame on the Spaniards for the sin of buying the Africans. In addition, the Spaniards were also responsible for God's judgment on the sins committed by both the Portuguese in distributing the slaves and the Africans themselves in capturing and selling other blacks.[39]

Thus the bishop of Chiapa now expanded his message to condemn not only enslavement of Indians and Africans, but also the slave trade itself. He no longer viewed the raids on the coast of Guinea as being just. Greed and the concurrent lust for wealth and power were the cause of these affairs. Christian evangelism, the main concern of Las Casas, suffered as a result of practices that had no justification. After the blinders fell from his eyes he equally condemned these injustices. He was also the first of his time to speak out against the institution of slavery. He presaged the movement to condemn slavery that would not begin until the end of the sixteenth century. As mentioned earlier, he was in conflict with the major theologians of his time concerning this issue, including the Salamancan School, which clung to the just war justification for slavery.[40] His message of repentance for the Spanish and justice for the oppressed matured and deepened as his understanding and knowledge increased. The priest had now progressed substantially since his first *remedios* in 1516 and, as a result of this enlightenment, asked forgiveness for his earlier position.

The Monarchy Responds

The result of the original remedies Las Casas issued was that Cardinal Cisneros, the regent who would rule Spain and the Indies until the arrival of the new Hapsburg king, appointed the Jeronymite friars to investigate the treatment of the natives in the Indies. These priests were selected because of their virtuous reputation and ability to administer economic enterprises. Cisneros's detailed instructions differed little from the original remedies of Las Casas. Despite the fact that Cisneros appointed him as advisor to the friars, Las Casas did not sail with the investigative team and arrived thirteen days after they did. This accented the differences between the Jeronymites, whom the colonists had already influenced, and the protector of the Indians, whose main concern was the Amerindians' welfare.[41]

According to Las Casas, the Jeronymites informed the colonists of their purpose immediately upon arrival. They were there as a result of a number of complaints concerning the treatment of the natives, and their main purpose for coming to the Indies was to see that the Indians were treated "like Christians and free men." Therefore, meetings of both *caciques* and Spaniards should be held to determine solutions they both could accept.[42]

Las Casas provided an interesting vignette as to how the cardinal came to admit that the Indians were indeed free and therefore worthy of equal treatment with the Christians. While speaking with Cisneros, he had avoided mentioning the free condition of the Amerindians, stressing instead their poor treatment. Finally, he asked the cardinal what could possibly justify the Spanish oppression and placing the Indians in such servitude. Cisneros curtly answered, "None, of course. Why? Are they not free men? Does anyone doubt this fact?" From that time on the priest spoke openly about the free nature of the natives.[43]

The exact authority of the Jeronymites has been an issue of discussion. They definitely had wide powers to carry out their directives. Las Casas believed they were not to form policy, but were there to administer royal instructions and listen to the counsel of Las Casas and other priests. According to the priest, they acted more like royal governors. They interviewed *encomenderos* and other colonists, who testified that the Indians were incapable of self-rule and needed to be under the tutelage of the Spanish. The authority of the protector of all the Indians was only in an advisory capacity, however, and he became furious with the friars for not immediately carrying out his plans. Because they did not respond to his directives, he quickly returned to Spain to complain of their actions. By this time, however, the cardinal was ill and gave him little attention.[44]

Basically, the Jeronymite mission failed to satisfy anyone. The reformers were not satisfied because the *encomienda* system remained in place. They accomplished few reforms to alleviate the plight of the natives. In fact, Las Casas, the prophet and spokesman for God, attributed to the judgment of God the fact that King Charles would not meet with the Jeronymites upon their return to Spain in 1520, because "they did so little to remedy the oppression of the Indians, they who could have done so much since they held the remedies in their hand." God also demonstrated his displeasure, according to the protector, with one of the friars, Luis de Figueroa, chief among the three, who later received an appointment as bishop of Santo Domingo. He died, however, before assuming the office.[45] The displeasure of God was demonstrated against those who carried his authority and responsibility but failed to carry out his purposes.

The colonists, on the other hand, did not appreciate the few reforms instituted by the friars. Unfortunately, after thirty villages were constructed for the relocation of the natives, an epidemic of smallpox broke out and killed about a third of the population. The resulting lack of laborers caused the Spaniards to begin asking for the importation of African slaves to replace the dying workers. A further recommendation that the Indians be exempted from working in the mines and used exclusively for agriculture was also proposed. Fear of losing their way of life caused the colonists to oppose all efforts by the Jeronymites. Caught between the two conflicting forces, the priestly mission accomplished little and suffered much frustration.[46] Also frustrated was the reformer, who now believed that the only way to prove his ideas was to create a colony unadulterated by the greedy Spanish. In an effort to accomplish this task he returned to Spain.

With the help of Fray Reginaldo Montesino, OP, the brother of the famous preacher Fray Antonio, his knowledge of Latin, and a letter of recommendation from the Picard Franciscans, Las Casas soon became the advisor on Indian affairs to the Flemish chancellor Jean le Sauvage. At his request, the priest drew up a series of plans for a new government in the Indies. Unfortunately for the reformers, Sauvage soon died, and Chief Minister Chievres placed the responsibility for the Indies in the hands of Juan Rodríguez de Fonseca, the bishop of Burgos and no friend of Las Casas.[47]

The initial plan called for incentives to be given to peasants who immigrated to the Indies. These benefits included free land, passage, animals, and seed. Even Las Casas was to receive a salary and a staff. This plan received approval in September 1518. Resistance to the plan, however, came from the grandees of Spain, who feared losing their tenants as these peasants migrated to the Indies. Resistance also came from the bishop of Burgos, who saw no financial benefit to the Crown. In addition, word arrived that the Indians of Hispaniola had all but been exterminated through disease, and the farms that were to support the peasants had been sold. Because of these difficulties, Las Casas abandoned this scheme, yet embarked upon the most ambitious plan to date and one that would occupy him for the next three years—Tierra Firme, a settlement on the coast of Venezuela.[48] This effort was a practical application of the ideal of Las Casas to merge the evangelism of the natives with the prosperity of the empire through a specific colonization technique.

The significance of this project in the life of Las Casas cannot be overestimated. Experience gained from this experiment proved invaluable for the future plans in his peaceful experiment in Verapaz. The failure of his plan led to what scholars have called his second conversion. For it is after this event, dejected and frustrated, that he entered the Dominican Order.[49] Here he deepened and broadened his message theologically, which led to future practical applications. No longer did he compromise evangelism for colonization. This became a significant change in attitude that subsequently affected the message of the future Dominican.

The desire to bring the missionary effort to the mainland from the islands was not new. As early as 1513, after viewing the destruction of the natives on the islands, the Dominicans considered a plan to reach the as yet relatively untouched Indians along the mainland coast. Pedro de Córdoba, in an agreement with King Ferdinand, planned to begin the colony on the coast of Paria. His license, which stipulated that no Spanish could even approach the areas of missionary activity, was the first of its kind. His vision of an entirely Indian community under the sovereignty of the Spanish king and administered by the mendicant orders was unique.[50] Unfortunately, however, this area, which Columbus had visited in 1498, quickly gained a reputation as having large quantities of pearls and Indians who desired to trade them for trinkets. Many traders, therefore, cruised the coast looking for wealth.[51] Thus, instead of becoming a missionary experiment, it became another opportunity for exploitation.

About the middle of 1518, Las Casas received a letter from Pedro de Córdoba.[52] He reported that Juan Bono (whom Las Casas sarcastically renamed "malo") had again raided the coast of Trinidad, killing and taking natives as slaves. In this letter, Córdoba instructed Bartolomé to request one hundred leagues of mainland territory from the king. This would include the Dominican monastery at Chiribichi and the Franciscan settlement at Cumaná. If he could not receive this total amount of land, he should seek at least ten leagues. If this was also not acceptable, he should negotiate for the Alonso islets, located some fifteen or twenty leagues out to sea. There they could establish a refuge for the Indians who were fleeing the tyrannies of the Spanish and attempt to save their souls as well as their bodies from destruction. The letter continued that if he could accomplish none of these goals, Córdoba would remove all the missionaries from Tierra Firme to Hispaniola because they could do nothing about the injustices. Las Casas was more concerned for the souls of the Indians than for his own comfort or ease. He wrote that because there was no one in that area who "knew God" or could teach the faith, he himself would go. Because, "according to the desire that God gave to the cleric, he strongly believed Christ should be preached by the friars, and even greatly desired to go there and labor with them and help them in this work, as a cleric."[53] Evangelism and the desire to bring the gospel to those who had not heard the message motivated the priest, and he immediately pressed for a new plan for colonization and missionary activity.

This message is revealed in the speech that "micer Bartolomé" made before the young King Charles, probably in late 1518, as he prepared for his plan of colonization. This account would be the second of three times that Las Casas referred to his prophetic call experience while in Cuba. This defining moment in his life had such an effect on him that it influenced the rest of his life. The final time he referred to this call would be in his Last Will and Testament.[54]

The first person to address the king on the subject of the Indians and the possibility of colonization was the bishop of Darién, Juan Cabedo. He believed that the Spanish had arrived at the right time and were doing the right thing in the Indies. His observation of the Indians of Darién as well as of those on the islands that he had visited was that "those people are servile *a natura,* and they hold in high esteem and have much gold, which they work hard to obtain."[55] After these observations, Las Casas addressed the court.

He began his words to King Charles by emphasizing the fact he had been in the Indies for many years, since the beginning of Spanish colonization. What he was about to recount were eyewitness accounts and not mere hearsay. The continual and obvious mistreatment of the Indians, which had resulted in their near extirpation, had one cause: "greed, the insatiable hunger and thirst for gold in our people." This lust for wealth resulted in the death of the natives. They died in two ways:

> The first, is through the unjust and extremely cruel wars against people who live, with no offense against anyone, in their own homes and lands. The people who died are numberless, both nations and races. Secondly, after killing the leaders and chiefs, they placed the Indians into servitude, dividing them up for each other, by hundreds, by fifties, and then sent them to the mines, where, in the end, due to unbelievable suffering at digging for gold, they all died. Wherever there are Spaniards I see the Indians dying in these two ways. One of those who helped in this tyranny was my very own father, though not anymore.[56]

After explaining what he had seen and indicating how this was the norm in the Indies, Las Casas recounted his own prophetic call, giving some valuable insights and demonstrating how he had matured. "Seeing all of this, I was moved, not because I was a better Christian than anyone else, but by a natural feeling of compassion which I had at seeing a people suffer terrible oppression and injustice, who did not deserve it."[57] Gone now was the self-righteous justifying attitude that singled him out as being a better *encomendero* than the rest who treated his Indians with such compassion and so well. Now he understood it to be God's grace that had opened his eyes and allowed him to see the suffering and injustice in a new way, a way in which he desired to become a part of the solution instead of being a part of the problem. This event, which had now happened four years previously, was what had caused him to change his life's mission and message and represent the natives before Ferdinand.

By informing and challenging the young King Charles, Las Casas demonstrated his loyalty to the Crown by telling it what it needed to hear, not what was popular or pleasing to the ears. He emphasized that the reason he was bringing this to the attention of the king was not for personal gain, unlike those who were taking advantage of the Indians, or even out of service to the king, but because it was God's will. He wrote, "The fact is I would not move from here to go to that corner to serve Your Majesty—with all due respect I owe as a subject—if I did not think and believe I was offering something great to God by so doing." The priest was more concerned with following the will of God than in serving the emperor. If Spain put God first and did what God required, the result would be profit and riches beyond what anyone could expect. Obedience to God would result in blessings, according to Las Casas, but disobedience would produce ruin.

In a further effort to assure that all those who were listening understood the difference between him and those exploiters, he then made it clear: "I state, I affirm, that I renounce any reward or recompense that Your Majesty could or would desire to make me."[58] If he should seek a reward, King Charles would then be justified in not believing him.

As a response to the bishop of Darién, Las Casas moved to the crux of his speech and the cry of his heart. He emphasized his basic message of evangelism and the capability, even desire, of the Amerindians to receive Christ. "Those Indian peoples, most powerful Lord, and the entire New World which is full of throngs of them, are supremely capable of the Christian faith, of all virtue, civilized behavior, tractable to both reason and revelation, and *a natura* free peoples."[59] Because the Indians have rulers and kings who govern them in a structured society, they are capable of reason and order and thus not subject to natural slavery, as Aristotle indicated in his *Politics*. Even if the bishop had interpreted the philosopher correctly and determined they were servile by nature, "Aristotle was a pagan, and is now burning in hell," so his teaching must be utilized as befits the Church, not the other way around. Then in an expression of universality for which the Catholic faith is justly named and proud, he said, "our Christian religion is for all. It adapts itself to every people in the world, accepting all equally, removing liberty from no one, sovereignty from no one and places none under servitude, especially by the rubric that some are servile *a natura*."[60]

Finally, Las Casas aimed the full force of his prophetic message at the monarch, as he gave him both a specific directive from the word of God and a veiled threat of what would occur in the future if he did not heed this word. "Therefore it is Your Majesty's responsibility to root out, at the start of his rule, the tyranny, monstrous and horrible before both God and the world, that causes such evil, such irreparable harm, involving the damnation of a major part of the human race." Las Casas demanded that the monarch remove these injustices so that "the Royal Kingdom of our Lord Jesus Christ, who died for those Indian peoples, might grow and prosper."[61] By not stopping the oppression, which was his responsibility as monarch and representative of God, Charles was in danger of bringing many to damnation, both Indian and Spanish, and holding up the progress of the Lord's kingdom. The goal of Christianity is to include nations in the family of God, not exclude or reject them en masse. In his presentation to the young King Charles, Las Casas interceded for the Indians and attempted to speak for God on their behalf. He also spoke for the nation as he attempted to avert disaster for its sinfulness. The monarch's response did not come immediately, however.

After nearly a year's struggle, during which time Bishop Fonseca and Secretary Francisco de los Cobos opposed Las Casas at every turn, the monarchy responded and Charles approved his grant late in 1519, during the last seven days the emperor was in Spain prior to his departure for Germany. Perhaps the plea of Cardinal Adrian of Utrecht, later elected pope, convinced him. Adrian stated that according to divine law, the church fathers, and natural laws, the

Indians were indeed free and should be evangelized in a peaceful manner and "not by Mohammedan methods." This convinced the king and the council and they decided"that the Indians were free men, should be treated as free, and attracted to the faith in the manner Christ established." They further determined that Las Casas should be in charge of this conversion process.[62] The amount of land he received, however, had shrunk to 260 leagues along the coast, but unlimited toward the interior. His responsibility was to erect Christian towns that were to be producing a certain amount of wealth within a number of years. As incentives to the colonists, they could import black slaves, be free from import duties, and receive appointments as knights of the Golden Spur. The Crown furnished no funds, however. Unfortunately, the colony turned into a disaster for Las Casas. This apparent failure, however, led to his entry into the Dominican Order.[63]

The Failure at Cumaná

Because he desired to build forts that could be utilized as trading posts, some have questioned the motivation of Las Casas in the Cumaná project. He certainly had little experience in the field of colonization and, more properly, his experience and not his motivation should be in question. Most likely Las Casas, the cagey veteran of court intrigues who understood the motivation of many in power, recognized that he must appeal to the profit motives of both Crown and investors in order for them to agree to his plan. As always, however, his ultimate goal was evangelism. He needed to give the appearance of a profitable venture to acquire support. His first and foremost goal, however, continued to be a peaceful settlement of Indians and Spanish peasants who prepared the way for future evangelization.[64]

Perhaps the clearest statement concerning his motives, however, came from Las Casas himself. While he was negotiating at the court of King Charles for the colony detailed above, a pious Catholic and a member of the Royal Council and the Inquisition named Aguirre came to the cleric and expressed his disapproval and concern over the deal that was being made. Basically he accused the priest of having ulterior motives. In his response to this man, Las Casas wrote what Gutiérrez called "one of the most impressive passages anywhere in his works."[65] In this passage Las Casas revealed his innermost thoughts and his concern for the natives, whom he identified with Christ. The negotiations made concerning the land were for the purpose of, as it were, buying or ransoming the natives and saving them from certain death. If they remained alive they would subsequently have the opportunity to receive the gospel and the sacraments, thereby becoming a part of the Body of Christ. This passage is significant as it revealed Las Casas's message clearly:

> Sir, if you were to see Our Lord Jesus Christ abused, with someone laying hands on Him, afflicting Him with all manner of calumny, would you not beg with the greatest urgency and with all your might that He be handed over to you instead, that you might worship, adore, and serve Him and do all that a true Christian ought to do? He replied, "Of course I would." And suppose they would not just give Him to you, would you not buy Him? He replied, "Indeed I would, I would purchase Him." Then the cleric added: Indeed, Sir, I have but acted in that very manner. Because I leave Our Lord, Jesus Christ in the Indies, scourged and afflicted and buffeted and even crucified, not just one time but millions of times, on the part of the Spaniards who ruin and destroy these people and deprive them of the space required for their conversion and repentance, depriving them of life before their time, so they die without the faith and without the sacraments. Many times I have asked the King's Council to provide them with the remedy and remove the stumbling blocks to their salvation, which is made up of the Spaniards holding in captivity those they already have, and where they still do not, to send Spaniards to go to a certain part of the continent where religious, servants of God, have begun to preach the Gospel. The Spaniards who cross that land with their violence and wicked example prevent them from doing so and make the name of Christ into a blas-

phemy. They replied there is no room there, that is if the friars were to occupy the land, the King would have no income from it. At the moment I saw they were asking me to sell the Gospel, and therefore Christ, and that they scourged Him and beat Him and crucified Him, I agreed to purchase Him, offering many goods, much income, and temporal wealth, to pay back the King, in the manner Your Mercy has heard.[66]

Thus, Las Casas might admit to the "sale of the gospel" but for the motivation of saving and rescuing the natives. As a man of action, he could not passively sit back while the colonists slaughtered the natives and at the same time endangered their own souls. In fact, those who "sell the gospel" in an effort to save the person are not guilty of any sin; it is those who look the other way and do nothing that have the greater guilt. They are guilty of the sin of omission and will ultimately receive their punishment from a just God.

Las Casas developed and expanded on this theme of the sin of omission in *The Only Way*. Here, drawing upon the authorities of both Augustine and Chrysostom, he interpreted the text from Matthew 25. This Scripture reads in part, "Whoever helps one of the helpless, helps me." The one who helps the poor and attempts to alleviate their suffering is an assistant or extension of Christ. In discussing another part of the same chapter of Matthew, Las Casas quoted from Augustine, who referenced the section of the verse, "I was starving. You fed me nothing. I was thirsty. You gave me no water." Augustine wrote, "They are damned, not for doing evil, but for not doing good."[67] Failing to do what is right in the presence of evil is the sin, not acting in accordance with one's desire to assist Christ in his ministry. After arriving in the Indies, however, the cleric had to make more concessions to the profit seekers in an effort to save the Indians, whom he henceforth identified with the crucified Christ.

Upon arrival in Puerto Rico early in 1521, the colonist-priest learned that the Indians along the coast of Tierra Firme had killed some Dominican priests at their convent at Chiribichi. They had attacked the priests as a consequence of a previous slaving expedition under the leadership of Alonso de Hojeda. The Audiencia ordered a punitive expedition to retaliate. This news caused Las Casas great pain, as this area was his first destination to begin evangelism. He attempted to stop the punitive expedition, under the leadership of Gonzalo de Ocampo, by showing him the order of the king for his settlement. This did not stop Ocampo. Las Casas proceeded to Santo Domingo in an effort to convince the Audiencia to stop the mission against the Indians.[68]

Although the authorities agreed that the priest had the proper papers, they would not halt the expedition of Ocampo, which had already begun. While discussions were taking place, Ocampo returned with the first group of slaves from the region where Las Casas was to go. Without a seaworthy vessel and without funds to continue, the cleric agreed to a business partnership with the ruling group of businessmen from Santo Domingo. They arrived at an agreement that would divide the spoils from pearl fishing, slave trading, and gains that resulted from establishing a profitable colony. Las Casas and his "knights" would each receive one-quarter of the profits, the Crown would also receive one-quarter, and the remainder would go to those pooling their resources. In a decision he later regretted yet justified, Las Casas agreed to this bargain. He even accepted the responsibility for deciding which groups of natives were capable of receiving the faith and which would become slaves because of their cannibalism. After making this arrangement, he set sail for Tierra Firme. First, however, he went to Puerto Rico to pick up the fifty knights he left there. Imagine his frustration when he learned they had already left on slaving expeditions![69]

The priest-colonist, now without colonists, finally arrived at Cumaná in late summer of 1521. He left behind little information about his life with the friars there. Apparently, there was little evangelization and not much contact with the natives. His main problems were with the nearby Spanish settlement. Unable to stop the raids, afraid that the outpost where he lived was going to be attacked, and sick at heart at how events turned out, he returned to Santo Domingo.[70] After his departure the Indians attacked the monastery and killed several servants, although the friars escaped. A month or so after this event Las Casas heard the news, including the rumor that he himself had been killed. The result of the news of this disaster was a period of intense soul searching.

He began to ask himself if this disaster at Cumaná was a result of God's judgment on him for not totally following spiritual principles and compromising with those of the world. He wrote:

> He began to believe and fear that everything he had worked for was now lost, and later, when he learned more he believed it to be a divine judgment aimed at punishing and causing him to suffer for joining in partnership with those he knew would not assist him, either out of dedication or love of God, to save the souls perishing in that province, but helped him only for the purpose of greed and getting rich. It seemed he had offended God, by making unclean the purity of that very spiritual goal, only intended for God, which was for him to go and assist the religious and with them to illuminate those people with the preaching of the Christian faith and doctrine. He had soiled this with the garbage and uncleanness of such earthly human, and even inhuman means, so antithetical to the methods used by Christ.[71]

While wondering what to do next and waiting for further royal orders, Las Casas experienced what has been called his second conversion.[72] He labored under the guilt that his partnership with those who were more concerned with worldly wealth than souls had caused the disaster to occur. Had God now punished him because of his poor judgment? Although he did not believe that he personally had caused the death of the individuals involved, the priest felt remorse that peaceful means had not worked and that those advocating armed conquest felt justified. Las Casas again sensed the need for repentance. Convinced that God had spared him, not because of his actions, which were reprehensible, but because of his intentions and underlying motivation, he sought aid and comfort from the Dominicans.[73]

While speaking with Fray Domingo de Betanzos, Las Casas came face to face with his own mortality. He realized that he must seek God and the divine will for his life and not do only what he himself desired to do. After he argued with Betanzos about waiting to receive a letter from the king with instructions on where to proceed, the friar challenged him by confronting him with the issue of what would happen to the instructions if he died. "These words stuck in the soul of the cleric Casas, and from then on he began to think more often of his condition and in the end he determined to consider himself dead to his own aims and desires."[74] After this experience, which he himself referred to as a conversion, he decided to enter the Dominican Order. There is nothing in this decision of Las Casas to indicate that it was insincere or that his motivation was anything less than an honest act of penance. Apparently, he again experienced an encounter with God. As in the previous conversion or prophetic call, he faced a crisis in his life. He believed he was acting according to God's will, yet he had failed. This failure brought him to the realization that if he were going to "speak for God," he would have to do it God's way. It was not a case of "playing dead," as suggested by some, but of a genuine death to self.[75] This process of refinement was typical of the biblical prophets and others chosen by God. Self and selfish goals and desires were being squeezed out of the priest, and he was learning to submit to God's will in his life.[76] This process of refinement was indicated also by the submission that he must now make to the order. He no longer would be a free agent, but would come under the authority of the prelate. Friar Betanzos encouraged him to abandon colonization as a means of accomplishing his goals and devote himself solely to evangelization. In other words, he should become single-minded and more directly focused. His continually deepening self-realization that his actions in speaking for God, and corresponding intercession between God and both the Spanish and Indians, were what gave continuity and meaning to his life. To best accomplish his mission, he decided that he should now become a member of a community, the Dominican Order, instead of attempting to achieve his goals by himself. This would provide him with the support and leadership he needed.[77] Thus, in 1522, he consecrated himself to a more ascetic and disciplined life in the Dominican Order in order to draw closer to God and purify his message.

It is indeed as if he "went to sleep" for a number of years, to the delight of his enemies and the fears of his friends. He would, however, awaken again, dead to self and alive to God's direction in his life.

This time his message would be deeper, more full of theological reflection, free of self-ambition, and even more committed to the good news he had to share. Gone would be the compromising attitude of the past, and he would become much more confrontational with the monarchy and direct in his words.

CHAPTER FIVE

The Message Is Refined and Deepened (1523–42)

The decision of Las Casas to enter the Dominican Order was one of the most significant of his life. The process of becoming a friar would forever transform the former diocesan priest. About April 1524, he completed the first year of his novitiate and formally entered the order.[1] He then began his four-year course of study in the Dominican monastery of Santo Domingo, on Hispaniola. Because he had already studied canon law and knew Latin well, he was exempt from those studies. He also began living the life of poverty and obedience required by his vows. Along with the others in his order, he practiced fasting, prayers, and vigils of the disciplined life.

It was difficult for someone like him, a man of action, to submit himself to the authority of another and discipline himself to the required studies. Nevertheless, this change in his status was necessary for the priest to deepen and refine his message. He now sought to justify theologically what he knew to be true practically, yet at the same time to be able to distinguish between the two. Compromising his message for the sake of appealing to the worldly interests of others could, he had learned, have tragic consequences. Yet, the transition from businessman to man of God would take time, and the new Dominican would not immediately renounce worldly means to accomplish heavenly goals. He still appealed to the potential profit of the Indies for the royal treasuries.[2]

In 1526, at the conclusion of his studies, the now Friar Bartolomé, on the orders of his superiors, went to Puerto de Plata on the northern coast of Hispaniola to build a monastery. It was here, in 1527, that he began the greatest work of his career, the *Historia gen-*

eral de las Indias, which occupied his attention for thirty-five years. It appears, however, that he had been collecting material since his initial arrival in the Indies in 1502. This work covered the history, natural history, and ethnography of the New World up to the year 1520.[3] His original manuscript also contained the material for his *Apologética historia.* He may have begun this work to give the perspective of the Native Americans that was missing from the work of Oviedo, who published a brief edition of his *Historia general* in 1526.[4] Las Casas's great themes in both of these works, which he separated from each other and revised in 1552, involved the proclamation of the gospel in both word and deed to both believers and pagans, and the defense of the life and freedoms of the Amerindians. He developed these doctrines out of his personal experience and was convinced that only by both teaching and example could evangelization take place and the truth of Christianity take hold.[5]

This chapter continues the examination of the prophetic message of Friar Bartolomé, emphasizing those aspects of the message that became more focused as a result of his studies in the Dominican monastery and that influenced those in power in both the secular and religious realms. He spoke in a more theologically refined and specific manner, and eventually criticized not only the colonists but also the monarchy. The seeds of his message, which we examined in the previous chapter, matured and began to bear fruit. He had an impact on the legislation of the Crown, specifically in the New Laws of 1542. For Las Casas the state was the representative of the Church on earth. Therefore, as the nation dedicated itself to the fulfilling of the divine mandate, it would reap the temporal rewards that accompany doing God's will. He also impacted the Church as his works formed the foundation for papal bulls. His prophetic judgments would be much more pronounced as he warned of God's judgment on the monarchy and the nation. He also began to expound on the theme of restitution whereby the Spanish should repay the Amerindians for past tyrannies. Thus, as a result of his studies, reflections, and experiences, he expanded, documented, and refined his words that would have an ever widening audience and an ever more judgmental and ominous tone. In his initial letter as a Dominican, however, he visited some old themes, albeit in a more theologically refined manner.

106

Chapter Five

On January 20, possibly in the year 1531, Las Casas wrote a long, somewhat rambling letter to the Council of the Indies. This epistle, which contained doctrinal treatises and Latin excerpts indicating that the author was writing in a monastery with access to its theological library,[6] broke his long silence and signaled his return to the fight for the rights of the Indians. He challenged the council members to consider and then to put themselves in conformity with the will of God, and to focus on the text of the letter rather than reject it because of its author. He viewed his role as reminding the council of their Christian responsibility and defending the faith that nominal Christians daily mocked by their unchristian actions. "But see the Christian faith, so vilified, affronted, and worldly in this New World, and the loss of such an infinite number of souls, growing greater each day, not only Spanish Christians but also those of these people, called by Christ in these final days for eternal salvation." If they could only keep their eyes on this fact, they would realize that it would not take "a lot of work, or require spending great amounts of money," for the greatest harvest of souls to occur since apostolic times. If they would attend first to saving the eternal souls of these individuals, the acquisition of temporal wealth would easily follow.[7] Thus, they could not only acquire wealth, but, according to the papal bull of donation of Alexander VI, from which he quoted a large section, also fulfill their evangelical mandate. He also quoted from the Last Will and Testament of Queen Isabella, which served to remind them that "our first purpose was…to convert them to our holy Catholic faith, and to send to the islands and Tierra Firme, prelates and religious…to teach the inhabitants our Catholic faith."[8] Las Casas thereby continued to remind the monarchy of its primary responsibility in the Indies, a message he reiterated until his death.

As in other works, the friar also gave remedies to alleviate the death of the natives, which he testified as numbering "two million dead souls from the surrounding area, a million, one hundred thousand from this island alone."[9] First of all, those in power should be removed and the Indians set at liberty. They also should bring African or other slaves to the Indies to alleviate the burden of work on the natives.[10] Forts should be constructed and soldiers placed in these forts, but only for self-defense and under the authority of bishops. Conversion of the natives is to be their prime duty. If the monarchy would follow this advice, the natives would more readily pay tribute to the Crown and the religious who actually collected the revenue would not steal, as the present authorities were doing.[11]

In this letter of 1531, Las Casas demonstrated that he had not only continued his studies in law and doctrine, but had also deepened his personal relationship with Christ. His message, though retaining its basic theocentrism, had matured theologically. He still recognized that any plan, in order to receive royal approval, must reward those who invested in such a project and provide for the Crown's needs. Therefore, his plans demonstrated a reality based on experience and appealed to the motivations he knew would get results. His emphasis, however, was the ending of oppression, not based solely on a new social order but on the gospel of Christ. God's word specifies that justice is to be given to the poor and the responsibility of the Christian is to live according to this directive. In an effort to communicate most effectively the seriousness of this message and its relevance to the hearers, he forces them into a confrontation with God and God's word.[12] Thus the "new" Las Casas, the Dominican friar, began his reformed ministry by utilizing the learning he had acquired and becoming more confrontational in his words. A specific practical event solidified much of his thinking and had a major impact on one of his most significant and revealing publications.

The Enriquillo Incident

The case of the Indian chief of Hispaniola, the so-called Enriquillo incident (Enriquillo is the Spanish diminutive form of Enrique, or Henry), demonstrates the further maturation of the message of the prophet as it became tempered with experience.[13] In this event Las Casas played a significant role in establishing peace between the natives and the Spanish. This incident provided the framework, or model, for what became one of his most significant evangelistic ideas—the peaceful conversion of the Indian. It also provided him with the opportunity to develop another theme—the concept of the just war. This doctrine had been utilized to justify the conquest of the New World, but now the friar contended that this had no validity in the case of the Spanish, and in fact the Indians were the ones justified in using this remedy. The story of Enriquillo is an example of a native who played by the rules but was still abused.

Enriquillo learned to read and write Spanish while still a youth in the Franciscan monastery of Verapaz. He became a Christian and was familiar with the doctrines of the Church. He and a woman named Lucía were married in the Church with its blessing. He served a Spanish man, "suffering his unjust servitude and the mistreatment he received on a daily basis with patience."[14] His master, however, stole his mare and then raped his wife. When the Indian protested this treatment, he was beaten and verbally abused. In accordance with the law, he then went to the magistrate in that town, who responded to his complaints by throwing him in jail. After his release, he went to complain to the *Audiencia*, who merely sent him back to the original official who had abused him. He then returned to his original master, Valenzuela by name, about whom Las Casas dryly remarked, "It would have been more just if he had been the servant and Enriquillo the master." Valenzuela continued to abuse him. Soon after this the Indian fled to the mountains and encouraged others to escape the colonists and join him there.[15]

While in the mountains, Enriquillo proved to be a difficult enemy for the Spaniards who attempted to capture him. Because of his ability as a leader and his mobility, he frustrated all Spanish attempts to take him prisoner. His forces, augmented by runaway Indians and black slaves, became well armed and well financed as they took weapons and money from the Spanish but killed few. After several serious attempts to apprehend Enriquillo, the Spanish government sent a force under the leadership of Francisco de Barrionuevo to bring the matter to a conclusion. After months of searching for Enriquillo in the mountains, in August 1533 Barrionuevo met with the chief and gave him a full pardon and the title of "don," which he used thereafter.[16]

Apparently Las Casas met with Enriquillo soon after this event, because the peace treaty needed to be cemented and Las Casas applied for the task. Because he was familiar with the chiefs, his superiors allowed him to go. With one other priest he made the secret journey into the mountains, where he met with the chief and his people.[17] Later, in a letter to the Council of the Indies, Las Casas explained what had happened during the month he was gone. In this letter we can see that the Dominican takes much credit for the peace and the submission of Don Enrique:

> I went—with only the grace of God and a companion friar, whom the Order furnished me—I went to Baoruco, and reassured Don Enrique and confirmed him in the service of the Emperor, our lord. I was with him a month, and confessed him and his wife and all his captains, and relieved them of all their very just fears. I would not come away from there, till I took him with me to the town of Azúa, where he was embraced by the citizenry and made merry [with them]; and I left him with the course agreed he was to follow, [namely] to go and be entertained at the other Spanish towns, and to bring to the service of His Majesty certain captains and people in rebellion, and particularly to establish his town seven leagues from Azúa; and he is to provide all that region with bread and other supplies. All of this he is actually fulfilling gladly. And in truth, noble sirs, had the Dominican Order not sent me, to serve God and His Majesty, and I had not gone there, it might be a hundred years before Don Enrique would be seen outside the impregnable peaks and highlands where he was born and possesses his patrimony. Because even though Francisco de Barrionuevo went there and commenced the peace, and it is not right he should be defrauded of what he did, yet he was there only one night and part of a midday, and then he came back; and this was not sufficient in a situation where such a capital and justly undertaken war had gone on for so many years previous. Since I saw the great harm and destruction of this island, and the inestimable good that would accrue to all the land from security and peace with Don Enrique, and the long experience I have in such matters, I persuaded the superior to send me; and it was necessary to keep my going a secret from the royal judges, on account of the hostile attitude I knew they had towards me. So I went, and I reas-

sured him; and I left him firmer in the service of His Majesty than the peak of Martos, and may it please God that they know how to keep him thus.[18]

From the tone of the letter it is obvious that Las Casas was pleased with himself and his successes. He not only affirmed the peace treaty, but also evangelized the natives and brought to them the sacraments. Thus, he joined the practical and the spiritual that were always so important to him. Even his rival, Oviedo, validated his success in this venture.

Oviedo added to his account of the story that the local judges, whom Las Casas failed to notify prior to setting out on his journey, were initially angry with him for his visit to the chief. They feared he might upset the fragile peace and frankly were not that convinced of his abilities to negotiate a lasting peace. If he were successful, their method of accomplishing peace would be proven inadequate. After they saw, however, that he had been successful in his efforts to bring about peace, they were content. Success usually brought approbation. Oviedo added that Don Enrique lived a little more than a year after this event, and then died as a Christian.[19]

Despite his self-references, this event demonstrated to the Crown and a doubting community that the Spanish could use peaceful means to bring about both peace and the evangelization of the natives. This event would prove to be a precursor to Las Casas's future project at Verapaz. If it worked with one *cacique,* could it not then work for a whole region? At last, Las Casas had a success to which he could point, an example he could show others to follow. Violence and the force of Spanish arms had not won the war with Enriquillo despite the nearly fifteen years it had continued and certainly had not facilitated the Christianization of the Amerindians. The way of Christ, however, the way of gentle, reasonable persuasion, had accomplished the desired result in both areas.

Helen Rand Parish believes that this event was the spark that ignited Las Casas to write one of his most significant and far-reaching works, a treatise concerning the evangelization of the Indians entitled *The Only Way to Draw All People to a Living Faith.* Written in 1534 while Las Casas was at the monastery, this work, originally in Latin with the title *De unico vocationis modo omnium gentium ad veram religionem,* was both religious and political. It contained references not only to biblical and patristic sources, but also to the ancient philosophers.[20] Las Casas therefore combined his theological knowledge with the practical experience he had gained in this incident and arrived at the conclusion that only peaceful means should be utilized to pacify and convert the Amerindians. From this point he further refined his message and abandoned such notions as establishing forts to protect the Spanish from contact with the natives as in Tierra Firme. Manuel Martínez has said of this work, "The first and most erudite treatise on missiology, which although aimed primarily at stimulating and beginning evangelization in America, is the mission code for all times…and anticipated the teaching of Vatican Council II, contained in the document *Ad gentes.*"[21] The message of the prophet finally had a concrete successful example to which it could point. The theoretical and theological had now come alive in the practical and it served as the model for future efforts at converting the natives and bringing peace to the area.

At the heart of this work of Las Casas, and of the gospel message itself, is the concept of teaching by example, or allowing a person's actions to speak for her or him. The Spaniards needed to earn the right to preach to the natives through Christian behavior and mode of conduct. This they clearly had not done. Just as Christ had given the apostles an example of how to live and thereby spread the gospel, so too did the apostles pass on this mode of teaching. As Bartolomé wrote, "Given that Christ, the model of all graces of the soul, taught, set the form of preaching His law, worldwide—not just by word, but also by deed, winning people over gently, persuasively, attracting them—then clearly the apostles kept to that form unswervingly."[22] Because even the apostles needed to follow the way of Christ in their teaching, so too did the Spanish. Las Casas concluded, "So Christ taught, Christ set the way, the form for preaching the Gospel: deeds first, words later."[23] No one is allowed to bring the gospel by a different way. The Dominican used the peaceful conversion of Don Enrique as a way to demonstrate that the Spanish should follow his example and bring about not only peace but also the conversion of the natives to the gospel of Christ. His words aligned with and supplemented his actions.

Within the retelling of the Enriquillo incident, however, Las Casas expounded on another theme that he repeated and developed many times in his writings. This was the idea that the natives, and not the Spanish, were conducting a just war. Inherent within this concept is the obvious corollary that warfare was not a valid way to spread the gospel of peace. This concept would be the heart of his work, *In Defense of the Indians,* which formed the basis for his famous dispute with Sepúlveda in Valladolid in 1550. The Spaniards called the actions of Don Enrique an uprising, and sought to put him and his followers down as rebels against the lawfully established government. To the Dominican, however, this was not the case because the Indians had never accepted the rule of the Spanish in the first place. They were merely defending themselves and their homes; the Spanish were the usurpers of authority.

Appealing to both history and Scripture, Las Casas wrote that the natives were just acting in self-defense and attempting to maintain their form of government:

> The war against the Spanish by him [Enriquillo] and his followers was a just one. He was chosen by his followers as the leader, as can be justly demonstrated. This justification is clear from both the history of the Maccabees in the Scripture, and the acts of D. Pelayo in Spanish writings. Not only was his a war of self defense, but by the same token and in the same manner of justification, Enriquillo and his Indians could avenge personal affronts, decimation, as well as territorial usurpation by war and punishment. This is in regards to natural law, and for the moment I am not even speaking of matters of faith which would add another right to self defense, Enriquillo and his few followers, had every justification to follow and destroy the Spaniards as their main enemy because of they had survived the cruelty and terrible tyranny of the Spaniards. They had destroyed all the great republics established by the natives on this island. In this regard they were justified by natural law, since this is not properly called, war, but an act of self-defense.[24]

Because the Indians had never recognized the Spanish king as the legitimate ruler, Don Enrique was the prince of the island. The natives may have been tyrannized *"de facto* but not *de jure."* Therefore that which the Spanish perpetrated on the island was not done according to reason but according to force and injustice. In a future writing, *Doce dudas* in 1564, Las Casas developed this theme even further. He wrote that the monarchy was obligated to punish the Spanish because they were destroying the Indians.[25] Therefore, even at personal risk to the king, he should not only wage war but even lead it himself, against the unjust who were tyrannizing other of his subjects. The bishop of Chiapa, acting in the role of prophet or spokesman for God because he here interpreted the specific will of God in the particular situation, wrote this to the king as a service to him, to apprise him of his responsibilities, and to assure him that as he fulfilled these duties he would conserve his soul and live a blessed life.[26] Thus we can see that although the Dominican repeated, refined, and strengthened his message throughout his life, the basics of that message remained constant.

To continue Las Casas's thought on this doctrine, in one of his last writings the bishop of Chiapa addressed another *memorial* to the Council of the Indies. In this document is found the culmination of his concept of the just war doctrine as it applied to the Indies, as well as other prophetic warnings. At the end of his life he spoke as clearly and as forcefully as possible. Gone now was any self-justification or attempt to appeal to worldly measures to achieve heavenly goals. In as clear and as strong a way as possible, he wrote: "The native peoples of all the lands in the Indies into which we have come, have the vested right to make war on us most justly and to expel us immediately from the land. This right will remain with them until Judgment Day."[27]

All of the wars fought against the Indians had been waged unjustly. Implied within the above statement of Las Casas, and spelled out specifically in another part of this *memorial,* was the fact that all those who had abused the Indians and did not make restitution for their action were in mortal sin, and therefore their eternal souls were in jeopardy. There would be a Judgment Day, even for the king himself, since he had done nothing to prevent the tyrannies and murders. The protection of the Indians, who were also royal subjects, was both his responsibility and mandate. He fulfilled none of these responsibilities.[28] As he aged, the prophet became increasingly confrontational with the monarchy. The message hardened not because Las Casas was disrespectful to the monarch, but because he was concerned for his eternal salvation. As previously explained, an important prophetic role is to force the hearer to view himself and his situation in light of Scripture. Las Casas attempted here, in a figurative manner, to hold a mirror up to the king and allow him to see his destiny if he did not repent and change his actions. He believed the eternal soul of the monarch to be in jeopardy because of his sin of omission or inaction in preventing the destruction of the natives.

Not only was it necessary for the Spaniards to cease doing evil and making war on the natives, but their souls were also in danger if they did not make restitution for all they had unjustly taken from the natives. They must return to them what they had stolen and destroyed. This concept was another one of Las Casas's favorite themes, introduced in *The Only Way*, which he continued to develop and repeat until his death. He challenged the authorities: "On peril of losing their souls, all who start wars of conversion...all are bound to restore to the devastated pagan peoples whatever they took in war, permanent or perishable and make up for whatever they destroyed. Make up totally."[29] Thus the conquerors must not only give back what they had taken but also make amends for all that they had consumed. The Dominican emphasized and expanded on this concept in the future after he was ordained bishop.

The incident with Don Enrique was, therefore, crucial to the development and maturation of the message of Las Casas. Out of this experience he deepened his conviction that there was only one method of spreading the gospel message. This consisted of peaceful persuasion and appeal to the reason of the hearers; war was never justified. This was the opening thought for his work *The Only Way*. "One way, one way only, of teaching a living faith, to everyone, everywhere, always, was set by Divine Providence." Thus he demonstrated his inductive Aristotelian logic that from examining the specifics, in this case the example of Enriquillo, one could then project the ideal, which would be valid at any time or in any circumstance. He continued to elaborate on how this could be done: "The way that wins the mind with reasons, that wins the will with gentleness, with invitation. It has to fit all people on earth, no distinction made for sect, for error, even for evil."[30] Thus, we observe the former *clérigo*, now as a

Dominican, deepening his theological justification for what he always knew to be true. Peaceful conversion through the use of example and reason was the only legitimate way to spread the message of Christ that was available to all. Salvation is universal, not restricted in any way. Las Casas's message now broadened to include his personal experiences with Enriquillo, which could be applied to all efforts at evangelization as well as to bring about peace, and the concept of restitution for past sins that must be made to all exploited individuals or nations.

After his experiences with Don Enrique, and the writing of *The Only Way*, Las Casas now decided to begin his own missionary venture in Peru. Traveling in 1535 with the newly appointed bishop of Panama, Fray Tomás de Berlanga, he soon arrived in that region but found it full of sickness and hunger. Because of these conditions, he left for Peru. After two and a half months becalmed at sea, however, he and his companions arrived in Nicaragua. There he found the natives to be suffering greatly.[31]

From Land of War to Land of Peace

Writing to an unnamed courtier in October 1535, Las Casas described the beauty of the land and the fact that it was God's will that had brought them there instead of to Peru. After describing how the Spanish had reduced the number of Indians from a total of perhaps 600,000 to perhaps 12,000 to 15,000, Las Casas proposed a plan that continued the goals of peaceful conversion as set out in *The Only Way* and also anticipated his future project of Verapaz. He wrote that beyond Lake Nicaragua there were a large number of tribes who were enemies of the Christians because of the atrocities committed in the area. If the Crown would send a *cédula,* or royal order, he and his companions would pacify these peoples and make them subjects. In order to accomplish this, however, the official document must specify that no Christian, "great or small," should have any contact with them. Also, they must not be subjected in any way to the Spanish. If these points were agreed to, "I and my companions, trusting in divine assistance and protection, for we undertake this mission for His honor and the salvation of their souls, would go among them, pacify them, and bring them to serve our sovereign, and to convert them so they may know their Creator." This is necessary, and "is the true way of having these people acknowledge God, as their God, and then the king as their sovereign. The goal of Your Majesty is to spread the faith. This is your primary authority and title to these lands."[32] This *cédula* had to stipulate that anyone violating these principles would be subject to death.

Thus, in an attempt to move from individual conversion by peaceful means, as in the case of Enriquillo, to the conversion of a number of tribes Las Casas developed his mission. Viewing his unexpected arrival in Nicaragua as God's provision, he sought to bring about God's will. He again brought up the theme that conversion to Christianity, by authority of the papal donation, was the main purpose and sole justification for the Spanish presence in the Indies. He wrote, "The whole purpose of the [papal] concession to the Spanish monarchs, its motivation and lordship that they exercise over these lands was for their life and for the conversion and salvation of their souls. Yet it has become a quick, miserable death, and final perdition."[33] To clarify and expand further on the lack of focus of the monarchy and to reinforce the blame it had for what was happening, as well as to offer a further admonition for his peaceful means, he ended this letter with the words, "This is not the way of Christ, nor of His preaching, nor His way of converting souls. This is the way of Muhammad, and even worse than his way…because after those he subjected by force of arms believed in his religion, he gave them their lives."[34] His message continued to emphasize the necessity of saving both the physical life on this earth and salvation of the soul through eternal life in the hereafter. Because he preached this kind of message and declared that he would refuse absolution to anyone who participated in a slave-raiding expedition of Governor Rodrigo de Contreras, Las Casas and his companions were not welcome in Nicaragua and therefore went to Guatemala.

Las Casas and his associates arrived in Santiago de Guatemala in the summer of 1536 as the guest of Bishop Marroquín, who instructed the preachers to learn the Mayan language because of their desire to begin a pastoral ministry among the natives. They were in need of instruction in the faith, and this the friars desired to do in the natives' languages.[35] There is some question as to whether or not Las Casas learned any of the local languages. Conflicting with the account of Remesal, the Franciscan Motolonía wrote in his 1552 letter to Charles V that Las Casas did not learn any native tongue.[36] Although he may not have learned any of the indigenous languages, he did consider this knowledge to be important for those religious actually working with the natives. For example, he recommended to the pope that any bishops coming to the Indies "learn the language of their sheep."[37] Also, in his 1516 *Memorial de remedios,* obviously considering how the *Requerimiento* was broadcast to the Indians in a way they could not understand, Las Casas urged that all new laws and information promulgated by the Crown be in the native languages so that the natives could clearly understand them.[38] He did not speak to the issue of whether or not he was fluent in any of the languages, but he certainly demonstrated his regard for those who were and recognized the importance of the Spanish identifying with the natives in their own tongue. This concern for the natives hearing the message in their own language, yet not learning it himself, would be consistent with his role as prophet.

The pastor must learn the "language of their sheep," but the prophet's main responsibility is to influence those in authority as he interprets God's message for the time. It is apparent from the letters of Las Casas from the 1530s that he desired to return to Spain and the seat of power. He believed he could influence royal policy more effectively there. While pastoring and teaching the Indians about the faith was important and needed to be done, he knew that his responsibility was elsewhere and that, in order to save the Indians, he had to influence those in authority who could pass legislation that would protect the native peoples. Just as the biblical prophets had pleaded their case before the kings of Israel, so too did the Dominican desire the royal ear. Soon Las Casas had a direct impact on the authorities in both the religious and secular arenas.

Prior to beginning his work on peaceful conversion in Guatemala, Las Casas received a summons from Bishops Juan de Zumárraga and Julián de Garcés to attend a conference in Oaxaca, Mexico. His companions remained in Guatemala. This meeting was very significant in that those who attended agreed on and sent specific suggestions to the pope on three themes: adult baptism of Indians, slavery of natives of the Indies, and, perhaps most important, the manner of their conversion. Bernardino de Minaya, a Dominican, took these petitions to Pope Paul III in Rome. He also carried notes from Las Casas that contained the initial ideas of *The Only Way.* Apparently after consulting these communications the pope promulgated the bull *Sublimus Deus* on June 2, 1537. This document follows the concepts outlined in *The Only Way.*[39] This decree emphasized the rationality of the Indians and the fact they should not be enslaved but brought to a knowledge of the faith. This bull was directly based on the message of Las Casas and demonstrated his influence with the pope.

The bull is addressed to "all Christ's faithful who will read these words." After the blessing, the pope wrote, "Sacred Scripture also testifies that we were created to attain eternal life and eternal bliss. And no one is able to reach life and bliss in eternity except through faith in Jesus Christ." Because all humans were created in God's image, "so we have perforce to admit that we humans are of such nature and condition that we can receive the faith of Christ. Anyone who is a human being is capable of receiving that faith." In an effort to thwart the designs of God, who desires that all individuals learn of him and his plan for their lives, Satan blinded certain ones with a lust for riches and had them proclaim that the Indians were incapable of receiving the faith because they were beasts. These lackeys of Satan "reduce them to slavery, they load them with afflictions they would never load on any beast of burden." The pope then expounded the heart of his message:

> We are the unworthy Vicegerent on earth of the Lord. We try with all our might to lead into the flock of Christ committed to our care, *those who are outside the sheepfold.* We are aware through what we have been told that those Indians, as true human beings, have not only the capacity for Christian faith, but the willingness to flock to it. We wish to provide apt solutions for the situation. *The Indians we speak of, and all other peoples who later come to the knowledge of Christians, outside the faith though they be,* are not to be deprived of their liberty or the right to their

property. They are to have, to hold, to enjoy both liberty and dominion, freely, lawfully. They must not be enslaved. Should anything different be done, it is void, invalid, of no force, no worth. And those Indians and other peoples are to be *invited into the faith of Christ by the preaching of God's word and the example of a good life.*[40]

Thus, incorporated within this papal bull are the two great themes of Las Casas, especially as espoused in *The Only Way.* The first of these was the universality of the gospel. Christ died for all, who were made in the image and likeness of God. All were equal in God's eyes. These peoples included not only those who were already within the family of faith but also those who have not yet heard the message or had the option of accepting or rejecting it. Thus, the Indians and any others who remain to be "discovered" have just as much a right to the gospel as the Spanish. They are free beings and may not be deprived of their liberty. The other theme is that Christians must proclaim this message by both word and deed. They must appeal gently and reasonably to the pagan in words and act out the message in their lives by example. One without the other will not produce the desired result, which is the attraction of all peoples to the message of Christ.[41] Thus, Las Casas had an influence on the highest spiritual authority in the Church.

Only days before issuing this bull, the pope issued two other pronouncements relevant to the question of the Indians. Both of these bear the mark of Las Casas. The brief *Pastorale Officium* (May 29, 1537) included the threat of excommunication for those enslaving the Indians. As the Amerindians were human beings, they could accept the faith and therefore must not be deprived of their liberty. The other bull, *Altitudo Divini Consilii* (June 1, 1537), addressed to the bishops in the Indies, dealt with the issue of baptism. Siding with the Dominicans against the Franciscans in an inoffensive and non-condemnatory way, the pope decreed that instruction in the faith should precede baptism. Unfortunately, Emperor Charles V soon officially forced the revocation of these documents by royal decree. Apparently, this action was really unnecessary because the *encomenderos* and royal officials were already ignoring the intent of the bulls.[42] Las Casas utilized these bulls as official Church documents, however, in his attempts to bring justice and the gospel to the natives in a peaceful manner.

After his conference in Oaxaca, Las Casas returned to Guatemala, where he embarked on another attempt to put into practice the principles he developed in *The Only Way*. To accomplish this task he needed the support of government officials. He entered into secret negotiations with Governor Alonso de Maldonado, who was sympathetic to his ideas. According to these plans, the Dominicans would enter into an area in northeastern Guatemala, known as Tuzulutlán, or "Land of War," which contained warlike peoples and subdue them by peaceful means. The inhabitants of this area had fiercely resisted three previous Spanish attempts at conquest. The Dominicans' mission was to bring the gospel slowly and deliberately to these peoples without the involvement of any other Spaniards and, at the same time, to make them subjects of Spain in a reasonable and peaceful manner.[43]

As Las Casas preached the doctrines he desired all Christians to practice, his message met with derision among the colonists. They actually believed that the Lord had brought this meddlesome Dominican to their area so that he would fail in his attempts at peaceful negotiations. Here in the Land of War he would fail once and for all, and he and his methods would be proven invalid. Perhaps the natives would even do the Spanish the favor of permanently doing away with the meddlesome priest. This action would, therefore, justify and reinforce their method of enslaving and slaughtering the warlike natives and set back the initiatives of the religious. Yet Las Casas was just as convinced that his methods would work, and he secretly worked out a plan with the governor.[44]

The agreements made between the Dominicans and Governor Maldonado were simple and to the point: only the Dominicans could enter the province for five years, and all the natives converted by peaceful means would be subject only to a small tribute and under the direct authority of the Crown and not be divided among the Spaniards. The purpose behind these agreements was to give the peaceful plan enough time to work and to keep secular Spaniards from interfering with the actions of the priests.[45]

The work began as the friars composed verses, religious songs, and Christian teaching in the local Quiché language. These lessons explained the basic biblical messages, such as creation and the coming of Jesus. They then taught these stories to some Indian merchants who traveled in that area. The Dominicans also provided them with some trinkets to excite the interest of the natives. Their efforts met with some success although the project took them a year to complete. Their first success was when Father Cáncer, a skilled linguist, went to the area of Zacapulas and began to rebuild a church previously destroyed in that area. Out of curiosity for the message and realizing that the Spanish were not as fearsome as they once believed, the Indians established contact with the friars.[46]

One of the most successful converts for the Dominicans was the *cacique* Juan. It was through his efforts that they rebuilt the church that had been burned in Zacapulas. He also provided safe passage for the friars throughout the area. Several other *caciques* received the faith and later received the title of "don" for their efforts. Now Las Casas was ready to go into the fiercest area, Cobán. With an escort of seventy warriors from the people of Chief Juan, Las Casas went throughout the area and received a warm reception. At the beginning of 1538, he returned to Zacapulas after a successful missionary and evangelization mission into the heretofore untouched areas.[47]

News of their success was a complete surprise as well as a disappointment to the colonists, who expected and desired the priests to fail. Upon his arrival back in Santiago de Guatemala, Las Casas began to preach about his activities and called for the peaceful conversion of the natives and restitution for past atrocities. It was obvious to the friars, however, that more clerics must come to the area to complete the project successfully. To accomplish this task, Las Casas left for Spain with instructions from Bishop Marroquín to induce fifty more friars to come to the region. They also carried letters of recommendation from Maldonado, the *adelantado* Pedro de Alvarado, and Bishop Zumárraga. Thus, after nearly twenty years, the Dominican was to return to the seat of power to continue his message and recruit new laborers for the field. He traveled to Spain with the twin successes of Enriquillo and the commencement of the pacification of the Land of War by peaceful means.[48] The Sevillian now embarked on another mission, that of influencing King Charles V to bring about legislation that would continue the peaceful conversion and halt, or at least modify, the hated *encomienda* system.

When Las Casas and his companions, Cáncer and Ladrada, arrived in Spain, they learned that the king was abroad. They then traveled to the Court at Madrid in order to obtain from the Council of the Indies royal *cédulas* that would allow for the mission in Tuzulutlán to continue. These documents took the form of obtaining royal financial support as well as official letters of gratitude to the *caciques* in Tuzulutlán, who assisted the Dominicans in the spreading of the gospel.[49] They then traveled to Seville, where it was publicly proclaimed from the steps of the Seville Cathedral that only friars could enter the Land of War. After this success Cáncer and other Franciscan religious returned to the Indies with the official documents. Las Casas and Ladrada, however, decided that they needed to meet personally with Charles V, whom the Dominican trusted, in order to state their case and seek support for a new series of attacks on those who were destroying the Indians.[50]

Because Las Casas was a Dominican and therefore subject to the authority of the order, he needed to respect Cardinal García de Loaysa, also a Dominican and head of the Council of the Indies. Fearful that Loaysa might attempt to prevent the meeting with the emperor, Las Casas wrote the monarch a letter. In this communication, dated December 15, 1540, he stressed he had some important matters to discuss personally with him. Also, he again made reference not only to the evangelism that was taking place in the Indies, but also to the future increase in royal revenues that would accrue to the royal coffers if his plans of peace could be accomplished. Furthermore, he requested that the king order him to remain in order for their meeting to take place when Charles returned from Flanders.[51] Thus did Las Casas bypass his Dominican superiors and Loaysa.

The emperor answered his letter almost immediately from Flanders and promised a meeting as soon as he returned to Spain. When Las Casas had this assurance, he ended his efforts at missionary recruitment in order to begin again lobbying for the Indians. Five years after influencing the pope to issue bulls and edicts, Las Casas prepared to lobby the secular realm of authority for legislation to bring about justice for his beloved Amerindians. As was his custom, while he awaited the monarch the ever-diligent Dominican kept busy by writing and preparing documents.[52]

The result of the request by Las Casas, combined with other complaints against the treatment of the Indies, such as those made by the Spanish Cortes of Valladolid in 1542, moved the emperor to convene a meeting with the Council of the Indies in April 1542. At the same time the monarch, perhaps suspecting some duplicity among the members of the council, ordered a *visita,* or inspection, of this body. As a consequence of this formal investigation, Ramírez de Fuenleal replaced the Dominican Loaysa, no friend of either Las Casas or the Indians, as president. Also, the *visita* removed Diego de Beltrán and Juan Suárez de Carvajal from office for receiving bribes. While this was going on Las Casas was busy strengthening his influence with Charles V, who respected him greatly and apparently listened to his counsel.[53]

Las Casas now brought forth two of his most powerful writings. He presented these to the council and they had a dramatic effect on both the immediate as well as the long-range situation. His "Octavo Remedio" and the *Brevísima relación,* both written in 1542, would become the basis for the New Laws.[54] The exact influence of the Dominican on the writing of the New Laws has been a subject for debate and will be treated below. All agree, however, that these two works, especially the latter, first published in 1552, ten years after its writing, with the complete name of *Brevísima relación de la destrucción de las Indias (A Short Account of the Destruction of the Indies),*[55] had a profound negative effect on the image of Spain among the rest of the world. Both works provided a platform for Las Casas to speak in a prophetic manner concerning Spain and its future.

In this *relación,* which Las Casas wrote for Crown Prince Philip, he began by explaining his unique, if unwilling, qualifications for writing such a polemical piece. The mood of the work was sensational, and its purpose was to shock the moral sensibilities of the monarchy. Spain had now been fifty years in the Indies and still had no official policy of stopping the slaughter. As the author writes about himself again in the third person, "Brother Bartolomé de Las Casas, or Casaus, came to the Spanish court...to give our Lord, the Emperor, an eye-witness account of these enormities, not a whisper of which had reached the ears of people here." From the beginning of this treatise, Las Casas made it known this was not something he had heard about, but he was personally present during the atrocities.

This was a *relación*, or formal historical relation, of what actually happened, not simply an opinion or summary of others' experiences.[56] He continued: "He also related these same events to several people he met during his visit and they were deeply shocked by what he had to say and listened open-mouthed to his every word." It is also obvious that one of his purposes for writing this was its shock value. He desired to provoke a reaction and cause a sensation. By means of this account he hoped to draw attention to the plight of his beloved Indians, who had nearly already perished from the islands, and the fate of those remaining was now in jeopardy in New Spain and Peru. As if he were an unwilling participant in this unfolding drama, he said, "They later begged him and pressed him to set down in writing a short account of some of them [the atrocities], and this he did." Finally, to speak his mind fully, and to keep from being ignored, he challenged those who had profited by the exploitation by invoking a biblical threat: "he observed that not a few of the people involved in this story had become so anesthetized to human suffering by their own greed and ambition that they had ceased to be men in any meaningful sense of the term,...so totally degenerate and given over to a reprobate mind, they could not rest content."[57] They were again seeking from the monarchy more license to exploit and "commit their dreadful deeds."[58] To frustrate these plans, the author addressed this work to the crown prince, who could intervene with the emperor.

The text of the work itself is a litany of the destruction of the Indians in each specific area that the Spanish now controlled. Not mincing words, Las Casas wrote concerning the cruelty of the Christians as they pacified Hispaniola: "They forced their way into native settlements, slaughtering everyone they found there, including small children, old men, pregnant women, and even women who had just given birth. They hacked them to pieces, slicing open their bellies with their swords."[59] In a condemnation of the *encomienda* system, a favorite theme as we have noticed, he wrote concerning Nicaragua, "Each of the settlers took up residence in the town allotted to him (or encommended to him as the legal phrase has it), put the inhabitants to work for him, stole their already scant foodstuffs for himself and took over the lands owned and worked by the natives." Concerning the mistreatment of the natives, he continued,

"The settler would treat the whole of the population—dignitaries, old men, women and children…and make them labour night and day in his own interests, without any rest whatever; even the small children, as soon as they could stand, were made to do as much as they could, and more."[60] The entire treatise was full of such condemnatory words. What broke the priest's heart, however, was the lack of evangelism and the attitude of the natives concerning Christianity.

In an effort to appeal to the Christian conscience of the monarchy Las Casas emphasized that evangelism was not taking place. "The Spanish have taken no more trouble to preach the Christian faith to these peoples than if they had been dealing with dogs or other animals." Not only have they not spread the gospel by word or deed, which is the formula from *The Only Way*, but, "indeed they have done their level best to prevent missionaries from preaching, presumably because they felt that the spread of the Gospel would in some way stand between them and the gold and wealth they craved." The result of this enmity to the preaching of the gospel must stand as an indictment to the Christian Spanish monarchy. Las Casas concluded, "Today, the peoples of the New World are as ignorant of God as they were a hundred years ago: they have no idea of whether He is made of wood, or of air, or of water."[61]

Las Casas insisted that the lust for wealth had blinded the Spanish and they had not fulfilled their mission before God. They had not brought the gospel to the infidel, had not demonstrated the faith by their conduct, and indeed had actually been a hindrance, as they had not allowed the true missionaries to complete their task. They acted less civilized than the pagans they came to convert to their way of faith. In fact, the natives referred to the Christians as *yares*, or demons, because of their actions that seemed to mock both God and God's word.[62] The representatives of Christ had now been identified as being of the devil and not of God. The irony was too much for the man of God. How painful this must have been for the Dominican whose sole desire was to bring Christ to these unbelievers! Because of these actions and omissions the judgment of God could not be far away.

At this point the prophet spoke for God. Las Casas emphasized that his motivation for bringing such a message was not for selfish or even punitive reasons, but "to help ensure that the teeming millions in the New World, for whose sins Christ gave His life, do not die in ignorance, but rather are brought to a knowledge of God and thereby saved." Because of his love for his native Castile, and his desire therefore not to see the wrath of God come upon it because of their sins by lack of following their divine mandate, he wrote, "For I do not wish to see my country destroyed as a divine punishment for sins against the honour of God and the True Faith."[63] There it is. The prophet finally warned his king and his nation that God would destroy them for their lack of obedience. The nation remained only as long as the mercy of God held out. At this point in his life Las Casas spoke as clearly and dramatically as he could. There could be no doubt as to his meaning and the authority with which he spoke from this time forward.

In the other work of 1542, the "Octavio Remedio," also known as "Among the Remedies," which Las Casas wrote at about the same time and utilized in the same way as *The Short Account,* he continued this prophetic theme. He expressed his love of his nation and the Crown, and his desire for their good fortune. If the Indians continued to die at the current rate, the royal treasury would lose "riches and treasures it rightly should have, both from the Indian vassals as well as the Spanish people." Therefore, the kingdom would suffer loss and not be as strong as it might.[64] Worse yet, the colonists in the Indies were in mortal danger of divine retribution. This punishment would also apply to those in Spain who did nothing to change the situation. After enumerating his complaints against the *encomienda* system and explaining why the emperor did not have power over the natives who did not voluntarily submit to him, and why he should release them from this system, Las Casas wrote that the monarchy could do a great service for those Christians living in the Indies. The Crown should attempt to make restitution for the sins of the colonists "in order to free them from the great sins of tyranny, robberies, violence, murders, which they commit every day, oppressing and robbing and killing those people." These actions will bring about divine condemnation and retribution unless atoned for. This the Crown itself must do to save its subjects.[65] The inhabitants of the Old World would have to pay for the sins of those in the New. Las Casas ended his tract with a prophetic warning: "and because of all these sins, and because of what I read in the Sacred Scripture, God must punish,

127

with terrible retributions, and perhaps even destroy all of Spain."[66] The entire nation must pay the price of the monarchy's refusal to obey the word of God.

For the first time the message of Las Casas became prophetic in the sense of prophesying the destruction of the nation. According to Menéndez Pidal, Las Casas meditated much on the book of the Bible written by the prophet Isaiah, especially chapter 30. In this chapter Isaiah prophesied against those who did not listen to the prophets, change their ways, and cease oppression. Judgment would come suddenly on the unjust and totally destroy them.[67] This was the first time the warning took on such drastic tones, but it would not be the last.

In a 1555 letter to the royal confessor Bartolomé de Carranza, Las Casas warned that because the monarchy had not punished the *conquistadores,* but in fact had rewarded them with Indians and land, "they [the monarchs] must be punished by God."[68] At the end of that same letter, he warned that because the emperor and his confessor at the time, Pedro de Soto, had revoked the Laws of Inheritance, a part of the New Laws discussed below, they would be in danger of judgment. Las Casas wrote, "On the day they both die they shall see what kind of candle they have obtained to light their way to heaven"[69] This judgmental theme will continue throughout the remainder of his writings and culminate in his Last Will and Testament. Judgment from an angry God would come to those who flaunt his justice toward the poor and oppressed. Those in authority were placed there by God, represented him, and were commanded to bring about justice and not exploit those incapable of defending themselves. Perhaps because of these writings, a new role of spiritual authority with its consequent privileges was about to come upon the Dominican.

CHAPTER SIX

Las Casas as Bishop and Beyond (1542–63)

In the midst of the deliberations that formed the backdrop for the publications that would result in the New Laws that were promulgated in late 1542 and officially printed in mid-1543, Las Casas received his appointment as bishop of Chiapas. During the years 1542–43, the Dominican was at the peak of his influence with the emperor. In November 1542, Las Casas apparently received a visit from the imperial secretary Francisco de los Cobos, who offered him the wealthy bishopric of Cuzco. This he refused. Subsequently, however, Las Casas accepted, under threat of a possible papal order, the poorer bishopric of Chiapa.[1] A new chapter in the life of Las Casas began. During his tenure as bishop, he continued to write and utilize his influence, in both Spain and the New World, for the benefit of the Indians. This chapter emphasizes the role of the works that he wrote during these years and the influence he wielded on both secular and religious authorities.

Upon his nomination, Las Casas composed a petition to the emperor in which he listed a number of requests. First of all, he desired that his boundaries be specifically defined to include the area south of Chiapa. This area contained the Land of War, which continued as his experiment in peaceful conversion. It was subsequently renamed Verapaz, or Land of Peace. He made it clear in this petition that the primary reason for his return to the Indies was to continue the project of pacification and evangelization.[2] In order to carry out these designs more competently he made other requests, among which was the strengthening of the religious authority that the civil powers should enforce in questions concerning the treatment of the natives. Finally, he requested financial backing from the Crown and, in an overtly political move, the removal of the Governor Montejo of the Yucatán region, who had opposed Las Casas and the Dominicans. Montejo had done nothing to end the repression of the natives in that region, which would be under the bishopric of Chiapa.[3]

The question arises as to why Las Casas would accept a bishopric in the New World since he was at the pinnacle of his influence with the aging Charles V and had the respect, and ear, of the crown prince. This issue was especially pertinent because Cardinal Loaysa, who had been demoted as the result of an investigation called for by Las Casas, was temporarily in charge of the council when it pressed Las Casas to accept the bishopric.[4] Also, the monarchy was pressuring him to leave for the Indies as soon as possible, even before the papal bulls announcing his appointment as bishop and the ordination rite. In several *cédulas,* the Crown exempted him from all taxes, requested local governmental financial assistance for him, and, in general, tried to smooth the way for him to leave as quickly as possible.[5] Yet, although he knew that his foes were pushing him into this bishopric, he accepted it.

The reasons for his acceptance seemed to outweigh the motivations of those pushing for it. Convinced that this appointment would be useful in his attempt to enlist the Church's assistance in the enforcement of the New Laws, Las Casas recognized the necessity of his presence in the New World. Also, by accepting the miter, he was relieved from his vow of obedience to the Dominican Order. For these reasons, along with his desire to continue putting into practice the peaceful methods of evangelism he had originated, he accepted the office. On March 31, 1544, in the Church of San Pablo in Seville, Las Casas was consecrated bishop.[6] His goal was to proceed to the New World and assist in the enforcement of the New Laws he had helped to write and publicize.

The New Laws enacted by Charles V in late 1542 resulted from an offensive by the defenders of the Indians, primarily Las Casas; they also coincided with the king's desire to limit the burgeoning colonial aristocracy. The goal of the emperor was not only to seize the wealth of the *encomenderos,* but also to secure his authority as much in the New World as he had in Spain. Specifically, he feared the ascension of a new hereditary nobility among the *encomenderos* like that which opposed Ferdinand and Isabella's centralization policies in fifteenth-century Spain.[7] Charles desired to be the only *encomendero* in the New World and by these laws he reaffirmed his authority.[8] Although they followed the pattern of the Laws of Burgos, promulgated in 1512, these laws were much more specific and written in stronger language; this demonstrated that Charles was not only more secure in his authority as monarch but also that the influence of the humanitarian reformers at court had grown.[9]

The specific influence of Las Casas on the writing of the New Laws is a matter of some question. Menéndez Pidal, probably the most outspoken critic of the Dominican, believed that Las Casas's theories (which he labeled "extremist") had little to do with their formulation and that the laws more reflected the influence of Vitoria. Therefore, the passage of the New Laws did not indicate a victory for the ideas of Las Casas, but for those of the reformist majority in the Church and high government authorities. Because he was the most outspoken supporter of the Indians and because at the time he was at the height of his influence with the Crown, it is natural that Las Casas would receive the credit for their passage, but he was not primarily responsible.[10]

Contemporaries of Las Casas and most current scholars, however, give him much more credit for the passage of the New Laws. Gómara, for example, wrote in his *Historia general* that Las Casas had obtained passage of the New Laws and that the colonists all blamed him for the changes dictated by these laws.[11] Modern scholarship seems to agree with this assessment. Parish, representative of this sentiment, writes, "At court, Bartolomé de Las Casas achieved the greatest legislative triumph of his career, the New Laws of 1542–1543, 'The Laws and Ordinances Newly Made for the Good Government of the Indies and the Preservation of the Indians,'" as they were formally entitled.[12] Concurring at least with the effect of the legislation is Hanke, who writes, "The Dominican friar...had set in motion as revolutionary a change in American society and in the administration of Spain's great empire overseas as...Copernicus had achieved in astronomical circles with his *De revolutionibus orbium coelestium* printed in the same year as the New Laws."[13]

There is no mistaking the influence of the Dominican on the New Laws. His ideas were at the heart of these mandates. Although many of the laws dealt with such topics as the meeting times and days of the Council of the Indies and other procedural matters, the most meaningful and, therefore, the most controversial were those regarding the welfare of the natives. Of the fifty-four articles, twenty-three have to do with the status of the Indian.[14] These provisions were designed to protect and provide freedoms to the natives as well as to curb the power of the *encomenderos*.

The most significant articles in the New Laws dealing with forced servitude were numbers twenty-six and twenty-seven, which prohibited enslavement of Indians and affirmed that they were vassals of the Crown and not private individuals. In the future, not even in the case of rebellion could the colonists enslave the natives. If an *encomendero* could not show legal ownership of an Indian, the Indian must be set free. The Crown would pay for the claim of and represent any Indian who argued for his freedom. In addition to these two significant articles, others dealt with the ending of forced labor and the sending of natives to the pearl fisheries.

The significant articles dealing with *encomiendas* were numbers thirty-one and thirty-five. The former abolished the holding of *encomiendas* by public officials, institutions, the secular clergy, and religious organizations. The latter, which was perhaps the most difficult for the colonists to accept, ended the inheritance of the *encomienda* at the death of the original owner. Many of the *conquistadores* who had originally obtained title to the property were aging or had died. The question arose as to what would happen to the *encomienda* at their death. In an effort to prevent any new type of hereditary nobility from forming, the Crown ordered that at the death of an *encomendero*, the property be reverted to the Crown. An evaluation would be made of the life of the deceased and if he had provided the Crown with some exceptional service, the Crown would provide his heirs with some type of support, but the property and Indians were not part of this. In addition to these provisions, the Indians were to receive instruction in the Catholic faith.[15]

These articles correspond almost directly with the "Eighth Remedy" proposed by Las Casas. Las Casas believed that the most important law that could be passed was the ending of the *encomienda* system. This institution was the center of all the other injustices in the Indies. For out of this system flowed the greed that infected every other aspect of life and blinded the Christians to their duty toward the natives. He wrote, "Your Majesty should order and command…that all the Indians in the Indies…should be incorporated into the royal Crown of Castile and Aragon, as free subjects and vassals, and that none should be encommended to Spanish Christians."[16] This ordinance must be permanent and apply to all others not yet in contact with the Spanish. Thus Las Casas again emphasized the Christian mandate of the bull of donation of Alexander VI and the responsibility that this donation placed on the Crown. The Crown's obligation was to evangelize, not to enslave. The influence of Las Casas was now at its apex among both the Church clergy and the state officials. His ideas were at the center of both the papal pronouncements and the New Laws. Unfortunately, however, it was one thing to enact legislation or promulgate bulls and quite another to enforce the policies in the New World. The problem that had plagued the monarchy since 1492 was how to obtain compliance with its desires half a world away. This predicament was especially acute when these laws were unpopular.

Another feature that distinguished these ordinances from the Laws of Burgos was that the emperor assigned specific individuals to enforce compliance with the legislation. Obviously those affected were not going to comply willingly with these provisions. Unfortunately, the arrival of Governor Blasco Núñez de Vela in Peru coincided with the rebellion of Gonzalo Pizarro, brother of the *conquistador.* Pizarro's forces captured and beheaded Núñez de Vela when he arrived and attempted to implement the New Laws. The same fate may have awaited Tello de Sandoval in New Spain had he not immediately suspended the most controversial provisions pending an appeal. Officials immediately left for Spain to inform the monarchy why these could not be carried out.[17]

Significantly, not only the *encomenderos* but also some of the clergy opposed the ending of the *encomienda* system. The clergymen who opposed the dissolution of this system included Bishops Motolinía, Marroquín, and Zumárraga. Even Domingo de Betanzos, the Dominican who had encouraged Las Casas to enter the order years before, argued against the abolition of the *encomienda* system. In a letter to the emperor, Betanzos and other religious contended that the placing of natives under the care of Christians allowed for the teaching of the faith in the most effective manner. He argued that the Spaniards treated the natives well, as if they were their own children, and that the close contact assisted in the Indians' conversion to Christianity.[18] Also, the *encomenderos* were necessary for the financial support of the poorer Spaniards and provided for the defense of the nation. With no real support among those in authority, the New Laws were bound to fail. No one felt this more strongly than the new bishop of Chiapa and the missionaries he had recruited to come to the New World to evangelize and work with the natives.

Back in the New World

If ever a person had the opportunity to doubt the direction of God and to compromise the message he felt he had received from God, it was the new bishop of Chiapa. As he returned to the New World and assumed his duties as bishop, he encountered much opposition. His entourage required almost a year of difficult travel to reach its destination of Ciudad Real in Chiapa. After innumerable delays and difficulties, Las Casas and the largest group of missionaries to travel to the New World at one time, forty-five, finally set sail on July 11, 1544.[19] Upon their arrival in Santo Domingo, the bishop and his entourage experienced what would be the first taste of the colonists' hostility and outrage.

As Las Casas and his group of friars processed through the streets of Santo Domingo, instead of rejoicing at their arrival, the onlookers jeered and mocked them. Furthermore, they refused to provide them with food or a place to stay. They even boycotted their religious services.[20] While on this island, Las Casas wrote to Prince Philip that the colonists were not observing the New Laws. Because of this failure their souls were in danger and the prince should do something about it or he would also be held accountable.[21] To make matters worse for the new shepherd, there existed dissension even among his own priests. While the missionaries celebrated their final Mass on Hispaniola, five of their number deserted.[22]

The reception in his own diocese was no better. Despite a hospitable reception in the town of Campeche, the residents would not pay him their tithe, release any of the Indians they held, or acknowledge him as their bishop. Similar events occurred in Mérida. These activities portended the difficulties Las Casas found when he finally arrived at the principal town in his district, Ciudad Real, in March 1545. In this town resided the majority of his Spanish flock.[23]

The new bishop of Chiapa expected to utilize his episcopal authority to enforce compliance with the New Laws. What he experienced, however, was resistance on every front. His clergy defied his authority, his flock refused to tithe, and crowds demonstrated against him. Once he had to face down threats from an armed mob.[24] In addition, he received no assistance from the Audiencia, or secular High Court, of Central America. Despite his success in having the New Laws promulgated in Spain, he faced defeat in their application in the New World as the colonists sensed that their very livelihood and way of life was coming under attack.

Finally, bowing to the pressure of civil war in Peru and needing the revenue of the Indies to satisfy his debts in Europe, Charles V revoked the heart of the New Laws. On October 20, 1545, he revoked the law of inheritance, which provided that on the death of the *encomendero* the Indians reverted to the Crown. Thus, in his quest to end the hated system, Las Casas faced both resistance in his diocese and lack of support from a vacillating monarch.[25]

In the midst of these challenges to his episcopal authority, Las Casas composed his most controversial tract, his "Twelve Rules for Confessors," also known as the *Confesionario*. This document circulated among the religious after 1547. Because this document threatened Church sanctions if confessors did not provide restitution to the natives, the Council of the Indies ordered its seizure and Viceroy Antonio de Mendoza publicly burned it in 1548. Because of the unfavorable reception, it was not printed and widely circulated until 1552.[26]

In this *Confesionario* Las Casas hardened his position and developed the theme of restitution, which he would include in his subsequent messages. Without restitution for what had been done in the Indies, there could be no salvation. He had begun to develop this theme on a theoretical level in *The Only Way*, but now he specifically applied this principle to the situation at hand and it became the center of his counsel to confessors.[27] Recognizing that the emperor had succumbed to the financial pressure of his worldly needs and, therefore, was not a reliable ally, the bishop utilized the spiritual power he possessed. If secular laws could not bring about the desired effect, the power of the Church could be brought to bear on the eternal souls of those who denied justice to the oppressed.

These "Twelve Rules" were to apply to all who desired absolution from sins. Trusted priests in his diocese received these guidelines, which contained "what was for him [Las Casas] the true conscience position of Christians, and the classical doctrine of restitution required of all who exploited and oppressed other peoples."[28] These applied "to *conquistadores, encomenderos,* slaveholders, and all others who made money from the Indians (including merchants who furnished supplies for the wars, and overseers of mines and plantations)."[29]

The document gave a detailed description of how priests were to conduct confessions. The first responsibility of a confessor was to determine the status of the penitent. He must place him in the category of *conquistador, encomendero,* or merchant. Then, if he were a *conquistador,*

> the confessor should make the conquistador declare, ordain, and grant the following things: First, he is to agree and say that he chooses so-and-so for his confessor, a secular priest or religious priest of x order. Then that the conquistador is a believing Christian and wants to depart this life free from offense to God and with a clear conscience, thus to stand before the judgment seat of God in a state of innocence. He gives his confessor complete power over all those matters the confessor judges to pertain to his salvation—insofar as the penitent is able and is obliged to by divine and human law in the discharge of his conscience. If the confessor should think, should judge it necessary for the man to give back all he owns in the manner the confessor judges best, leaving nothing at all to his heirs, the confessor is free to do so. It is what the sick man, penitent man should do, would do freely, if he were still alive, for the safety of his soul. As a dying man, he submits all he

owns to his confessor's best judgment, without condition, without limit of any kind.[30]

Those who still owned slaves were to set them free immediately. As for those merchants who had profited by importing weapons of destruction, "they are guilty of all the damage done by those things, they are bound to restitution for whatever they stole, for whomever they terrorized, killed, destroyed."[31]

Thus did the bishop link eternal salvation with the restoration of stolen property. He now merged the secular world of possessions with the spiritual world of salvation. He attempted to use the Church to bring temporal justice and to right the wrongs of those who called themselves followers of Christ. According to Las Casas, the responsibility of the Church was to confront injustice and utilize its influence to bring about political change through the force of its moral arguments. Las Casas soon recognized, however, that the monarchy was either powerless to bring about the changes he desired or uninterested in doing so. In fact, in subsequent writings he expanded the idea of restitution to make the monarch responsible for the actions of its subjects.

Faced with disrespect and rebellion in his diocese, the bishop complained to Prince Philip. In a letter dated October 25, 1545, Las Casas and Bishop Antonio de Valdivieso protested that the authorities, especially his old ally Governor Maldonado, were not obeying the New Laws. Furthermore, they were not providing the priests with their maintenance support. Perhaps the most interesting comment in this letter is that if the prince could not bring about some kind of changes in the situation, "we are determined to leave our bishoprics and to return to those lands [Spain], and seek justice and aid from Your Majesty, and not to return here until you uproot this tyranny, both for the Indians and for the Church."[32] In this letter Las Casas not only demonstrated his increasingly confrontational manner with the monarchy but also his desire to return to the seat of power.

Smarting under the hostile attitude of his parishioners, the government officials, and even other members of the clergy, Las Casas decided to attend a convocation of bishops in Mexico City in January 1546. As he left Ciudad Real, the aging bishop must have realized that he would not return, because he appointed the Mercedarian

Fray Hernando de Arbolancha as vicar.[33] Although the other bishops at the meeting wanted only to focus on the conversion of the Indians—that is, spiritual matters—Las Casas quickly brought them back to the secular issues he desired to discuss. He agreed that the instruction of the Indians was important and then moved into the heart of his message, which was restitution by the *encomenderos*. The bishops unanimously approved this recommendation as well as others dealing with Indian rights. Viceroy Mendoza refused to accept the resolutions of condemning personal service by Indians to the Spaniards and the question of slavery itself. This did not deter Las Casas, however, as he spoke with the authority of God's word. Parish writes, "He would have to get these by other means. Once more, like the Old Testament prophets and the Kings of Israel, he must force the Viceroy to submit before the moral authority of the Law of God."[34]

At a packed cathedral, Las Casas preached a powerful prophetic sermon from Isaiah 30:8–11, in which he challenged the secular authorities to heed the voice of the prophets.[35] He concluded the message with a call to end mistreatment and enslavement of the Indians. Everyone knew the message was directed at the viceroy. After this service, Mendoza agreed to another meeting of religious, which immediately condemned slavery and abusive personal service.[36] Unfortunately for the Indians, no provision was made for the enforcement of these pronouncements. Making resolutions cost nothing and achieved little. Having accomplished what he could in the Indies, Las Casas made preparations to leave Mexico and return to Spain.

In Defense of the Indians

Upon his return to Spain, Las Casas became embroiled in defending his *Confesionario*. Although this directive had some results, in that several *encomenderos* and others who held properties freed their Indians and made restitution, the majority of the colonists opposed the measure and many died without receiving absolution. If universally applied, this doctrine threatened the wealth of many.[37] The Council of the Indies received many complaints about this doc-

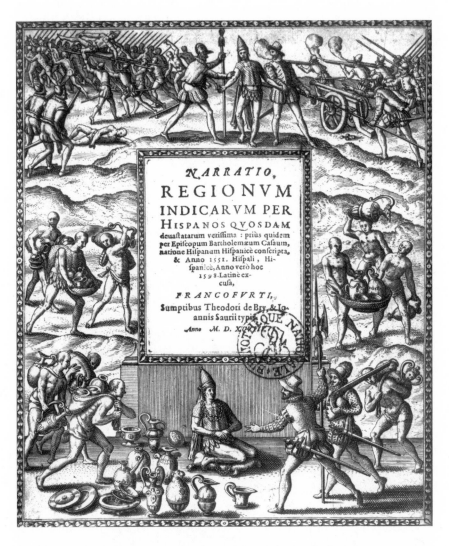

Theodore de Bry and Joannis Sauri, *Bartolomé de las Casas stigmatizes the cruelties committed by the conquistadores.* Frontipiece of *Narratio regionum indicarum per Hispanos.* Bibliotheque Nationale, Paris. Giraudon/Art Resource.

trine and consequently had to respond to it. After an investigation, they issued an order to collect and burn all copies of this document in the Indies. Furthermore, the council alleged that Las Casas had challenged the right of the monarchy to possession of the New World by declaring that all that had been done there was illegal and void of any authority. Therefore, they ordered him to present his views concerning the royal title to these lands.[38]

In his first attempt to explain his position, Las Casas composed another document, probably in 1548–49. "Thirty Propositions," published in 1552, defended his controversial *Confesionario*. After explaining that what he was about to say was the product of his nearly fifty years of experience in the Indies, Las Casas stated that these propositions were a brief summary of his position in the matter at hand. This significant document revealed that Las Casas's reasoning had not changed. Although he had refined and deepened his message, and his beliefs had become more legally astute and confrontational in their presentation, his basic motivation and theology remained the same. In the seventeenth proposition, he affirmed that the Spanish monarchy was the rightful ruler of the Indies. This authority resulted, however, from "the authority, concession, and donation of the Holy Apostolic See, and therefore by divine authority."[39] This authority extended to the proclamation of the faith and not to the usurpation of property. Their sole juridical right of possession depended on evangelism and nothing else. In subsequent propositions he clarified that the natives were required to submit to the authority of the Spanish monarchy after they had, of their own free will, accepted the holy faith and received baptism. The responsibility of the Crown was to provide the gospel and teaching in the faith, and these must be offered peacefully.[40]

In his first written document of 1516, the *Memorial de remedios para las Indias,* Las Casas began his ministry of intervention with the Crown with the same theme he now repeated. Although at that time he did not mention the Alexandrine bull of donation of 1493, the substance of the message remained the same. He wrote, "The principal goal for which all should be aimed and ordered...is the salvation of those Indians...this must be the best return for your labors."[41] He summarized this *memorial,* "That the first and last aim that must motivate us in a solution for those poor souls must be God, and how to attract them to heaven; because he did not redeem them nor discover them so that they might be cast into hell [by the Spanish] caring only for the acquisition of gold."[42] Nearly forty years after his conversion, or prophetic call, Las Casas reiterated his message for a new monarch. This time he spoke with more authority and specifically mentioned the papal decree, but his ultimate goal of bringing the natives to a knowledge of Christ and his Church had not varied or wavered. Again, Las Casas called the Crown to its primary responsibility of evangelism. This mission was the sole authority for the Spanish presence in the New World, and to this goal they must adhere or their claim had no validity, either legally, morally, or spiritually. This was his message from the beginning and would be his final word to his beloved sovereign.

At the same time as he was composing these propositions, Las Casas became embroiled in yet another struggle for the rights of the Indians. Upon his return to Spain in 1547, he learned of a tract written by Juan Ginés de Sepúlveda, which he believed was full of lies and exaggerations about the nature of the Indians that would cause irreparable harm if published. Therefore, he "opposed him with all his might, discovering and declaring the poison which filled it, and ways to bring about its end."[43] This struggle was to culminate in the famous disputations of 1550–51 in Valladolid.[44]

In 1544 Sepúlveda had written a tract entitled *Democrates alter*, which was intended to justify the Spanish conquest of the Indies and explain the natural inferiority of the natives. This work, which justified Indian subordination to the Spanish and was supported by those who profited from the existing system, caused concern among certain members of the Council of the Indies. Therefore, they submitted the work to the examination of the scholars at the Universities of Alcalá and Salamanca. Both institutions condemned the work and recommended against its printing. Although it is unclear exactly why they withheld approval, Sepúlveda believed it to be the influence of Las Casas and the theologians who followed Vitoria.[45] Thus the stage was set for a theological and moral battle over Spain's actions in the New World.

In an effort to resolve the continuing question of the justice of the wars in America and the treatment of the natives, in July 1550 Charles V called for a special council meeting to take place in

Valladolid. Furthermore, the Holy Roman Emperor, the strongest monarch in Europe at the time, in a unique decision ordered all conquests stopped until this issue could be resolved.[46] The significance of this order has not been lost to historians. This was the first time in history a monarchy halted its own military conquest to discuss the morality of its actions.[47] Perhaps to be free from all spiritual duties and participate more fully in this junta, Las Casas resigned his bishopric in August 1550.[48] At stake in this dispute was the very legitimacy of Spanish presence and actions in its New World empire.

In mid-August 1550, the sessions of the Council of Fourteen began. Among this group were theologians who already had indicated their support of Las Casas's position, Domingo de Soto and Melchor Cano, and a supporter of Sepúlveda, Dr. Moscoso. Unfortunately, Vitoria had died in 1546.[49] The council chose Domingo de Soto to condense and record the discussions. He characterized the purpose of the sessions as "to discuss and determine the best form of government and the best laws which will permit the most favorable preaching and extension of the Holy Catholic Faith in the New World, which God discovered for us." They also were to determine the best form of government to assure the natives' obedience to the emperor "without doing damage to the royal conscience, and in accordance with the Bull of Pope Alexander."[50]

Both men agreed that the preaching of the faith in the Indies was necessary and proper. They also agreed that Spain exercised sovereignty in the New World. They disagreed, however, on the methods of spreading the faith and establishing Spanish dominion.[51] On the first day, Sepúlveda gave his position in a speech lasting about three hours, based on his work *Democrates alter.* The next day Las Casas appeared and read from his *Apologia.* He continued to do so for five straight days until the council was exhausted.[52] After Sepúlveda received a copy of the former bishop's *Apologia,* he wrote a rebuttal consisting of twelve points. Las Casas then responded with twelve points of his own. After hearing both individuals, the members of the council departed, agreeing to meet again in January 1551 for their final decision. For the next few months they considered both sides of the debate.[53]

Sepúlveda, who had no firsthand knowledge of the American Indian and whose mind Pagden describes as "rigidly orthodox and highly chauvinistic," based his arguments on information in Oviedo's *Historia general.*[54] He argued that Spain was justified in its military conquest of the Indians because their subjugation facilitated the spread of the gospel. He reasoned that the Spanish waged a just war in an effort to evangelize most effectively and in accordance with the papal bulls of donation. Because Indians were culturally inferior and practiced cannibalism, human sacrifice, and idolatry, they were barbarians and should submit to their cultural and religious superiors. Sepúlveda wrote, "Now compare their [Spanish] gifts of prudence, talent, generosity, temperance, humanity, and religion with those semi-humans (*homunculos*) in whom one can scarcely find traces of humanity."[55] According to Aristotle, who was Sepúlveda's model, the natives were natural slaves. Consequently, they deserved to be under Spanish *dominium.* Sepúlveda also argued that Augustine had demonstrated that slavery was the punishment for the sins of which the Indians were guilty. Warfare, therefore, was justified to bring these peoples out of darkness and into the light of the gospel and Spanish control.[56]

Las Casas then read from his *Apologia,* which he wrote "at the cost of much sweat and many sleepless nights" and had dedicated to Prince Philip. In his dedicatory introduction he indicated the purpose for his writing. Speaking against the words of Sepúlveda, whose "poisons are disguised with honey," he wrote, "Therefore I considered the many misfortunes, the great harvest of evils so deserving of rebuke, and the severest punishment which will arise from his teaching." Always mindful, however, that he must link together the offenses against God, the faith, and God's secular representative, the monarchy, he continued, "[The Crown's]...offense against God [has led to] ill repute and hatred for our most holy religion, irreparable damage, and the loss of so many believing souls, and the loss of the right of the kings of Spain to the empire of the New World." Because he feared these things happening to his beloved nation and monarch, Las Casas could not remain quiet. He continued writing, and here the order of the titles he used to describe himself is significant: " Mindful that I am a Christian, a religious, a bishop, a Spaniard, and a subject of the King of Spain, I cannot but unsheathe the sword of my pen for the defense of the truth."[57] Always Las Casas was mindful of the perspective from which he wrote. He recognized his calling to spread the gospel within the context of the Christian nation of Spain.

Las Casas then attacked the doctrines of Sepúlveda one by one, utilizing his *Apologia* and *Apologética historia.* The underlying basis for his arguments, however, was *The Only Way.*[58] Drawing upon church fathers, Scripture, philosophers, and Church tradition, he argued that the Amerindians were not barbarians. Furthermore, just because they worshiped idols and were guilty of pagan practices, including sodomy, did not justify the Spaniards' use of warfare against them. He wrote, in clear reference to *The Only Way,* "Therefore there is no crime so horrible, whether it be idolatry or sodomy or some other kind, as to demand that the Gospel be preached for the first time in any other way than that established by Christ"—and, just in case they had forgotten the way of Christ, he added, "that is, in a spirit of brotherly love, offering forgiveness of sins and exhorting men to repentance."[59] Finally, he contended that force was not a way of bringing individuals into the fold of God. This was not the way of Christ. "Leading to faith by massacre and terror is Mohammedan."[60] Thus did Las Casas dispense with the accusations of Sepúlveda. The priest then left the fate of the natives in the hands of the council.

The Council of Valladolid never rendered a definitive verdict on the "winner" of this debate. As late as 1557, one judge had not even made a decision.[61] The fact is that they never did approve of the printing of *Democrates alter,* and this tract was never published. Las Casas took credit for stopping this publication and therefore declared victory. On the other hand, no official changes in policy were forthcoming. Spain received much revenue from its colonies, and any change in this status threatened its income. Thus, realistically, no policies could change. The *encomienda* system was too well entrenched and would continue until the nineteenth century.[62]

In 1551, Las Casas and his constant companion, Fray Ladrada, moved into the Dominican College of San Gregorio at Valladolid. He received three rooms for himself and his books and the college provided him with the essentials of life. He had no responsibilities and could travel freely. The Dominican paid the college from an annual pension furnished him by the Crown. He busied himself during this period by recruiting missionaries for the Indies and, of course, by writing.[63]

Later Works of Las Casas

During the years 1552–53, while waiting for a fleet to sail to America with a number of missionaries he had recruited and was training, Las Casas utilized his time in Seville to publish a number of his most famous tracts. The purpose of these tracts was "to summarize and consolidate all his past arguments, and lay a foundation for his future advocacy of Indian rights with the new administration."[64] He published these works without a license; because of this fact someone, probably Sepúlveda, denounced him to the Inquisition. Although this organization did not institute formal proceedings against him, it did block the printing of one of his tracts.[65] Finally, the former bishop had the time to organize, collate, and publish the collection of works he had been utilizing during the past decades. These writings became some of his most famous (or, to his detractors, infamous), as they circulated in both America and the rest of Europe.[66]

Published in late 1552 and early 1553, these writings encapsulated Las Casas's thought. First he published the *Octavo remedio*, which was part of a treatise he had presented in 1542. This work called for the Indians to reside under the direct authority of the Crown and not in the *encomienda* system. Next, he published a tract probably written for the bishops' meeting in Mexico City in 1546, an attack on the enslavement of the Indians entitled *Tratado sobre los esclavos*. Certainly the best known and perhaps the most controversial of his works came next, the *Brevíssima relación*. He dedicated this work to Prince Philip, and he intended it to inform the monarchy of how the Spanish had decimated the natives. The fourth work was the summary completed by Domingo de Soto of the controversy with Sepúlveda, *Aquí se contiene una disputa o controversia con Sepúlveda*. The next tract was the *Treinta proposiciones muy jurídicas*, and on September 20, 1552 the controversial *Avisos y reglas para confesores*. These six were published and brought with the missionaries to the New World when they departed in November 1552.[67]

In 1553 Las Casas completed the last two of his doctrinal works. Replying to the criticisms of his *Treinta proposiciones*, he wrote the *Tratado comprobatorio del imperio soberano*, published in January. Finally, the only work not printed in Spanish was the Latin *Principia quaedam.* This tract dealt with the responsibility that the stronger have in their governance over the weaker. After publishing these works, Las Casas returned to Valladolid.[68]

In 1555, Emperor Charles V abdicated his throne and Prince Philip came to power. With the kingdom came the burden of debt accumulated by Charles. Recognizing his need for funds, the Peruvian *encomenderos* approached Philip with an offer to buy perpetual rights to the Indians. This would solve his debt problem and once and for all answer the question of what to do with the Amerindians. When Las Casas learned of this offer he sent a letter to his friend, the confessor to the emperor Bartolomé de Carranza, urging him to use his influence to intervene against the sale.[69]

In this letter Las Casas continued to develop his theme of the responsibility of the monarch for the actions of his subjects. He spoke out boldly, stating that one cannot be a Christian and act in an oppressive manner. By placing the Indians in perpetual *encomienda,* the monarchy was placing its own salvation in jeopardy. He asked Carranza:

> Father, is there no one who can dissuade these our Catholic monarchs, and make them understand that they cannot receive a single *real* from the Indies and have a clear conscience if they as much as consent—I am not even saying permit—but just consent—…to the subjugation of such a large number of tribes and Indian people to the bitter and hopeless lives they lead in these captivities of the present, not even counting the murders and losses of the past?[70]

In this letter, Las Casas broadened his prophetic pronouncements against the monarchy to judge not only its actions, or lack thereof, but also its intentions and motivations. In fact, Las Casas now emphasizes that those who have the most authority also bear the greatest responsibility. This position represented the more confrontational and direct approach that had now become one of his standard themes.[71]

Despite the efforts of Las Casas and Carranza, on September 5, 1556, the now King Philip II wrote that he had made up his mind.

He would accept the offer of the *encomenderos* and grant them the Indians in perpetuity. Fortunately for them, however, this decision was never carried out. Bureaucracy and Las Casas prevented it from occurring. By the time the announcement was to be sent to Peru, Las Casas, in conjunction with his religious allies, especially the Dominicans Fray Domingo de Santo Tomás and Alonso Méndez, offered a counterproposal. In this offer they stressed the harm that would befall not only the Indians but also the monarchy. They would top any financial offer the *encomenderos* would make. In addition, Las Casas stressed that the enslavement of the Indians would result in their further decline in population and thus in an even greater loss of revenue to the Crown. In an effort to remind the monarchy that there existed in the colonies a danger of a new class of hereditary nobility, the Dominican played on Philip's concerns. Without funds and personnel, the king could not gather and pay for an army that he might need if there was a rebellion in the Indies. Also, to appeal to the financial need of the monarchy, knowing that he needed funds to repay the debts acquired by his father, the priests alluded to tombs full of treasure. The natives had refused to uncover these sites lest the Spanish steal it. Perhaps this wealth might be turned over to a just ruler, such as Philip. These burial sites were filled with treasure by the Incas and hidden from the Spanish *conquistadores*. Although the king did not accept their proposal, his indecision proved valuable and the deal granting perpetual ownership of the Indians by the *encomenderos* was never consummated.[72]

Out of the dispute concerning Peru came the final works of Las Casas. His treatise, *Los tesoros del Peru*, written in 1563 and presented to the king in 1565, argued that the treasures buried with the Inca rulers did not belong to the Spaniards even if they uncovered them. To remove the gold and silver from the *guacas*, or tombs, without permission would constitute a mortal sin. Even the Spanish king could not take possession of these treasures unless the Inca rulers, or their heirs, had first given them to him. Furthermore, the Spanish legal claim to Peru, based on the papal donation, was valid only as long as the Spanish peacefully presented the gospel. The use of force invalidated this bull.[73] To this treatise Las Casas added another just as polemical.

The brief yet powerful "Tratado de las doce dudas," also written in 1563 and framed in the form of twelve "doubts," concerned moral questions posed to Las Casas by an anonymous Dominican preacher about the situation in Peru. The priest asks if the conditions he views in this nation are in accordance with law. He questions not only the validity of the Spanish presence in Peru but also the legality of the tribute extracted from the natives. Las Casas responded to these questions with eight principles, including his final and most demanding word on the topic of restitution.[74] In his response to the sixth problem, the priest concluded that "the King of Spain and the Spanish hold the mines of Peru against the wishes of the chiefs and people of that area." The proof of this sentiment is that "they hold the Spanish as public enemies and destroyers of their nation, and the King of Castille likewise, because they believe all the injustices and tyrannies they have suffered are due to his will and command." Las Casas concluded by saying that possession of Peruvian treasure was a mortal sin. Furthermore, "the King of Castile and León" may not possess anything of value from Peru unless the rightful owners give it to them, and that which the Spanish rulers have allotted to others is not rightfully theirs. Therefore, all who own mines or have removed riches from Peru must give them back. If they do not make restitution, they are under eternal damnation.[75]

This restitution concerned not only the land and treasures of Peru but political domination as well. In a response to the eleventh problem, or "doubt," Las Casas wrote that the king of Spain, "if he desired to save his own soul," must give the nation back to the legitimate heir of Guainacápac, the last Inca ruler, who had secluded himself in the mountains to escape Spanish capture. In order to return the title to Peru, the monarch must make every effort necessary to draw him out of his mountain hideout. If the colonists should rebel against the monarch for giving back their wrongfully obtained possessions, "the King of Spain is obligated to fight them and die if necessary, to liberate those oppressed peoples."[76] If the rightful ruler, Tito Inca, comes down from the mountains and becomes a Christian, which, according to the Dominican, he most surely would if the gospel were properly presented to him, then the rest of the nation would also join the Church. The people could then present to the king of Spain the legal title to Peru. Until this action is done, the title to the land is invalid.[77] Of course, what was valid for Peru would also apply to the rest of the Indies.

In this work, Las Casas confronted King Philip concerning his responsibilities toward his subjects in the New World. At this time in his life the retired bishop spoke as plainly and as forcefully as possible. His message in this, his last major treatise, included the themes he had developed and refined over fifty years of ministry. They had not significantly changed since the moment of his conversion and prophetic call; they only deepened and became more forceful. His last writing of significance, however, is his Last Will and Testament. In this document he included and summarized all the major themes of his life, including the prophetic element of predicting what would happen to Spain in the future if the leadership of that nation did not heed God's message as spoken through his messenger. In this work Las Casas not only "spoke for God" in the sense that he interpreted God's will for the people at that time in history, but he also prophesied future destruction based on the principles of God's written Scripture. Because of the significance of this writing and because it summarizes the life of Las Casas so well, we examine it in some detail.

The Climax of Las Casas's Message (1564)

Sometime during the end of February 1564 Fray Bartolomé wrote his will and delivered it to a notary on March 17, 1564. Even though he was ill, the Dominican continued his fight for the Indians and their salvation until the very end. He continued to write and speak on their behalf to anyone who listened. He died on June 20, 1566, in the monastery of Antocha, Madrid. On July 31, Church officials opened and read his Last Will and Testament.[78]

He began by confessing the Christian faith. Above all else Las Casas considered himself a Christian. He lived his life in an attempt to demonstrate his faith and represent the Christ whom he served. All other aspects of his life revolved around this central theme, and he never varied from this direction or forgot its application. His life's message was that the Christian must not only articulate his faith, based on biblical and Church authority, but also live that faith in such a way that others could see the gospel through the life. He continued to espouse and demonstrate these articles of faith until the end. He wrote:

> In the name of the Most Blessed Trinity, Father and Son and Holy Spirit, one God and true. I, Bishop Fray Bartolomé de Las Casas, knowing that every believing Christian must lay bare his soul at the time he comes to die, insofar as he can by the grace of God, and knowing that many things can prevent this at the hour of death: I wish to say solemnly before I see myself at that point that I will live and die as I shall have lived, in the holy Catholic faith of the Most Blessed Trinity, Father, Son, Holy Spirit, believing and holding, as indeed I do, all that the holy Church of Rome believes and holds. I wish to live the rest of my life in that faith, right up to and including death, and I want to die in that faith.[79]

It is evident that Las Casas had a very definite sense of his own call. He was convinced that God had chosen him for a special purpose, and he was constantly aware of this fact during the course of his life. The success or failure of his mission was, in a sense, irrelevant. He was compelled to do what he did regardless of the consequences or the response from those he challenged. It was this call that gave meaning to his life; now at the end of that life, he emphasized and reiterated for the last time how he had received it. The emphasis of his message was to speak for God and to interpret God's will on behalf of those unable to do so on their own, whom Gutiérrez labels "the poor of Jesus Christ." Las Casas attempted to act as mediator and intercede between the powerful, represented by the Crown, and the weak, the Amerindians who died on a daily basis before his eyes. He was at home in both worlds. This mediation was his duty as a Christian and as a spokesman for the Lord he desired to represent and serve. This sense of mission is what motivated him to action for the more than fifty years since his call in 1514. He had no other goal or desire, and this work had attempted to demonstrate the consistency of his beliefs and actions and unselfish dedication to fulfill his call. He continued in his will:

> And *I testify that it was God in his goodness and mercy who chose me as His minister*—unworthy though I was— to act here at home on behalf of all those people out in what we call the Indies, the true possessors of those kingdoms, those territories. To act against the unimaginable, unspeakable violence and evil harm they have suffered from our people, contrary to all reason, all justice, so as to restore them to the original liberty they were lawlessly deprived of, and get them free of death and violence, death they still suffer, they perish still the same way. Thousands of leagues of land were thusly depopulated; I witnessed a great deal of it. For almost fifty years I have done this work, in the court of the kings of Castile, back and forth between the Indies and Castile, Castile and the Indies, often, since 1514. *I have done it for the sake of God alone,* out of compassion of seeing the deaths of so many human beings, rational, civilized, unpretentious, gentle, simple human beings who were most apt for accepting our holy Catholic faith and its entire moral doctrine, human beings who already lived according to sound principles. As God is my witness, *I had no other motive.*[80]

Las Casas may not have called himself a prophet. He did, however, by interpreting God's will for evangelism and justice in the specific experiences of his own life and times, fulfill the role of one.[81] As one who spoke on behalf of God and represented God's word to God's people, the Dominican had functioned in the mold of a prophet since his life-changing experience in 1514. He tried to bring to the rest of the nation the repentance he felt at that moment. Always his goal was to bring the monarchy and the nation to repentance; they needed to change how they viewed the Indians, seeing them as rational human beings, and change how they acted toward the Indians, stopping their exploitation and murder. He argued that the reason for this act of contrition was not only for the benefit of those being slaughtered and abused, but also for the eternal salvation of his fellow followers of Christ. To make their offering—their lives—acceptable to God, they must demonstrate justice to the oppressed. The eternal destiny of their souls depended on what they did here on earth.

In addition to his role as spokesman for God, Las Casas also, in the prophetic tradition, warned of the impending wrath of God should they fail to heed his words. In this he predicted the downfall of the nation. He was not functioning as a seer who foresaw the future in some mystical way, but rather as one who knew and understood the Scripture. Throughout the Bible disobedience to God's principles brought judgment. Therefore it took no special discernment on his part to recognize what would happen to his beloved Spain. In this same vein, he knew that repeated failures to listen to God caused one's heart to grow hard, as had happened to Pharaoh, and one's eyes to be blinded to the truth, as Jesus said happened to the Pharisees. The wrath of God followed this occurrence. It was the fear of this happening that compelled him to plead as he completed his Last Will and Testament:

> What I say next I hold as certain doctrine, I judge it certain, it is what the Holy Roman Church holds and values as a norm of belief for us. All that the Spaniards perpetrated against those [Indian] peoples, the robbery, the killing, the usurpation of property and jurisdiction, from kings and lords and lands and realms, the theft of things on a boundless scale and the horrible cruelties that went with that—*all this was in violation of the whole natural law, and a terrible blot on the name of Christ and the Christian faith. It was all an absolute impediment to faith, all a mortal damage to the souls and bodies of those innocent peoples.* And I think *that God shall have to pour out His fury and anger on Spain* for those damnable, rotten, infamous deeds done so unjustly, so tyrannically, so barbarously to those people, against those people. *For the whole of Spain has shared in the blood-soaked riches,* some a little, some a lot, but all shared in goods that were ill-gotten, wickedly taken with violence and genocide—and all must pay unless Spain does a mighty penance. And

I fear it will be too late or not at all, because there is a blindness God permits to come over sinners great and small, but especially over those who drive us or are considered prudent and wise, who give the world orders—a blindness because of sins, about everything in general. But especially that recent blindness of understanding which for the last seventy years has proceeded to shock and scandalize and rob and kill those people overseas. A blindness that is not even today aware that such scandals to our faith, such defamations of it, such robbing and injustice and violence and slaughter and enslavement and usurpation of foreign rule and rulers, above all such devastation, such genocide of populations, have been sins, have been monumental injustices.[82]

It is probably fitting that in his final work Las Casas made reference to the fact that the actions of the Spanish had made "a blot on the name of Christ and the Christian faith" and that this would be "an impediment to the faith." Undoubtedly he was thinking back to that day in 1514 when the light came to him and he realized he had to give up the Indians he held in order to be a witness to others of the faith. Though ordained a priest, he realized that his words and actions were not consistent with his calling. Above all else, Las Casas desired to be an example. He demonstrated his virtue by his actions. Despite the fact that the destruction of the New World continued almost unabated, Las Casas, like the prophet Amos, announced that the Lord was dropping a verbal plumb line. The nation must align itself with God's word or receive divine judgment. The monarchy, the people, the nation as a whole may not choose to hear and obey, but they could not say they had not heard about or seen the injustice. They could not say they did not have an example to follow. They had been forced to view the results of their actions as if a mirror were held up to them. Like the children of Israel in the Bible, when the prophets confronted them with God's truth, they either had to kill the prophet, line up to his words, or suffer the consequences.

Conclusion

This work has emphasized the development of Bartolomé de las Casas from priest-*encomendero* to prophetic spokesman for God to both the Amerindians and the Spanish nation. His conversion experience changed Las Casas from one who accepted the Spanish colonial policy of commending the Amerindians into the care of the Spaniards and enjoyed the material benefits thereof to a dedicated and persistent advocate for its modification. As he studied and meditated on Scripture, Las Casas became acutely aware of both his mission and his message. He realized the moral inconsistency of his own life and actions and recognized that Spain's official policies were inconsistent with Catholic beliefs and practices. Within the context of this calling, he became aware of his self-identity. This work has traced both the stages and elements of this process, building on the historical interpretations of Las Casas as prophet in the biblical mold.

Las Casas was a product of the political, intellectual, and spiritual milieu of the sixteenth century. He believed that Spain had a legal and moral right to colonize and convert the inhabitants of its new possessions, as described in the Alexandrine decrees. In an effort to facilitate this dual purpose, the colonists initiated the *encomienda* system. The termination of this arrangement became the focal point of Las Casas's life. Initially, however, he participated in Spanish colonization as an instructor of religious doctrine and *encomendero*. He saw no dichotomy in using Native Americans for forced labor while simultaneously attempting to convert them to the Christian faith. In fact, he justified his own actions by emphasizing the benign treatment of those under his care. Experiences and events, however, played on his conscience. On one hand, the Dominican priests in America preached the need for Christian love and treatment of the Amerindians. On the other hand, the colonists who profited from their labor emphasized the natives' inferior nature, thereby justifying their exploitation for the benefit of the Spaniards.

As Las Casas prepared a sermon for Pentecost Sunday, 1514, he studied Ecclesiasticus 34:18ff. and reflected on what he had heard and seen in the New World. At this moment, his first conversion occurred. He experienced an inner change of heart that resulted in an outward change of behavior. This self-awareness was not a political change, but recognition that his actions were not consistent with his beliefs. This experience was not a conversion in the radical sense that he changed from nonbeliever to Christian, in the style of St. Paul, but rather it was an awakening of conscience and realization of the message he must now proclaim. Modern analyses of the psychology of conversion concur with this assessment. Las Casas believed that God had chosen him to proclaim Christianity in both word and deed, to preach the gospel peacefully, and to demonstrate its application by social justice.

Las Casas's life became an example of moral consistency. For the nearly fifty years that he wrote, labored, and spoke on behalf of his beloved natives, his basic message did not change. From his first written tract, the *Memorial de remedios,* to his Last Will and Testament, he emphasized that the sole legal and moral justification for Spain's claim to the New World was evangelization, not material gain. The institution that became the focal point for his anticolonial activities was the *econmienda* system from which he had initially profited. Although his methods changed as he aged and became wiser, his emphasis and goals never varied.

Las Casas spoke in the tradition of the Hebrew prophets and emphasized that his was more a mission of confrontation with political authorities than a priestly ministry among the natives. During the first stage of his prophetic ministry, his goal was to initiate in others the same behavioral change he himself had experienced. This effort was evident in his initial written work, the *Memorial de remedios* (1516). In an effort to promote this change, he initially appealed to the self-interest of the Crown. He even justified slavery at the time as a result of the prevalent concept of the just war. His failure at Cumaná, which was a practical attempt to merge economic colonization with spiritual conversion, forced him into a period of introspection and a reexamination of his own motivations.

While undergoing this protracted time of self-condemnation and introspection, Las Casas entered the Dominican Order. Many refer to this experience as his second conversion. The prophetic ministry of Las Casas entered a deeper and more significant stage after his involvement in the Enriquillo incident. The success he achieved in resolving this dispute provided him with the practical experience he needed to refine and deepen his message. He now realized that the conversion of the natives must be accomplished by peaceful means alone. Christ, who offered the gospel without coercion, became his model. There could be no compromise between evangelism and material gain. The only effective way of spreading the gospel message was by coupling reasonable proclamation with loving example. According to Las Casas, this method would result in the conversion of the Amerindians to Christianity and their transformation into loyal subjects of the monarchy. His most ambitious project, turning the Land of War into the Land of Peace, achieved positive results and convinced him that his concepts were correct. He articulated these ideas in his work *The Only Way*.

Las Casas's desire to continue his successful policies in America led to his acceptance of the office of bishop of Chiapa. As bishop, and working within the framework of the Church, he moved to institutionalize and fulfill his pronouncements. Increasingly, his writings reflected a condemnation not only of those who profited by the *encomienda* system but also of the monarchy and even all of Spain. His works became polemical and direct. He wrote perhaps his most controversial work, *A Brief Account of the Destruction of the Indies* (1542), in an effort to expose what he considered Spanish atrocities. Las Casas also expanded his denunciations. Now the Crown had to both end this hated use of the Indians and make restitution for all past offenses. This would be the only way the natives could come to a true knowledge of the gospel and Spain could maintain its favor with God.

In his Last Will and Testament, Las Casas repeated and summarized the themes he had developed throughout his life: God had chosen him for this mission. He had no other motivation than the propagation of the gospel. The entire nation would suffer for the monarch's rejection of the prophetic words from God. The salvation of the Indians was the principal reason and justification for Spain's presence in the New World. Thus, the basic message had not changed, but the context and manner in which it was shared had.

An examination of the prophetic call and message of Las Casas reveals both a completed event and the inception of an evolutionary calling. Several times throughout his life he made reference to this event. In a way, the life of this now-converted priest was an act of penance for his previous actions and profession. His constant and consistent actions on behalf of the poor and weak against the oppression and injustice of those in power must be viewed within the context of his sense of mission and calling. This self-awareness, initiated at his first conversion, grew as Las Casas matured and achieved success. His ultimate goal was to initiate within the monarchy a similar conversion experience, an event that would lead the nation also to do penance and make restitution to their Amerindian subjects.

In order for Christian Spain to live up to the gospel message it professed and for which it had fought, Las Casas believed it must act as Christ had acted. The Crown had to value the physical lives and eternal souls of its New World subjects more than the acquisition of wealth. The monarchy also had to act in an ethically consistent manner and align its practices with its doctrines. As the prophet sought to fulfill his calling, he challenged all to a life of consistency, persistently seeking justice for the oppressed and dedicated to the achieving of God's will. In this he was without equal and served as an example for all who seek to reconcile humanity with God.

Notes

Introduction

1. For a complete description of this event and the reception that the Catholic monarchs gave Columbus, see Bartolomé de Las Casas, *Historia de las Indias,* 3 vols. (Mexico City: Fondo de Cultura Económica, 1951), 1:332–35. Helen Rand Parish, Introduction to Bartolomé de Las Casas: The Only Way, trans. Francis Patrick Sullivan (Mahwah, NJ: Paulist Press, 1992), 11–12, also describes this scene.

2. Marvin Lunenfeld, ed., *1492: Discovery, Invasion, Conquest* (Lexington, MA: D. C. Heath and Co., 1991), xvii. Lunenfeld writes that *Amerindian* is the term ethnohistorians currently prefer because it has less negative connotations than others. In this work *Amerindians, Native Americans, natives,* and *Indians* will all be used interchangeably.

3. Lewis Hanke, *Bartolomé de Las Casas: Historian* (Gainesville: University of Florida Press, 1952), 2.

4. Simpson, *The Encomienda in New Spain* (Berkeley and Los Angeles: University of California Press, 1950), xi. Simpson quotes the Congreso de Americanistas that met in Seville in 1935 and voted Las Casas "the authentic representative of the Spanish conscience." Simpson believes that, despite this, Las Casas had very little impact on the policies of the Crown concerning the forced labor system.

5. A tireless and disciplined writer, Las Casas produced more than three hundred works during his career. The best known of these are the three-volume *Historia de las Indias* (History of the Indies); the *Apologética historia sumaria; Short Account of the Destruction of the Indies;* the guide for missionary activity, *The Only Way; De regia potestate o derecho de autodeterminación,* published posthumously in 1571; and *In Defense of the Indians,* written ca. 1552, which reviews his defense before the Council of Valladolid. Of these sources, I utilize mainly the *Historia, The Only Way,* the *Short Account,* and *In Defense of the Indians.* These provide the basis of his work.

6. Las Casas, *Historia,* 3:93.

Notes

7. Las Casas is said to have had two conversion experiences. The first occurred on Pentecost Sunday, 1514, and the second after his failure at Cumaná in 1522. The distinction between the two events is clearly made in Manuel Giménez Fernández, "Fray Bartolomé de Las Casas: A Biographical Sketch," in *Bartolomé de Las Casas in History: Toward an Understanding of the Man and his Work,* ed. Juan Friede and Benjamin Keen (DeKalb: Northern Illinois University Press, 1971), 74–84. He also calls this event a "road to Damascus" experience, comparing it with the similar sudden and distinct event in the life of St. Paul, *Bartolomé de Las Casas: Delegado de Cisneros para la Reformación de las Indias (1516–1517),* vol. 1 (Seville: Escuela de Estudios Hispanoamericanos de Sevilla, 1953), 50. Also, Demetrio Ramos Perez, "La 'Conversion' de Las Casas en Cuba: El Clérigo y Diego Velázquez," in *Estudios Sobre Fray Bartolomé de Las Casas* (Seville: University of Seville, 1974), 247–57, emphasizes the fact that this decision was made over a period of months. Gustavo Gutiérrez, in *Las Casas: In Search of the Poor of Jesus Christ* (Maryknoll, NY: Orbis Books, 1993), 482, n. 1, states that Las Casas continually refers to this event as the "originating moment in his life," and labels it a "prophetic call." In his article, "Las Casas and Indigenism," in *Las Casas in History,* 132, Juan Friede calls this a conversion from "a preacher to…a political man."

8. Probably the two most specific articles outlining the place of Las Casas in the prophetic tradition of the Church are by Pérez Fernandez: "El pérfil profético del Padre Las Casas," *Studium* 15 (1975): 281–359; and "La fidelidad del Padre Las Casas a su carisma profético," *Studium* 16 (1976): 65–109. A discussion of Las Casas's prophetic call with a description of the French school viewing him in this tradition is found in Parish, ed., *The Only Way,* 185–86.

9. Bartolomé de Las Casas, Last Will and Testament, in *Opúsculos, cartas, y memoriales. Obras Escogidas de Bartolomé de Las Casas* (Madrid: Biblioteca de Autores Españoles [BAE], 1958), 110:539–40. Emphasis added.

10. Francisco López de Gómara, *Historia general de las Indias,* 2 vols. (Madrid: Calpe, 1922), 1:4. It was first published in 1552.

11. For an account of the life of Columbus and a description of his voyages by one who has retraced them, see Samuel Eliot Morison's *Admiral of the Ocean Sea: A Life of Christopher Columbus* (Boston, Toronto, London: Little, Brown & Co., 1970), *Christopher Columbus, Mariner* (New York: Meridian, 1983), and *The European Discovery of America: The Southern Voyages, 1492–1616* (New York: Oxford University Press, 1974).

12. Las Casas, *Historia,* 1:28–29.

13. For a discussion of the religious motivations of Columbus, see David M. Traboulay, *Columbus and Las Casas* (New York: University Press of

America, 1994). This book emphasizes the Christian mission of the colonization of America. For an interesting discussion of the judgment of history on Columbus, see Lunenfeld, 1492, 100–113.

Chapter One

1. Charles Gibson, *Spain in America* (New York: Harper Torchbooks, 1966), 4–5.

2. For a translation of the treaty itself, see Charles Gibson, ed., *The Spanish Tradition in America* (New York: Harper & Row, 1968), 17–26.

3. Hernando Colon, "The Life of the Admiral by His Son," in *The Four Voyages of Christopher Columbus,* ed. and trans. by J. M. Cohen (London: Penguin Classics, 1969), 127.

4. Colin MacLachlan, *Spain's Empire in the New World: The Role of Ideas in Institutional and Social Change* (Berkeley and Los Angeles: University of California Press, 1988), 1–5.

5. Henry Kamen, *Spain 1469–1714* (London and New York: Longman, 1983), 45.

6. Ibid., 1–3. For a discussion of the two papal bulls issued on May 3, 1493, and how these led to the Treaty of Tordesillas, see Arthur Phelps, *The Spanish Conquest in America,* 4 vols. (New York: AMS Press, 1966), 91, n. 1. Also see "Alexander VI," in *The Christopher Columbus Encyclopedia,* vol. 1, ed. Silvio A. Bedini (New York: Prentice Hall, 1995). This article emphasizes that both bulls were backdated after the arrival of a Spanish delegation to the pope in June 1493.

7. Gibson, *Spanish Tradition,* 36–39, provides us with the complete text and translation of "Alexander VI: Donation and Demarcation."

8. J. H. Parry and R. G. Keith, eds., *The Conquest and the Conquered,* 4 vols. (New York: Times Books, 1984), 1:274, contains the text of *Dudum Siquidem.*

9. J. H. Parry, *The Spanish Theory of Empire in the Sixteenth Century* (Cambridge: Cambridge University Press, 1940), 4.

10. Richard Konetzke, *America Latína: II, La época colonial* (Mexico, D.F.: Siglo XXI, 1981), 209.

11. Parry, *Spanish Theory,* 4.

12. Matías de Paz, in his treatise, "Concerning the Rule of the King of Spain over the Indies," written in 1512, basically upheld the authority of Ostiensis. He did, however, stipulate that the Indians are not slaves in the Aristotelian sense, nor infidels who have heard the gospel but rejected it. They are placed in the third category of the ignorant, or those who, according

to Aquinas, have never heard the gospel or have forgotten it. Juan Lopez de Palacios Rubios, in his treatise, "Of the Ocean Isles" (1512), basically agreed with Matías de Paz in that the title for Spanish dominion rests on the papal declarations. Las Casas praised Palacios Rubios for his concern for the Indians. Both of these works are in *Las doctrinas de Palacios Rubios y Matias de Paz,* ed. Silvio Zavala (Mexico City: Fondo de Cultura Económico, 1954). For a more complete discussion of the ideas of these two individuals, see Lewis Hanke, *The Spanish Struggle for Justice in the Conquest of America* (Philadelphia: University of Pennsylvania Press, 1959), 27–30.

13. Silvio Zavala, *New Viewpoints on the Spanish Colonization of America* (Philadelphia: University of Pennsylvania Press, 1943), 6–7.

14. For a translation of this document, see Sir Arthur Phelps, *The Spanish Conquest in America,* 4 vols. (New York: AMS Press, 1966), 1:264–67. See also Las Casas, *Historia* 3:26–7, and for his reaction to the document, 3:31.

15. Parry, *Spanish Theory,* 15.

16. Zavala, *Viewpoints,* 14–15.

17. Venancio D. Carro, OP, *La teología y los teologos-juristas español ante la conquista de America* (Salamanca, 1951), 291–92.

18. Quoted in Parry, *Spanish Theory,* 18. López de Gómara affirmed this belief as he wrote in his two-volume work, *Historia General* (Madrid: Calpe, 1922), "You [the monarchy] began the conquest of the Indies after finishing that of the Moors, because the Spanish will always war against the infidels" (1:5).

19. Bartolomé de Las Casas, *In Defense of the Indians,* trans. Stafford Poole, CM (DeKalb: Northern Illinois University Press, 1992), 339, 329. Originally published ca. 1552.

20. Sepúlveda, trans. J. L. Phelan, reprinted in Lunenfeld, *1492,* 218.

21. Lewis Hanke, *Aristotle and the American Indians: A Study of Race Prejudice in the Modern World* (Bloomington and London: Indiana University Press, 1959), 41.

22. Sepúlveda, in Lunenfeld, *1492,* 218.

23. For a complete summary of this disputation, in which the two men never actually confronted each other face to face, and which ground to a rather inconclusive result, see Hanke, *Aristotle and the American Indians,* especially chapter 6.

24. Anthony Pagden, *The Fall of Natural Man: The American Indian and the Origins of Comparative Ethnology* (London and New York: Cambridge University Press, 1982), 60.

25. Ibid., 61.

26. Justo L. González, *A History of Christian Thought,* 4 vols. (Nashville: Abingdon Press, 1975), 3:191. This theme that Vitoria attempted

to turn speculation into practicality, as well as a good brief biography of the man, is found in Bernice Hamilton, *Political Thought in Sixteenth-Century Spain: A Study of the Political Ideas of Vitoria, De Soto, Suárez, and Molina* (Oxford: Clarendon Press, 1963), 170–76.

27. David M. Traboulay, *Columbus and Las Casas: The Conquest and Christianization of America, 1492–1566* (London and New York: University Press of America, 1994), 94.

28. Ibid., 95.

29. Francisco de Vitoria, *Relectio de Indis et de Iure Belli,* ed. Ernest Nys (Washington, DC, 1917), 119.

30. Ibid., 126.

31. Ibid., 128–39.

32. Ibid., 146. Here Vitoria brought the discussion from a legal to a moral and theological level and therefore within the realm of the theologians, since "only theologians were equipped to discuss the divine law." See Pagden, *Fall of Natural Man,* 66.

33. Vitoria, *Relectio,* 150–54.

34. Ibid., 160–61.

35. For a discussion of their relative ideas, see Traboulay, *Columbus,* 110–15.

36. González, *Christian Thought,* 194, and Carro, "The Spanish Theological-Juridical Renaissance," 265, argue that Vitoria influenced Las Casas. Parish, in *Bartolomé de Las Casas: The Only Way,* trans. Francis Patrick Sullivan (Mahwah, NJ: Paulist Press, 1992), 55–56, however, believes the school began with Las Casas. The materials used in coming to this conclusion are fully discussed in her book, *Las Casas in Mexico: Historia y obra desconocidas* (Mexico City: Fondo de Cultura Económica, 1992).

37. Las Casas, *Historia* 1:13. Emphasis added.

38. Gibson, *Spanish Tradition,* 40–41.

39. Lesley Byrd Simpson, *The Encomienda in New Spain* (Berkeley, 1950), 3–4. Simpson writes that the queen was more upset at the usurpation of her power by Columbus than by a disapproval of slavery. In any case those remaining were returned (see n. 10).

40. Bernal Diaz del Castillo, *The True Account of the Conquest of New Spain,* ed. Ramon Iglesia (Mexico, 1943), 2:394. Quoted in Lewis Hanke, *The Spanish Struggle for Justice in the Conquest of America* (Philadelphia: University of Pennsylvania Press, 1949), 7.

41. Simpson, *Encomienda,* 2.

42. The two best general sources of information concerning the *encomienda* system are Silvio Zavala, *La encomienda indiana,* 2nd ed. (Mexico, 1973), and Simpson, *Encomienda.*

Notes

43. Simpson, *Encomienda*, 7.
44. Las Casas, *Historia*, 2:86–90.
45. Cited in Simpson, *Encomienda*, 7.
46. Las Casas, *Historia*, 2:86–90.
47. Las Casas, *Historia*, 1:263. In his final evaluation of Columbus, Las Casas declares that he cared more about serving the monarchy than going to heaven, and that he received his just rewards.
48. Traboulay, *Columbus and Las Casas*, 27. Also, Las Casas, *Historia*, 2:204.
49. Las Casas, *Historia*, 2:204, and Simpson, *Encomienda*, 10. Also included in this same order was the directive that heretics, even those reconciled to the Church after punishment by the Inquisition, Jews, Moors, or "New Christians," were not permitted in the New World.
50. *Colección de documentos inéditos relativos al descubrimiento, conquista y organización de las antiguas posesiones españolas de América y Oceanía, sacados de los archivos del reino y muy especialmente del de Indias* [DII], 42 vols. (Madrid, 1864–84), 31:156–74. Also discussed in Simpson and Zavala.
51. Zavala, *La encomienda indiana*, 15.
52. Simpson, *Encomienda*, 13.
53. "Provisión Real para que los indios de la Española sirven a los cristianos" (December 20, 1503), in *Cedulario Cubano (Los Orígenes de la Colonización): Colección de Documentos Inéditos Para La Historia de Hispano-America*, vol. 6, ed. José M. Chacón y Calvo (Madrid, 1929), 85–87. A large portion of this document is translated in Simpson, *Encomienda*, 13.
54. Parish, ed., *The Only Way*, 77.
55. Ibid.
56. Cited in Simpson, *Encomienda*, 14–15.
57. Cited in Robert Ricard, *The Spiritual Conquest of Mexico: An Essay on the Apostolate and the Evangelizing Methods of the Mendicant Orders in New Spain: 1523–1572* (Berkeley: University of California Press, 1966), 18. Significantly, Governor Velázquez of Cuba gave instructions to Cortés—Ricard adds these were probably the only orders Cortés obeyed—to "bear in mind from the beginning that the first aim of your expedition is to serve God and spread the Christian faith." Ricard believes these were the true desires of the monarchy and the pope. Ibid., 16.
58. Charles Gibson, "The Problem of the Impact of Spanish Culture on the Indigenous American Population," in *Latin American History: Select Problems*, ed. Frederick B. Pike (New York: Harcourt, Brace, and World, 1969), 67.
59. Ibid., 68.

60. Gibson, in Pike, *Latin American History*, 70–71. See also Sherburne F. Cook and Woodrow Borah, *The Indian Population of Central America 1531–1610* (Berkeley: University of California Press, 1960). By the same authors, *Essays in Population History: Mexico and the Caribbean* (Berkeley: University of California Press, 1971).

61. Las Casas's *Brevísima Relación* was published in 1552. Other European countries translated this book and it became the basis for the so-called Black Legend.

Chapter Two

1. For centuries the birthdate of Las Casas was set at 1474. Helen Rand Parish and Harold E. Weidman, SJ, demonstrate in "The Correct Birthdate of Bartolomé de Las Casas," *Hispanic American Historical Review* 56 (1976): 385–403, that his birthdate is 1484, probably on November 11.

2. For conflicting accounts concerning his ancestry, see Manuel Giménez Fernández, "Fray Bartolomé de Las Casas: A Biographical Sketch," in *Bartolomé de Las Casas in History: Toward an Understanding of the Man and His Work*, ed. Juan Friede and Benjamin Keen (De Kalb: University of Illinois Press, 1971), 67–68, and Henry Raup Wagner, with Helen Rand Parish, *The Life and Writings of Bartolomé de Las Casas* (Albuquerque: University of New Mexico Press, 1967), 1–3.

3. Las Casas, *Historia*, 1:347–48. Because of its significance, I use his *Historia* as the basis of the chronicle of events in the Indies and the activities of Las Casas. Written over a period of forty years, this contains not only a history of Spain in America, but also insights into the thought and action of Las Casas. As Hanke writes in *Bartolomé De Las Casas, Historian: An Essay in Spanish Historiography* (Gainesville: University of Florida Press, 1952), "His [Las Casas] claim to the title of historian must rest upon the *History of the Indies*. The *History* not only is the principal historical work of Las Casas: it also includes almost all of the ideas and propositions he set forth concerning the Indians during his long and turbulent life" (10–11). Also, "No one today, whether as supporter or opponent of Las Casas, doubts that the *Historia* has exercised a greater influence on the formation of world opinion of the Spanish conquest than any other historical work, with the possible exception of *A Brief Account of the Destruction of the Indies*, which can scarcely be considered history" (31). Of course most biographers of Las Casas use this as their primary text. I endeavor to utilize texts not emphasized by other authors, or to reinterpret these texts in a new light. Information concerning Juanico is from Helen Rand Parish, ed., *Bartolomé de las Casas: The Only Way*, trans. Francis

Patrick Sullivan (Mahwah, NJ: Paulist Press, 1992), 12–13. This was confirmed in a telephone interview with Parish on October 13, 1998, in which she said that she was still working on a biography of Las Casas and possessed previously unknown and unpublished material. Her manuscript has a working title of: "Bartolomé de Las Casas: The Suppressed Truth."

4. Las Casas, *Historia*, 1:173. Las Casas consistently speaks well of the monarchy and their policies toward the Amerindians. He blames their destructive policies, or those with which he does not agree, on bad counsel received from trusted advisors. For example, later in this same chapter, he wonders why the queen only freed the three hundred slaves distributed by Columbus, and responds that "the only reason I find is that the Queen believed that those taken previously were taken in a 'just war.' This because of misinformation given by Columbus." 1:173. Also Manuel Giménez Fernández, "A Biographical Sketch," in Friede and Keen, eds., *Las Casas in History*, 69, specifies that his slave was one of the twenty survivors of the original three hundred.

5. Las Casas, *Historia*, 2:213–15. Also, Giménez Fernández, ibid.

6. Las Casas, *Historia*, 2:214. The information concerning Las Casas as student and businessman is from the telephone interview with Parish.

7. Ibid., 2:215.

8. Ibid., 1:467.

9. Ibid., 2:387.

10. Ibid., 2:226.

11. Raymond Marcus, "El primer decenio de Las Casas en el Nuevo Mundo," *Ibero-Amerikanisches Archiv* 3, no. 2 (1977): 100.

12. Las Casas, *Historia*, 2:230.

13. Ibid., 2:231.

14. Ibid., 2:233.

15. Ibid., 2:263.

16. Ibid., 2:266.

17. Anthony Pagden, "*Ius et Factum:* Text and Experience in the Writings of Bartolomé de Las Casas," in *New World Encounters*, ed. Stephen Greenblat (Berkeley: University of California Press, 1993), 90.

18. Las Casas, *Historia*, 2:232.

19. Ibid., 2:238.

20. Parish, ed., *Bartolomé de Las Casas*, 15.

21. Las Casas, *Historia*, 2:385–86. Parish interview.

22. Hanke, *Spanish Struggle for Justice*, 11.

23. Las Casas, *Historia*, 3:321.

24. Gonzalo Fernández de Oviedo, *Historia general y natural de las Indias*, ed. Juan Pérez de Tudela y Bueso, 5 vols. (Madrid: Biblioteca de

Autores Españoles, 1959 [1535]), 1:lv–lvi. In the introduction, the editor pictures Oviedo as ambitious and opportunistic.

25. Oviedo, *Historia general*, extracts from several sections cited in Hanke, *Spanish Struggle for Justice*, 11.

26. Gonzalo Fernández de Oviedo, *Natural History of the West Indies*, trans. Sterling A. Stoudemire (Chapel Hill: University of North Carolina Press, 1959 [1526]), 43. Although his purpose in writing was primarily to describe the natural world, he makes some observations of the natives.

27. Oviedo, *Historia general*, 111.

28. Ibid., 168.

29. Las Casas, *Historia*, 3:324–25. Las Casas reproduces the words of Oviedo in this chapter. He then asks, "What then of the sin of Oviedo and what will be his restitution for having brought such destruction upon so many people?" Ibid., 3:325. In regards to their not having received the faith, he reminds him, "He should consider the status of his ancestors and all others before the Son of God came to this earth to remove the darkness, sending through Him the light of His Good News." Ibid., 3:326.

30. Oviedo, *Historia general*, 168–69.

31. Hanke, *All Mankind is One*, 43.

32. Las Casas, *In Defense of the Indians*, 343.

33. Ibid., 344.

34. Ibid., 348. Also in his *Historia*, Las Casas refutes his views of their being *mal inclinados*. He writes, "He has studied little philosophy and has had even less experience with them, nor does he have any experience with any of their languages to know of their bad inclinations, to so fearlessly judge them of something he has no knowledge unless it came by divine revelation." 3:330.

35. Ibid., 3:345. This expedition began in the province of Darién.

36. Ibid., 3:346. Las Casas had been actively involved in the pacification of Cuba, and for his part received his *encomienda* and *repartimiento* of Indians.

37. Ibid. The aspect of repentance will be developed below.

38. Ibid.

39. Las Casas, *Historia*, 3:92–94.

40. Las Casas, *In Defense of the Indians*, 347.

41. Ibid., 344. Here also Las Casas mentions that Oviedo had the effect of "lessening the zeal of godly men who thought they were preaching the Gospel, not to men, but to wild beasts." For this his judgment will be greater.

42. Hanke, *Spanish Struggle for Justice*, 17. In *All Mankind is One*, Hanke reiterates this theme and adds, "[This sermon] is also a turning point in the history of Christianity. Henceforth the *people*, not merely ecclesiastics, were to participate actively and responsibly in the conversion of the heathen."

Gutiérrez points out that according to Pérez de Tudela, Cristóbal Rodríguez, known as La Lengua because of his ability in Indian languages, was the first to protest their treatment. Gutiérrez, *Las Casas*, 476, n. 31.

43. Las Casas, *Historia*, 2:381. We must rely heavily on Las Casas as his is the principal primary source concerning the Dominicans and their early days in the New World. He also has the only copy of Montesino's sermon, discussed below.

44. Ibid., 2:382. Gutiérrez adds the detail that this was the center of internal reform within the Dominican Order, bringing it back to the foundations of contemplation and poverty. *Las Casas*, 27.

45. Parish, ed., *The Only Way*, 196. She calls him the "spiritual father" of Las Casas.

46. Las Casas, *Historia*, 2:383.

47. Ibid., 2:384. One has to agree with Simpson, who explains, "Their horror may well have been given an edge by the unexplained silence of the Franciscans in the face of such wickedness, for the two great Mendicant orders were centuries-old rivals." *Encomienda*, 31.

48. *Historia*, 3:438–439. Las Casas writes that in 1508, there were only 60,000 people living on Hispaniola, both native and Spanish. This was down from 3 million in 1494, when they arrived. They had perished from "war, slavery, and the mines. Who in future generations will believe this?" *Historia*, 2:346. Simpson, on the other hand, believes there could not have been more than 500,000 in 1492. He gives the figure of 29,000 natives in 1514. *Encomienda*, 30, n. 1. Cook and Borah give a figure closer to that of Las Casas, putting it between 2,500,000 and 5 million. Their figure in 1514 is 27,800, and by 1570, they report only 125 left. Sherburne F. Cook and Woodrow Borah, *Essays in Population History, Mexico and the Caribbean* (Berkeley, 1971), 410.

49. Las Casas, *Historia*, 2:439. This is in absolute violation of the papal donation of Alexander VI.

50. Ibid., 440.

51. Ibid.

52. Ibid.

53. Ibid. There is some dispute over the exact date of this sermon. Giménez Fernández ("A Biographical Sketch," 74) lists the dates of the two sermons as November 30 and December 7, 1515. Las Casas's account, "the fourth week in Advent," would place the date in that year, according to Pérez Fernández ("La fidelidad del Padre Las Casas a su carisma profético," 85–89 n.), on December 21. A discussion of this dispute occurs in Gutiérrez, *Las Casas*, 476, n. 33. Carro (*La teología y los teólogos-juristas*, 1:35, n. 32) indicates the text as being on the third Sunday in Advent according to Dominican ritual.

54. Giménez Fernández, "A Biographical Sketch," 74. Carro, *La teología y los teólogos-juristas,* 1:35.

55. Las Casas, *Historia,* 3: chapter 4, contains the text of the sermon. Translation is from Gutiérrez, *Las Casas,* 29.

56. Las Casas, *Historia,* 2:442. Las Casas, with his typical sarcasm, adds the detail that the *encomenderos* probably had a hard time digesting their dinner that day!

57. Hanke, *Spanish Struggle for Justice,* 17.

58. Carro, *La teología y los teólogos-juristas,* 1:18.

59. Las Casas, *Historia,* 2:442.

60. Castro, "Another Face of Empire," 68.

61. Gutiérrez, *Las Casas,* 30.

62. Las Casas, *Historia,* 2:443.

63. Ibid., 2:444.

64. Ibid., 2:445.

65. "Alonso de Loaysa to the Dominican Fathers in Española," Manuel Serrano y Sanz, *Orígenes de la dominación española in America* (Madrid, 1918), 1:349–50. Serrano y Sanz dates this letter as mid-1511, using as a basis for this the dating of Montesino's sermon during Lent, 1511. In his *Historia,* Las Casas dates the letter as the last Sunday of Advent, 2:440–41. The second letter is, "Message from the Provincial of the Dominicans to the general Vicar of the Indies, about certain sermons," dated March 16, 1512, in Chacon y Calvo, *Cedulario Cubano,* 425–26.

66. "Royal Cédula in reply to the Admiral and royal officials," March 20, 1512, in Chacon y Calvo, *Cedulario Cubano,* 427–31.

67. Simpson, *Encomienda,* 29.

68. Zavala, *La encomienda indiana,* 18.

69. Las Casas, *Historia,* 2:445.

70. Traboulay, *Columbus and Las Casas,* 46.

71. Simpson, *Encomienda,* 30; Las Casas, *Historia,* 2:446.

72. Las Casas, *Historia,* 2:447.

73. Ibid. The complete story concerning the formation of the Laws of Burgos from the perspective of Las Casas is found in *Historia* 2:448–89.

74. The complete translated text of the Laws is in Gibson, *Spanish Tradition in America,* 61–84.

75. Ibid., 61.

76. Las Casas, *Historia,* 2:476. Las Casas will change his position over the years as he becomes more critical of the monarchy. Juan Friede describes the Laws of Burgos thusly: "Considering the times, [the Laws of Burgos] may be regarded as the first practical measures directed at protecting the Indians. "Las Casas and Indigenism," in Friede and Keen, eds., *Las Casas in History,* 142.

77. Las Casas, "Representación a los regentes Cisneros y Adriano," in *Opúsculos*, 5, dated 1516.

78. Las Casas, "Memorial de remedios para las Indias," in *Opúsculos*, 6, dated 1516.

79. Las Casas, *Historia*, 2:478.

80. Simpson, *Encomienda*, 36.

81. Las Casas, *Historia*, 3: chapter 25.

82. Las Casas, *Brief Account*, 27.

83. Ibid., 28.

84. Ibid., 30.

85. Las Casas, *Historia*, 3: chapter 29 for the events at Caonao. Serrano y Sanz interprets the events at Caonao, which he identifies as Cibao, as the primary motivating factors for the conversion of Las Casas. Miguel Serrano y Sanz, *Orígenes de la dominación española en América* (Madrid: Nueva Biblioteca de Autores Españoles XXV, 1918), 1:340.

86. Las Casas, *Historia*, 3: chapter 32. Obviously these events made a lasting impression on Las Casas. He recorded the events concerning the slaughter in Cuba in both the *Historia* and the *Brief Account*. They are also recorded in "Entre los remedios," Razón Oncena, *Opúsculos*, 110:103–7.

87. Las Casas, *Historia*, 3:91.

88. Ibid.

Chapter Three

1. Alan Redpath, *The Making of a Man of God* (Old Tappan, NJ: Revell, 1962), 2.

2. Bernard Spilka, R. W. Hood Jr., and Richard L. Gorsuch, *The Psychology of Religion: An Empirical Approach* (Englewood Cliffs, NJ: Prentice Hall, 1985), 202.

3. G. A. Coe, *The Psychology of Religion* (1916; reprinted 2005, Kila, MT: Kessinger Publishing), 152. Cited in ibid., 203.

4. Ibid., 205. The authors summarize views from a number of noted psychologists, such as Coe, E. D. Starbuck, W. James, and F. L Strickland. Lewis Rambo, in *Understanding Religious Conversion* (New Haven, CT: Yale University Press, 1995), 1, agreed, calling conversion usually a "process not an event," though allowing that sudden conversion is also possible.

5. William James, *Varieties of Religious Experience* (New York, 1902), cited in Spilka et al., *Psychology of Religion*, 200.

6. Las Casas, *Historia*, 2:92–93. This translation is from Parish, ed., *The Only Way*, 187–89. As we will see in the following chapter, this Scripture

will have special meaning for the priest the rest of his life. He will refer to it when his blindness leaves him concerning the enslavement of Africans and Guanches of the Canaries, *Historia* 1:130 and 1: chapter 18.

7. Gutiérrez also makes this point: "Death is the inevitable consequence of oppression. Las Casas censures the Royal Council for not seeking to be duly informed regarding the Indians' situation, and thus condemning the latter, "to perpetual servitude, and to the death necessarily ensuing therefrom to this day." *Las Casas,* 476, n. 30. He quotes Las Casas, *Historia,* 3: chapter 14. I must also point out here that Las Casas also condemns self-imposed ignorance.

8. Las Casas, *The Only Way,* 63.

9. Quoted from Gutiérrez, *Las Casas,* 241.

10. Las Casas, *Historia,* 1:13–15.

11. Gutiérrez, *Las Casas,* 224.

12. Anton Peter, "Bartolomé de Las Casas y el tema de la conversión en la teología de la liberación," *Páginas* 116 (July 1992): 49.

13. Las Casas, "Carta a Carranza" (1555), in *Opúsculos,* 444.

14. Las Casas, "Respuesta al obispo de Las Charcas" (1553), in ibid., 428.

15. This point is made in Gutiérrez, *Las Casas,* 239.

16. Peter, "Tema de la conversión," 50–56.

17. Gutiérrez, *Las Casas,* 61.

18. Peter, "Tema de la conversión," 61.

19. Las Casas, " Entre Los Remedios" (1542), in *Opúsculos,* 88b.

20. Gutiérrez, *Las Casas,* 48.

21. Las Casas, *Historia,* 3:93. Translation is from *The Only Way,* 189–90.

22. Ibid. This is in fact what happened.

23. Ibid. Emphasis added.

24. Ibid., 191.

25. Ibid.

26. According to the *Expository Dictionary of Bible Words,* ed. Lawrence Richards (Grand Rapids, MI: Zondervan, 1991), 522, the Old Testament Hebrew word for repent, or change, is *shuv.* One use of this word indicates a physical turning away from past practices and going a new way. The word literally means to be walking in one direction and then to turn completely around and go in another. At times change of direction comes about after a long struggle and precedes an "about face" in the way of life. The Greek New Testament word is *metanoia.* This word involves a change of mind and attitude about something. The person who has experienced repentance no longer looks at the world in the same way. Thus the totality of the biblical concept of conversion, changing both the actions and attitude of the one who

repents, is present in the life of Las Casas. The proof of this action is then demonstrated in one's life, and others are able to see the change. Thus we can see the classic definition of a penitent in Las Casas's life. He not only changed his life's direction but also his conviction about the injustices practiced by his fellow peninsulars.

27. I. Pérez Fernández, *Cronología documentada,* 227, fixed this date as August 15, 1514.

28. Las Casas, *Historia,* 3:95. As before I have used the translation found in *The Only Way,* 191. Emphasis added.

29. I. Pérez Fernández, *Cronología documentada,* 227. He labels this sermon "the culmination of his 'first conversion.'"

30. Manuel Giménez Fernández, "Fray Bartolomé de Las Casas: A Biographical Sketch," in Friede and Keen, eds., *Las Casas in History,* 74.

31. Las Casas, *Historia,* 3: chapters 80–81. For the "Información" of his services to the Crown, *ad perpetuam rei memoriam,* see Wagner and Parish, *Life and Writings,* 259.

32. For a summary of these events, Parish, ed., *The Only Way,* 22.

33. Las Casas, *Historia,* 3:106–7.

34. For the text of these Laws of Burgos, see Gibson, ed., *Spanish Tradition in America,* 61–82. Las Casas also provides an inside account of the Junta of Burgos in *Historia,* 3: chapters 6–18.

35. Wagner and Parish, *Life and Writings,* 11.

36. Las Casas, *Historia,* 3:108.

37. Ibid., 3:110.

38. Ibid.

39. Wagner and Parish, *Life and Writings,* 18.

40. Kamen, *Spain 1469–1714,* 89. According to Kamen, until 1530 the main source of wealth from the New World was gold coming from the Caribbean Islands. After this date, silver from Potosí and Mexico became more profitable.

41. "*Representación hecha al Rey por el clérigo Bartolomé de Las Casas, en que manifiesta los agravios que sufren los indios de la isla de Cuba de los españoles*" (ca. 1516) in *Colección de Documentos inéditos, relativos al descubrimiento, conquista y organización de las antiguas posesiones españolas de América y Oceanía sacados de los Archivos del Reino y muy especialmente del de Indias,* vol. 7:11, ed. Luis Torres de Mendoza (Madrid, 1867). Hereafter cited as DII.

42. Ibid., 5–12.

43. The complete text of these is in Bartolomé de Las Casas, "*Memorial de remedios para las indias*" (1516), in Opúsculos, cartas y memoriales, BAE, 110.

44. Las Casas, *Historia*, 3:117.

45. Giménez Fernández, "A Biographical Sketch," 76. Also by the same author, *Bartolomé de Las Casas: Delegado de Cisneros para la Reformación de las Indias (1516–1517)* (Seville: Escuela de Estudios Hispanoamericanos de Sevilla, 1953), 168–71.

46. Las Casas, *Historia*, 3:136.

Chapter Four

1. This is the expression utilized by Gutiérrez, *Las Casas*, 482, n. 1. I hope to make clear the prophetic nature of his message in this chapter and therefore I utilize the term throughout.

2. Las Casas, *Historia*, 3:278.

3. Ibid., 3:279.

4. There is a lively discussion of the prophetic role of Las Casas. Parish, ed., introduction to Las Casas, *The Only Way*, 20, and in addendum 1, 185. Parish cites Abraham Heschel's prologue in *The Prophets* (New York, 1962), and wrote, "he describes the classic call of the Hebrew prophets; the description fits Las Casas's experience." Ibid., 21, n. 21. Carlos Soria, "Fray Bartolomé de Las Casas, historiador, humanista, o profeta?" *Ciencia Tomista* 101 (1974), concurs that Las Casas demonstrated a "prophetic character." Isacio Pérez Fernández, in "La Fidelidad del Padre Las Casas a su Carisma Profético," *Studium* 16 (1976), argues that because he is a priest, he therefore, in fulfilling this role, fulfills the role of prophet. Marie-Dominique Chenu, "El evangelio en el tiempo," *Estela* 9 (1966), agrees that Las Casas was a prophet in the biblical and evangelical sense of the word. On the opposing side of this issue are Marcel Bataillon, "Las Casas, un profeta?" *Revista del Occidente* 47, no. 141 (1974), who concludes that Las Casas is a "quasi-prophet" because he was not opposed by the Crown. For an extreme view disputing the prophetic nature of Las Casas, as well as his mental stability in general, consult Ramón Menéndez Pidal, *El Padre Las Casas: Su Doble Personalidad* (Madrid: Espasa-Calpe, 1963). Finally, those who place Las Casas in the role of a prophet for liberation theology include Enrique Dussel, *A History of the Church in Latin America: Colonialism to Liberation (1492–1979)*, trans. Alan Neely (Grand Rapids, MI: Eerdmans, 1981), 315, and Luciano Pereña, "Fray Bartolomé de las Casas, profeta de la liberación," *Arbor*, 89, no. 347 (1974): 21.

5. Geoffrey W. Bromiley, *Theological Dictionary of the New Testament* (Grand Rapids, MI: Eerdmans, 1988), 953.

6. Ibid., 954–57.

Notes

7. Ibid. This discussion is also carried out by Pérez, "El Perfil Profético," 296–324.

8. Laird R. Harris, ed., *Theological Wordbook of the Old Testament*, 2 vols. (Chicago: Moody Press, 1980), 2:1275–76.

9. David Atkinson, "Prophecy," in *Eerdmans Handbook to Christian Belief*, ed. Robert Koeley (Grand Rapids, MI: Eerdmans, 1982), 316–17. This is also discussed by Pérez, "El Perfil Profético," 296ff. A very interesting discussion connecting the beginnings of the gift of prophecy in the New Testament Church to the beginning of the Roman Christian Church is found in Jose Luis Espinel, "Aspecto profético de la vida cristiana según el Nuevo Testamento," *Ciencia Tomista* 98 (1971): 7–53.

10. Las Casas, "Memorial de remedios para las Indias" (1516), in *Opúsculos*, 20.

11. Ibid.

12. Ibid., 27.

13. Las Casas, "Memorial de remedios," in *Opúsculos*, 5.

14. Ibid.

15. Ibid., 7. The last line of this *remedio* made reference to an attached sheet with specific recommendations for these communities. If this was written, no copy of it is extant.

16. This experiment, much more successful then Cumaná and begun in 1536, is detailed in Benno Biermann, "Bartolomé de Las Casas and Verapaz," in Friede and Keen, eds., *Las Casas in History*, 443–84. It will be discussed below.

17. Las Casas, *Opúsculos*, 9.

18. Ibid., 17.

19. Las Casas, *Historia*, 3:177.

20. There are many books dealing with the issue of African slavery. Among these are David Brion Davis, *The Problem of Slavery in Western Culture* (Oxford: Oxford University Press, 1966), which contains a good history of the institution. Also, John Hope Franklin, *From Slavery to Freedom: A History of Negro Americans* (New York: Alfred A. Knopf, 1974).

21. Gutiérrez, *Las Casas*, 322, detailed the position of a number of the contemporary scholars both in Spain and in America concerning the issue of African slavery. His point is that serious questions concerning the legitimacy of the institution of slavery itself do not arise until late in the seventeenth century.

22. Isacio Pérez Fernández, *Bartolomé de Las Casas: Contra los Negros* (Madrid, 1991), 71–121. Pérez wrote this book to counter the so-called black legend concerning Las Casas and his alleged anti-Negro attitudes and identifying him as the founder of black slavery in America. He concludes that Las

Casas was the first to denounce African slavery once he realized the full impact of it and became acquainted with the people and their culture. He has also written *Bartolomé de Las Casas: Brevísima relación de la destrucción de África* (Salamanca, 1989), which also detailed the involvement by Las Casas in denouncing the African slave trade.

23. "Parecer de los religiosos de Santo Domingo," undated, *DII* 11:214.

24. Las Casas, "Carta al Consejo de Indias" (January 20, 1531), in *Opúsculos*, 54b.

25. Ibid., 55a.

26. Las Casas, "Memorial de Remedio," (1542), in *Opúsculos*, 121a.

27. Helen Rand Parish, *Las Casas as Bishop*, bilingual edition (Washington, 1980), 9.

28. Pérez, *Contra los Negros?* 262.

29. Ibid., 191–92. Pérez believed he went to Lisbon for just this purpose. Among those Portuguese historians studied and later quoted by Las Casas are Gomes Eanes de Zurara, *Crónica dos feitos da Guiné;* Garcia de Resende, author of *Crónica del D. João ll de Portugal;* and João de Barros, *Décadas da Asia*. All published between 1545 and 1552.

30. Ibid., 196. He dates these as having been written around 1554 at the latest. These chapters do not contain the customary summaries typical of the others.

31. Las Casas, *Historia*, 1:129.

32. Ibid., 1: chapter 25.

33. Ibid., 1:130.

34. Ibid.

35. Pérez Fernández, *Contra los Negros?* 188, fixed the date of these chapters as 1560, but believed his actual repentance came earlier, perhaps 1545–47.

36. Las Casas, *Historia*, 3:177.

37. Ibid., 3:275.

38. Ibid.

39. Ibid.

40. Gutiérrez, *Las Casas*, 329.

41. Giménez Fernández, "A Biographical Sketch," in *Bartolomé de Las Casas in History*, 76.

42. Las Casas, *Historia*, 3:122.

43. Ibid., 3:123.

44. Simpson, *Encomienda*, 43.

45. Las Casas, *Historia*, 3:360.

46. Simpson, *Encomienda*, 52–55.

47. Giménez Fernández, "A Biographical Sketch," 78.

48. Wagner and Parish, *Life and Writings*, 42–45.

49. For example, Bataillon, "The Clérigo Casas," 410, and Giménez Fernández, "A Biographical Sketch," 82. Both in Friede and Keen, eds., *Las Casas in History*.

50. Manuel Giménez Fernández, *Bartolomé de Las Casas: Capellán de S.M. Carlos l, Poblador de Cumaná (1517–1523)* (Sevilla, 1960), 675.

51. S. E. Morison, *Southern Voyages*, 153. Columbus visited this area during his third voyage.

52. Wagner and Parish, *Life and Writings*, 46, provided the dating of this letter.

53. Las Casas, *Historia*, 3:187–88.

54. An interesting note is that the conversion of St. Paul, also called his "Road to Damascus" experience, is retold three times in the Acts of the Apostles. The summary of his experience is found in chapters 9, 22, and 28. The Last Will and Testament is found in *Opúsculos*, 539–40. The Flemish officials used the title "micer" for priests.

55. Las Casas, *Historia*, 3:341. Las Casas notes the contradiction between the natives' natural laziness and subservience, on the one hand, and their working hard for the gold, on the other.

56. Ibid., 3:342.

57. Ibid.

58. Ibid., 3:343.

59. Ibid.

60. Ibid. Las Casas received a good deal of criticism for his statement about Aristotle, who was a favorite of the theologians of the day.

61. Ibid., 3:344.

62. Ibid., 3:361.

63. Wagner and Parish, *Life and Writings*, 57–60.

64. Refer to Las Casas, *Historia*, 3: chapter 130, mentioned above.

65. Gutiérrez, *Las Casas*, 54.

66. Las Casas, *Historia*, 3:308–9.

67. Las Casas, *The Only Way*, 138. A discussion of this is also in Gutiérrez, Las Casas, 63.

68. An account of the events leading up to the destruction of Cumaná are found in the *Historia*, 3: chapters 156–59. I am summarizing this account.

69. Hanke, *Spanish Struggle for Justice*, relates, "A sorry and impossible alliance, Las Casas recognized later, but it was a desperate effort to salvage some part, no matter how small, of his original plan." 67.

70. Las Casas, *Historia*, 3: chapter 159. In his *Apologética*, he informs us of some of the customs of the natives around Cumaná. Wagner and Parish indi-

cated that this knowledge, contained in chapters 245 and 247, was secondhand, learned from the friars who lived there. *Life and Writings,* 67.

71. *Historia* 3:382.

72. See Bataillon, "The Clérigo Casas," 410, and Giménez Fernández, "A Biographical Sketch," 82. Both are found in Friede and Keen, eds., *Las Casas in History.*

73. Las Casas, *Historia,* 3:382.

74. Ibid., 3:387.

75. Bataillon questions the motivations of Las Casas at this point. For example, "We would not distort his conversation with Betanzos if we said that he agreed *to play dead*" ("The Clérigo Casas," 413, emphasis added).

76. Biblical examples include Moses, Job, and, of course, Jesus in the Garden of Gethsemane.

77. Isacio Pérez Fernández, "El perfil profético del Padre Las Casas," 331, n. 117.

Chapter Five

1. Marcel Bataillon, "The Clérigo Casas," in Friede and Keen, eds., *Las Casas in History,* 414.

2. Giménez Fernández, "A Biographical Sketch," in Friede and Keen, eds., *Las Casas in History,* 83.

3. Hanke, *Bartolomé de Las Casas: Historian,* 30.

4. Wagner and Parish, *Life and Writings,* 72.

5. *Gutiérrez, Las Casas,* 191.

6. Hanke and Giménez Fernández, *Bibliografía crítica,* 43.

7. Las Casas, "Carta al Consejo de Indias," in *Opúsculos,* 43b–44a.

8. Ibid., 50b.

9. Ibid., 48a.

10. Specific examples of Las Casas calling for African slaves are discussed above.

11. Wagner and Parish, *Life and Writings,* 73. Although Las Casas specifically rejected any personal profit from this venture, Wagner believed he was angling for the job of bishop.

12. Gutiérrez, *Las Casas,* 81. Gutiérrez labeled this letter one of Las Casas's germinal texts, the other being his "Memorial de remedios" of 1516.

13. The story of Enriquillo is detailed in Las Casas, *Historia,* 3:259–70. The same events are dealt with by Oviedo, *Historia general,* 1:124–37. Obviously Las Casas does not play quite as large a role in the entire affair in

this account, but basically the facts are the same. The Franciscans who had trained him from a child gave him this name.

14. Las Casas, *Historia,* 3:260.

15. Ibid. Oviedo, *Historia general,* 1:124, gave the date when the conflict began as 1519.

16. Las Casas, *Historia,* 3:269.

17. Parish, ed., *The Only Way,* 33.

18. Las Casas, "Carta al Consejo de Indias" (1534), in *Opúsculos,* 57. The English translation, used in this work is in Wagner and Parish, *Life and Writings,* 77–78.

19. Oviedo, *Historia general,* 1:139.

20. Parish, ed., *The Only Way,* 34. For a complete discussion of other views on the dating of this work, refer to ibid., 211–21. Only chapters 5, 6, and 7 of the original are extant.

21. This point is made by Manuel Martínez, "El padre Las Casas, promotor de la evangelizacion de America," *Anuario de Estudios Hispanoamericanos* 23 (1966): 6. He also wrote that evangelism arrived late in America and was poorly done.

22. Parish, ed., *The Only Way,* 85.

23. Ibid., 90.

24. Las Casas, *Historia,* 3:262.

25. Las Casas, "Doce dudas" (1564), in *Opúsculos,* 532b.

26. Ibid., 532–34.

27. Las Casas, "Memorial al Consejo de Indias" (1565), in *Opúsculos,* 538b.

28. Ibid., 537–38. Gutiérrez made the point that Las Casas did not systematically develop the just war doctrine, so fully dealt with by Aquinas. Vitoria does deal with all aspects of the doctrine in his *Relectio de Iure Belli.* This was, of course, because Las Casas was not involved in writing doctrine but in applying doctrine to specific situations.

29. Parish, ed., *The Only Way,* 171.

30. Ibid., 68.

31. Las Casas, "Carta a un personaje de la corte" (October 15, 1535), in *Opúsculos,* 59–60. Gutiérrez wrote, "It is thought, with good reason, that the personage of the Court, to whom the letter was addressed, must be Juan Bernal Díaz de Luco, a person of influence when it came to questions of the Indies, and Las Casas's good friend." *Las Casas,* 471, n. 3. Giménez Fernández wrote that Las Casas had written this letter to the king and the Council of the Indies. "Unfortunately, the council, which despite the good intentions of the new counselors Bernal Díaz de Luco and Mercado de Peñalosa was still dominated by the corrupt spirit of the deceased Fonseca,

did not act on this proposal of Las Casas." "A Biographical Sketch," in Friede and Keen, eds., *Las Casas in History*, 87.

32. Las Casas, *Opúsculos*, 67a. Wagner listed the companions accompanying Las Casas as Rodrigo de Ladrada, Pedro de Ángulo, and probably Luís Cáncer. Wagner and Parish, *Life and Writings*, 83.

33. Las Casas, *Opúsculos*, 62a.

34. Ibid., 68a.

35. Antonio de Remesal, OP, *Historia general de las Indias Occidentales y particular de la gobernación de Chiapa y Guatemala*, ed. Carmelo Saenz de Santa María, SJ (Madrid, 1964–66), I, 206. This belief is challenged by Wagner and Parish, *Life and Writings*, 85.

36. "Father Fray Toribio de Motolinía to Charles V" (January 2, 1555). This letter is translated and included as appendix 5 in Simpson, *Encomienda*, 234–43.

37. Las Casas, "Petición a su santidad Pio V" (no date), in *Opúsculos*, 542a.

38. Las Casas, "Memorial de remedios para las Indias" (1516), in *Opúsculos*, 8a.

39. Helen Rand Parish and Harold E. Weidman, SJ, *Las Casas en México: Historia y obra desconocidas* (México, D.F., 1992). They have pieced together details of this meeting, especially in chapter 2, emphasizing the role of Las Casas. She wrote, "point by point these principles [of *De Unico Modo*] coincide with what will be later promulgated in the historic encyclical," 32.

40. Papal bull *Sublimus Deus*, in Parish, ed., *The Only Way*, 115. Emphasis added. This bull was included in a later version of *De Unico Modo*, and obviously not in the original 1534 version. Refer to ibid., 211–31.

41. This is a summation of the first lines of the work, refer to n. 36 above.

42. Gutiérrez, *Las Casas*, 302–8, has a complete discussion of these pronouncements and their effects in America.

43. Benno Biermann, "Bartolomé de Las Casas and Verapaz," in Friede and Keen, eds., *Las Casas in History*, 452–53. Biermann translated and included a letter from Maldonado to Charles V, October 16, 1539, in which he detailed the influence of Las Casas and the progress being made.

44. Hanke, *Spanish Struggle for Justice*, 77.

45. Ibid., 78.

46. Bataillon, *Estudios Sobre Bartolomé de Las Casas*, 204–5.

47. Wagner and Parish, *Life and Writings*, 91–92.

48. Giménez Fernández, "A Biographical Sketch," 92–93.

49. A brief summary of these *cédulas* is found in Hanke and Giménez Fernández, *Bibliografía crítica*, 59–62.

Notes

50. Giménez Fernández, "A Biographical Sketch," 93–94.

51. Las Casas, "Carta al emperador" (December 15, 1540), in *Opúsculos,* 68–69.

52. Wagner and Parish, *Life and Writings,* 107. The authors hint that perhaps this was why Las Casas desired to leave the Indies and come to Spain.

53. Giménez Fernández, "A Biographical Sketch," 96. Also refer to Hanke, *Spanish Struggle for Justice,* 93–94, in which he indicates that Las Casas had a hand in everything that transpired on the council, and that the emperor did nothing without seeking his advice. Ernesto Schaefer, *El Consejo Real y Supremo de las Indias,* 2 vols. (Seville, 1935), 1:63, suggests that the emperor called the *visita* because he suspected impropriety among some of its members.

54. Gutiérrez, *Las Casas,* 288.

55. There are several translations of this work. I have used the translation by Nigel Griffin, *A Short Account of the Destruction of the Indies* (London, 1992). There is an introduction to this work by Anthony Pagden.

56. In the introduction to *A Short Account,* Pagden provided an interesting summary of a *relación.* Comparing this work with the *Letters of Account* of Cortéz, Pagden writes, "Unlike the *History,* the *Short Account* is, by implication at least, a *relación*—the name given to the official report, witnessed and authenticated by a notary, which every royal officer in the Indies was expected to provide of his activities." xxx–xxxi. Las Casas was not present, however, at the destruction in Central Mexico and Peru, and therefore needed to rely on other eyewitnesses to these. Refer to xxxvi–xxxvii.

57. This biblical reference is to Romans 1:28 (KJV): "And even as they did not like to retain God in their knowledge, God gave them over to a reprobate mind, to do those things which are not convenient."

58. Las Casas, *A Short Account,* trans. by Griffin, 3–4.

59. Ibid., 15.

60. Ibid., 39.

61. Ibid., 127.

62. Ibid., 82. Because of this the Indians "scoff at God and His words."

63. Ibid., 127.

64. Las Casas, "Entre Los Remedios" (1542), in *Opúsculos,* 110a.

65. Ibid., 117a.

66. Ibid., 119b.

67. Ramón Menéndez Pidal, *El Padre Las Casas,* 328, notes that "in this tract he tells us, as far as I can see, the first instance that his great accusatory message also includes a prophetic aspect; it is the first time he threatens horrible punishment and perhaps complete destruction of all Spain."

68. Las Casas, "Carta al Maestro Fray Bartolomé Carranza De Miranda," in *Opúsculos*, 435a.

69. Ibid., 450a.

Chapter Six

1. Helen Rand Parish, *Las Casas as a Bishop: A New Interpretation Based on His Holograph Petition in the Hans P. Kraus Collection of Hispanic American Manuscripts* (Washington, 1988), xi–xii. Giménez Fernández, "A Biographical Sketch," 96, indicates that Las Casas was offered the miter to get him out of Spain and end his influence with Prince Philip.

2. Las Casas, "El Obispo electo Bartolomé de Las Casas al Emperador Carlos V," in Parish, *Las Casas as a Bishop*, 18.

3. Ibid., 19–23.

4. Ibid., xiii–xiv.

5. Four Royal Ordinances, dated February 13, 1544, translated and printed in appendix III, Francis A. MacNutt, *Bartholomew de Las Casas, His Life, Apostolate, and Writings* (Cleveland, 1909), 432–38.

6. Parish, *Las Casas as Bishop*, xiv. For the date of consecration, see Parish's preface to *The Only Way*, 41. Wagner and Parish (124) *Life and Writings*, list the date as Passion Sunday, March 30, 1544.

7. Gibson, *Spain in America*, 58.

8. Simpson, *Encomienda*, 129.

9. Gibson, *Spain in America*, 59. Schaefer emphasizes the sincerity of Charles V in promulgating these laws as he points out that the Spanish were to print these in all of the Indies, have the missionaries translate them into the native languages, and provide for a fine of one thousand *castellanos* for their violation. *El Consejo Real*, 1:69.

10. Menéndez Pidal, *El Padre Las Casas*, 151.

11. A discussion of the contemporary accounts of the influence of Las Casas is found in Wagner and Parish, *Life and Writings*, 108–13. This particular citation of Gómara is on 113.

12. Parish, ed., *The Only Way*, 40.

13. Hanke, *Spanish Struggle for Justice*, 95. This specific claim is disputed by Menéndez Pidal in *El Padre Las Casas*, 151; he sees it more as an evolution than a revolution.

14. Simpson, *Encomienda*, 129.

15. For those articles dealing with the Indians, see Simpson, *Encomienda*, 129–32. For the entire text of the New Laws in English, see Gibson, *Spanish Tradition in America*, 109–12.

Notes

16. Las Casas, "Octavo Remedio," in *Opúsculos*, 69b–70a.

17. Zavala, *La encomienda indiana,* 83.

18. Excerpts of this letter are found in Simpson, *Encomienda,* 134. The entire original is in *DII,* 7, 532–42.

19. Remesal, *Historia general,* 1:327b.

20. Giménez Fernández, "A Bibliographical Sketch," 100.

21. Las Casas, "Carta al príncipe Don Felipe" (September 15, 1544), in *Opúsculos,* 214.

22. Giménez Fernández, "A Biographical Sketch," 100.

23. Wagner and Parish, *Life and Writings,* 130–31.

24. Parish, ed., introduction to *The Only Way,* 42.

25. Wagner and Parish, *Life and Writings,* 157.

26. Juan Friede, "Las Casas and Indigenism," in Friede and Keen, eds., *Las Casas in History,* 188–89, see n. 243.

27. Gutiérrez, *Las Casas,* 365.

28. Francis Patrick Sullivan, *Indian Freedom: The Cause of Bartolomé de las Casas, 1484–1566* (Kansas City: Sheed and Ward, 1995), 281.

29. Wagner and Parish, *Life and Writings,* 167.

30. Las Casas, *Rules for Confessors,* trans. F. P. Sullivan, *Indian Freedom,* 282–83. For the Spanish, refer to *Opúsculos,* 235–49.

31. Las Casas, *Rules,* trans. Sullivan, 288.

32. "Carta de Fray Bartolomé de las Casas, Obispo de Chiapa, y de Fray Antonio de Valdivieso, Obispo de Nicaragua, al Principe Don Felipe" (October 25, 1545), in *Opúsculos,* 223.

33. Giménez Fernández, "A Biographical Sketch," 104. Pedro A. Vives Azancot, "El Pensamiento Lascasiano en la Formación de una Política Colonial Española, 1511–1573," in *En el quinto centenario de Bartolomé de las Casas* (Madrid, 1986), 35, stated that things were so bad for Las Casas in his diocese that "he was considered nothing less than a kind of antichrist."

34. Parish, *Las Casas en México,* 58–59.

35. Ibid. Isaiah 30:8–11, reads, "Go now, write it before them on a tablet, and inscribe it in a book, so that it may be for the time to come as a witness forever. For they are a rebellious people, faithless children, children who will not hear the instruction of the LORD; who say to the seers, 'Do not see'; and to the prophets, 'Do not prophesy to us what is right; speak to us smooth things, prophesy illusions, leave the way, turn aside from the path, let us hear no more about the Holy One of Israel.'"

36. Parish writes, "Never before had the Laws of God thundered so powerfully in the City of Mexico, and never before had the role of prophet been so clearly expounded." *Las Casas in Mexico,* 61.

37. Gutiérrez, *Las Casas,* 365–56.

38. Wagner and Parish, *Life and Writings*, 172–73. The specific article in question was probably the reason given by Las Casas for the seventh rule of confessors. This reason stated, "all that has been done in the Indies, from the arrival of the Spanish into each area as in the subjection of and enslavement of the inhabitants...has been contrary to all natural law, the laws of nations, and also against divine law; therefore it is totally unjust, iniquitous, tyrannical and worthy of hell's fire, and consequently null and void, invalid, without any worth and totally illegal." From "Rules for Confessors," in *Opúsculos*, 239b.

39. Las Casas, "Aquí se contiene treinta proposiciones muy jurídicas" (1552), in *Opúsculos*, 253. In another work on this same theme, "Tratado Comprobatorio" (which Wagner and Parish described as "massive and almost unreadable"), written probably the next year but also published in 1552, Las Casas further explained his propositions. This is found in *Opúsculos*, 350–423.

40. Ibid., 253–55.

41. Las Casas, "Memorial de remedios para las Indias" (ca. 1516), in *Opúsculos*, 20a.

42. Ibid., 27a.

43. Las Casas, "Aquí se contiene una disputa o controversia" (1552), in *Opúsculos*, 294a. This is the official summary of the Valladolid disputation written by Domingo de Soto, which Las Casas printed the following year.

44. Wagner and Parish think it probable that the *Confesionario* and subsequent propositions were the cause of the Valladolid meeting, because the emperor's conscience bothered him. *Life and Writings*, 177.

45. Pagden, *Fall of Natural Man*, 109–10.

46. Hanke, *All Mankind is One*, 67.

47. Angel Losada, "The Controversy between Sepúlveda and Las Casas," in Friede and Keen, eds., *Las Casas in History*, 279. Hanke, in *Spanish Struggle for Justice*, 117, also made this point.

48. Pedro Borges, *Quién Era Bartolomé de Las Casas* (Madrid, 1990), 222.

49. Hanke, *Spanish Struggle for Justice*, 117–18, provides a more complete list of the participants.

50. Domingo de Soto, printed in Las Casas, "Aquí tiene una disputa," in *Opúsculos*, 294a–b.

51. Losada, "The Controversy," 279.

52. Hanke, *Spanish Struggle for Justice*, 118.

53. Wagner and Parish, *Life and Writings*, 177.

54. Pagden, *Fall of Natural Man*, 109. As discussed in a previous chapter, Las Casas had much to say about Oviedo and his descriptions of the

Indians. For a complete discussion, refer to Hanke, *All Mankind is One*, 34–45.

55. In 1550, this booklet appeared in Rome in a shortened form, entitled *Apologia*. In 1892 it was first published in Spanish in fuller form, under the title *Tratado sobre las causas justas de la guerra contra los Indios*, by M. Menéndez Pelayo. This work was also known as *Democrates alter*, *Democrates II*, and *Democrates secundum*. The most complete recent edition is Juan Ginés de Sepúlveda, *Democrates segundo o de las justas causas de la guerra contra los Indios*, ed. and trans. Angel Losada (Madrid, 1951), 35.

56. Ibid., 110–22.

57. Las Casas, *In Defense of the Indians*, 20–22.

58. Parish, ed., introduction to *The Only Way*, 47.

59. Las Casas, *In Defense of the Indians*, 96.

60. Ibid., 297. I have summarized these arguments briefly because there are a number of books dealing specifically with this controversy, and as Hanke writes in his monograph concerning the subject, "the arguments of Las Casas require little detailed examination. He made a few simple points over and over, with numerous examples and references from the copious literature he had studied, and there is no real question on what he meant to say." *Aristotle and the American Indians: A Study in Race Prejudice in the Modern World* (Chicago, 1959), 41. In a more recent work Hanke also writes, "The multiplicity of citations and repetition of basic thoughts in a bewildering variety of situations leads the reader to believe at times that one of Las Casas's methods was to wear down his opponent by the very weight and reiteration of the argument." *All Mankind is One*, 99. Gutiérrez also has much to say on Sepúlveda and his beliefs in *Las Casas*.

61. Hanke identified this judge as Melchor Cano in *Aristotle and the American Indian*, 74.

62. Hanke and Giménez Fernández, *Bibliográfica crítica*, 141.

63. Wagner and Parish, *Life and Writings*, 183–84.

64. Ibid., 186.

65. Ibid., 187–90.

66. Hanke and Giménez Fernández, *Bibliografía crítica*, 140–41.

67. Giménez Fernández, "A Biographical Sketch," 111–12.

68. Ibid., 112.

69. Parish, ed., introduction to *The Only Way*, 50–51.

70. Las Casas, "Carta a Carranza," in *Opúsculos*, 431b.

71. Gutiérrez, *Las Casas*, 234.

72. Las Casas, "Memorial del obispo Fray Bartolomé de Las Casas y Fray Domingo de Santo Tomás" (1560), in *Opúsculos*, 465–468. English translation of this passage is found in F. P. Sullivan, *Indian Freedom*, 328–32.

73. Las Casas, *Los tesoros del Perú,* ed. and trans. Angel Losada García (Madrid, 1968).

74. Gutiérrez, *Las Casas,* 393.

75. Las Casas, "Doce dudas," in *Opúsculos,* 522–24.

76. Ibid., 531–32.

77. Ibid., 534–35

78. Wagner and Parish, *Life and Writings,* 236–38.

79. Las Casas, "Clausula del testamento que hizo el obispo de Chiapa, Don Fray Bartolomé de Las Casas," in *Opúsculos,* 539. I have used the translation by F. P. Sullivan in *Indian Freedom,* 353.

80. Ibid., 354. Emphasis added.

81. Alain Milhou, "Las Casas, profeta de su tiempo. Profeta para nuestro tiempo," in *Las Casas Entre Dos Mundos* (Lima, 1992), 177.

82. Las Casas, *Indian Freedom,* 355. Emphasis added.

Bibliography

Primary Sources

Colección de documentos inéditos, relativos al descubrimiento, conquista y organización de las antiguas posesiones españolas de America y Oceanía sacados de los Archivos del Reino y muy especialmente del de Indias (DII). 40 vols. Luis Torres de Mendoza, ed. Madrid: Imprenta de Frias y Compañia, 1867.

Díaz del Castillo, Bernal. *Historia verdadera de la conquista de la Nueva España.* 14th ed. Joaquin Ramirez Cabañas, ed. Mexico: Editorial Purrúa, S.A., 1986.

Fabié, Antonio María. *Vida y escritos de Fray Bartolomé de Las Casas, obispo de Chiapa.* 2 vols. Madrid: Imprenta de Manuel Ginesta, 1879.

Gómara, Francisco López de. *Historia general de las Indias.* 2 vols. Madrid: Calpe, 1922. First published in Zaragoza 1552.

Las Casas, Bartolomé de. *A Short Account of the Destruction of the Indies.* Translated by Anthony Pagden. New York: Viking, 1992.

————. *Apología de Bartolomé de Las Casas contra Juan Ginés de Sepúlveda.* In *Apología de Juan Ginés de Sepúlveda contra Fray Bartolomé de Las Casas y Fray Bartolomé de Las Casas contra Juan Ginés de Sepúlveda,* edited and translated by Angel Losada García. Madrid: Editora Nacional, 1975.

————. *Apologética historia sumaria.* Edmundo O'Gorman, ed. Vols. 1–11. Mexico: UNAM, Instituto de Investigaciones Históricas, 1967.

————. *Bartolomé de Las Casas: The Only Way.* Helen Rand Parish, ed.; Francis Patrick Sullivan, SJ, trans. Mahwah, NJ: Paulist Press, 1992.

————. *Brevísima relación de la destrucción de las Indias*. Buenos Aires: Ediciones Mar Océano, 1953. First published 1552.

————. *De Regia Potestate o derecho de autodeterminación*. Luciano Pereña, J. M. Pérez-Prendes, Vidal Abril, and Joaquín Azcárraga, eds. Madrid: Corpus Hipanorum de Pace, vol. VIII. Consejo Superior de Investigaciones, 1969.

————. *Diario del primer y tercer viaje de Cristobal Colón*. Consuelo Varela, ed. Vol. 14. Obras Completas. Madrid: Alianza Editorial, 1989.

————. *Doce dudas*. J. B. Lassegue, ed. Vol. 11.2. Obras Completas. Madrid: Alianza Editorial, 1992.

————. *Historia de Las Indias*. Agustin Millares Carlo, ed. 3 vols. Mexico: Fondo de Cultura Económica, 1951.

————. *Obras Escogidas de Fray Bartolomé de Las Casas*. Juan Pérez de Tudela Bueso, ed. 2 vols. Madrid: Biblioteca de Autores Espanoles (BAE) Vols. 95, 96, 1957.

————. *Opúsculos, cartas y memoriales. Obras escogidas de Fray Bartolomé de Las Casas V*. Vol. CX. Juan Pérez de Tudela Bueso, ed. Madrid: BAE, 1958.

————. *Los tesoros del Perú*. Angel Losada García, ed. and trans. Madrid: Consejo de Investigaciones Científicas, 1968.

————. *A Short Account of the Destruction of the Indies*. Nigel Griffin, ed. and trans. London: Penguin Books, 1992.

————. *Tratados de Fray Bartolomé de Las Casas*. Agustín Millares, Carlo and Rafael Moreno, trans. 2 vols. Mexico and Bueno Aires: Fondo de Cultura Económica, 1965.

————. *Tratados de 1552 impresos por Las Casas en Sevilla*. Ramón Hernández and Lorenzo Galméz, eds. Vol. 10. Obras Completas. Madrid: Alianza Editorial, 1992.

Losada, Angel, ed. and trans. *Apología de Juan Ginés de Sepúlveda contra Fray Bartolomé de Las Casas y de frey de Las Casas y de Fray Bartolomé de Las Casas contra Juan Ginés de Sepúlveda*. Madrid: Editoria Nacional, 1975.

Oviedo y Valdés, Gonzalo Fernandez de. *Historia general y natural de las Indias, islas y tierra del mar océano*. 4 vols. Madrid: Real Academia de a Historia, 1851–55. First published 1547.

————. *Historia general y natural de las Indias*. J. Pérez de Tudela, ed. Madrid: BAE, 1959.

Parish, Helen Rand, ed.; Francis Patrick Sullvan, SJ, trans. *Bartolomé de las Casas: The Only Way.* Mahwah, NJ, and New York: Paulist Press, 1992.

————. *Las Casas as a Bishop: A New Interpretation Based on his Holograph Petition in the Hans P. Krause Collection of Hispanic American Manuscripts / Las Casas, Obsipo: Una nueva interpretación a base de su petición autografía Hans P. Krause de Manuscritos Hispanoamericanos.* Washington: Library of Congress, 1980.

————, and Harold E. Weidman, SJ. *Las Casas en México: Historia y obra desconocidas.* México, D.F.: Fondo de Cultura Económica, 1992.

Pérez Fernandez, Isacio. *Inventario Documentado de las Escritos de Fray Bartolomé de Las Casas.* Baymón, Puerto Rico: Centro de Estudios de los Dominicos del Caribe (CEDOC), 1981.

Remesal, Antonio de. *Historia general de las Indias Occidentales y particular de gobernación de Chiapa y Guatemala.* P. Carmelo Saenz de Santa Maria, SJ, ed. 2 vols. Madrid: BAE, Vols. CLXXXV, CLXXXIX, 1964, 1966.

Sepúlveda, Juan Ginés de. *De las justas causas de la guerra contra los indios.* 2nd ed. México: Fondo de Cultura Económica, 1941. First published 1780.

Victoria, Francisco de. *Relacciones del estado de los indios, y del derecho de la guerra.* Antonio Gómez Robledo, ed. México: Editorial Porrúa, S.A., 1974.

————. *Relectio de Iure Belli.* Madrid: CSIC (CHP), 1981.

Secondary Sources

Andrien, Kenneth J., and Rolena Adorno. *Transatlantic Encounters: Europeans and Andeans in the Sixteenth Century.* Berkeley, Los Angeles, Oxford: University of California Press, 1991.

Avalle-Arce, Juan Bautista. "Las Hipérboles del padre Las Casas." *Revista de la facultad de Humanidades* 2, no. 1 (January–March 1960): 33–55.

Baptiste, V. *Bartolomé de las Casas and Thomas More's Utopia: Connections and Similarities*. Culver City, CA: Labyrinthos, 1990.

Bataillon, Marcel. *Estudios sobre Bartolomé de Las Casas*. Barcelona: Ediciones Península, 1976. First published in French 1965.

————. "Las Casas, un profeta?" *Revista de Occidente* 47 (December 1974): 279–91.

————, and André Saint Lu. *El Padre Las Casas y la defensa de los indios*. Barcelona: Editorial Ariel, 1976. First published in French 1971.

Bennassar, Bartolomé. *The Spanish Character: Attitudes and Mentalities from the Sixteenth to the Nineteenth Century*. Berkeley, Los Angeles, London: University of California Press, 1979. First published in French 1975.

Biermann, Benno M. "Bartolomé de Las Casas and Verapaz." In *Bartolomé de Las Casas in History: Toward an Understanding of the Man and His Work*, edited by Juan Friede and Benjamin Keen, 443–484. DeKalb: Northern Illinois University Press, 1971.

————. "Lascasiana, Unedierte Dokumente von Fray Bartolome de las Casas." *Archivum Fraturnam Predicatorum* 27 (1957): 337–58.

Bolaños, Felix Alvaro. *Panegírico y libelo del primer cronista de Indias Gonzalo Fernández Oviedo*. Bogotá: Instituo Caro y Cuervo, 1990.

Borah, Woodrow. "Representative Institutions in the Spanish Empire in the Sixteenth Century: The New World." *The Americas* 12 (1955–56): 246–56.

————, and S. F. Cook. *The Aboriginal Population of Central Mexico on the Eve of the Spanish Conquest*. Berkeley and Los Angeles: University of California Press, 1963.

Borges, Pedro. *Quién Era Bartolomé de Las Casas*. Madrid: Ediciones Rialp, S.A., 1990.

Bourne, Edward Gaylord. *Spain in America, 1450–1580*. New York and London: Harper and Brothers Publishers, 1904.

Boxer, C. R. *The Church Militant and Iberian Expansion, 1440–1770*. Baltimore and London: Johns Hopkins University Press, 1978.

Bibliography

Brading, D. A. *The First America: The Spanish Monarchy, Creole Patriots and the Liberal State 1492–1867*. Cambridge: Cambridge University Press, 1990.

Bromiley, Geoffrey W. *Theological Dictionary of the New Testament*. Grand Rapids, MI: Eerdmans, 1988.

Carbia, Rómulo D. *Historia de la Leyenda Negra hispano-americana*. Buenos Aires: Ediciones Orientación Española, 1943.

Carro, Venancio D. *España en America...Sin Leyendas...*Madrid: Librería Ope, 1963.

————. *La teología y los teólogos-juristas españoles ante la conquista de América*. 2nd ed. Salamanca: Biblioteca de Teólogos Españoles, 1951.

Castro, Daniel. "Another Face of Empire: Bartolomé de Las Casas and the Restoration of the Indies." Unpublished doctoral dissertation, Tulane University, 1994.

Chacón y Calvo, J. M. *Cedulario Cubano: Los orígenes de las colonización (1493–1512)*. Vol. 1. Madrid: Compañia Ibero-Americana de Publicaciones, SA. 1929.

Chenu, Marie-Dominique. "El evangelio en el tiempo." *Estela* (1966): 191–201.

Comas, J. "Las realidad del trato dado a los indígenas de América entre los siglos XV y XX." *América Indígena* 11 (1951): 323–70.

Congreso Teológico Internacional. *Las Casas entre dos mundos*. Lima, Perú: Instituto Bartolomé de Las Casas-Rimac-Centro de Estudios y Publicaciones, 1993.

Contreras, Juan de. *Los Orígenes del Imperio de Fernando e Isabel*. 2nd ed. Madrid, México, Buenos Aires, Pamplona: Ediciones Rialp, S.A., 1966.

Crosby, A. W. *The Columbian Exchange: Biological and Cultural Consequences of 1492*. Westport, CT: Greenwood Press, 1975.

Davis, David B. *The Problem of Slavery in Western Culture*. Ithaca, NY: Cornell University Press, 1966.

Durán Luzio, Juan. *Bartolomé de Las Casas ante la conquista de América: Las voces del historiador*. Heredia, Costa Rica: Editorial de la Universidad Nacional, 1992.

Dussel, E. "Sobre la historia de la teología en América Latina." In *Desintegración de la Cristiandad Colonial y Liberación*. Salamanca: Sígueme, 1978.

Elliott, J. H. *Imperial Spain 1469–1716.* New York: St. Martin's Press, 1964.

———. *The Old World and the New, 1492–1650.* New York and London: Cambridge University Press, 1972.

———. *En el quinto centenario de Bartolomé de Las Casas (1484–1566).* Madrid: Ediciones Cultura Hispánica, Instituto de Cooperación Iberoamericana, 1986.

Erickson, Millard J. *Christian Theology.* Grand Rapids, MI: Baker Book House, 1983.

Espinel, José Luis. "Aspecto Profético de la vida cristiana según el Nuevo Testamento." Ciencid Tomista, 98, 1971, 7–46.

Fabíe, A. M. *El Padre Fray Bartolome de Las Casas.* Madrid: Ateneo de Madrid, 1892.

Franklin, J. H. *From Slavery to Freedom: A History of Negro Americans.* New York: Alfred A. Knopf, 1974.

Friede, Juan. *Bartolomé de Las Casas.* Bogotá: Carlos Valencia Editores, 1974.

———. *Bartolomé de Las Casas, precursor del anticolonialismo: su lucha y su derrota.* México and Buenos Aires: Siglo Veintiuno Editores, 1974.

———. "Las Casas y el movimiento indigenista en España y América en la primera mitad del siglo XVI." *Revista de Historia de América* 34 (December 1952): 339–411.

———, and Benjamin Keen, eds. *Bartolomé de Las Casas in History: Toward an Understanding of the Man and his Work.* DeKalb: Northern Illinois University Press, 1971.

Gibson, Charles. *Spain in America.* New York and San Francisco: Harper Torchbooks, 1966.

———. *The Spanish Tradition in America.* New York: Harper & Row, 1968.

Giménez Fernández, Manuel. *Bartolomé de Las Casas: Delegado de Cisneros para la Refomación de las Indias (1516–17).* Vol. 1. Seville: Escuela de Estudios Hispano-Americanos de Sevillo, 1953.

———. *Bartolomé de Las Casas: Capellán de S. M. Carlos I, Poblador de Cumana (1517–1523).* Vol. II. Seville: Escuela de Estudios Hispano-Americanos de Sevillo, 1960.

Bibliography

————. "Fray Bartolomé de Las Casas: A Biographical Sketch." In *Bartolomé de Las Casas in History: Toward an Understanding of the Man and his Work*, edited by Juan Friede and Benjamin Keen, 67–125. DeKalb: Northern Illinois University Press, 1971.

Greenblatt, Stephen, ed. *New World Encounters*. Berkeley, Los Angeles, Oxford: University of California Press, 1993.

Greenleaf, Richard E. *The Roman Catholic Church in Colonial Latin America*. Tempe, AZ: Center for Latin American Studies, Arizona State University, 1977.

Gutiérrez, Gustavo. *Las Casas: In Search of the Poor of Jesus Christ*. Translated by Robert R. Barr. Maryknoll, NY: Orbis Books, 1993.

————. *Teología de la liberación de la liberación*. 7th ed. Lima: CEP, 1990. Eng. trans.: *A Theology of Liberation*. Rev. ed. Maryknoll, NY: Orbis Books, 1988.

Hanke, Lewis. *All Mankind is One: A Study of the Disputation Between Bartolomé de Las Casas and Juan Gines de Sepulveda in 1550 on the Intellectual and Religious Capacity of the American Indians*. DeKalb: Northern Illinois University Press, 1974.

————. *All the Peoples of the World are Men*. Minneapolis, MN: The Associates of the James Ford Bell Library, 1970.

————. *Aristotle and the American Indians: A Study in Race Prejudice in the Modern World*. Bloomington: Indiana University Press, 1959.

————. "Bartolomé de Las Casas, an Essay in Hagiography and Historiography." *Hispanic American Historical Review* 33, no. 1 (1953): 136–51.

————. *Bartolomé de Las Casas: Historian*. Gainsville: University of Florida Press, 1952.

————. "Bartolomé de Las Casas historiador." In *Historia de las Indias*, edited by Agustin Millares Carlo, ix–lxxxvi. Mexico and Buenos Aires: Fondo de Cutura Económica, 1951.

————. *Estudios sobre Fray Bartolomé de Las Casas y sobre la lucha por la justicia en la conquista español de América*. Caracas: Universidad Central de Venezuela, 1968.

————. Introduction to Las Casas, *Del único modo de atraer a todos los pueblos a la verdadera religión.* Mexico City: FCE, 1942. XV–XLIV.

————. "Las Casas historiador." Introduction to *Historia de las Indias.* Mexico City and Buenos Aires: FCE, 1961.

————. "More Heat and Some Light on the Spanish Struggle for Justice in the Conquest of America." *Hispanic American Historical Review* 44, no. 3 (August 1964): 293–340.

————. *La lucha por la justicia en la conquista de Améric.* Buenos Aires: Editorial Sudamericana, 1949.

————. "A Modest Proposal for a Moratorium on Grand Generalizations: Some Thoughts on the Black Legend." *Hispanic American Historical Review* 51, no. 1 (1971): 112–27.

————.*The Spanish Struggle for Justice in the Conquest of America.* Philadelphia: University of Pennsylvania Press, 1959. First printed 1949.

————, and Manuel Giménez Fernández. *Bartolomé de Las Casas, 1474–1566. Bibliografía critica y cuerpo de materiales para el estudio de su vida, escritos, actuación y polémicas que suscitaron durante cuatro siglos.* Santiago de Chile: Fondo Histórico y Bibliografico José Toribio Medina, 1954.

Harris, R. Laird, ed. *Theological Wordbook of the Old Testament.* Vol. 2. Chicago: Moody Press, 1980.

Help, Arthur. *The Life of Las Casas: Apostle of the Indies.* Philadelphia: J. P. Lippincott and Co., 1868.

Heschel, Abraham. *The Prophets.* New York: Harper & Row, 1962.

Huerga, A. "Bartolomé de Las Casas, dominico." *Communio* 7, fasc. 1 (1974): 5–31.

————. "El humanismo profético de Bartolomé de Las Casas." *Horizantes* 28, no. 55 (October 1984): 31–48.

Kamen, Henry. *Spain 1469–1714: A Society of Conflict.* London and New York: Longman Group UK Limited, 1982.

Keely, Robin, ed. *Eerdmans' Handbook to Christian Belief.* Grand Rapids, MI: Eerdmans, 1982.

Keen, Benjamin. "Approaches to Las Casas, 1535–1970. In *Bartolomé de Las Casas in History: Toward an Understanding of the Man and his Work,* edited by Juan Friede and Benjamin Keen, 3–63. DeKalb: Northern Illinois University Press, 1971.

Bibliography

————. "The Black Legend Revisited: Assumptions and Realities." *Hispanic American Historical Review* 49, no. 4 (1969): 703–19.

————. "The White Legend Revisited: A Reply to Professor Hanke's 'Modest Proposal.'" *Hispanic American Historical Review* 51, no. 2 (1971): 336–55.

Klein, H. *African Slavery in Latin America and the Caribbean.* New York: Oxford University Press, 1986.

Konetzke, R. *América Latina II: La época colonial.* Mexico City: Siglo XXI, 1972.

————. *Colección de documentos para la historia de la formación social de Hispanoamérica, 1493–1810.* 4 vols. Vol. 2: *La época colonial.* Madrid: CSIC, 1958–62.

Leonard, Irving A. *Books of the Brave: Being an Account of Books and Men in the Spanish Conquest and Settlement of the Sixteenth-Century New World.* New York: Gordian Press, 1964. First published 1949.

León-Portilla, Miguel. *Aztec Thought and Culture: A Study of the Ancient Nahuatl Mind.* Translated by Jack Emory Davis. Norman: University of Oklahoma Press, 1990.

Lességue, Juan Bautista. *La larga marcha de Las Casas: Selección y presentación de textos.* Lima: Centro de Estudios y Publicaciones (CEP), 1974.

López Martínez, H. *Diego Centeno y la rebelión de los encomenderos.* Lima, 1970.

Losada, Angel. "Bartolomé de Las Casas y la bula 'Inter Caetera.'" *Communio* 7, no. 1 (1974), 95–110.

————. "Introducción." In *Ginés de Sepúlveda, Demócrates segundo o de las justas causas de la guerra contra los indios.* Madrid: CSIC, 1951.

————. "The Controversy between Sepúlveda and Las Casas in the Junta of Valladolid." In *Bartolomé de Las Casas in History: Toward an Understanding of the Man and his Work,* edited by Juan Friede and Benjamin Keen. DeKalb: Northern Illinois University Press, 1971.

————. *Fray Bartolomé de Las Casas a la luz de la historia moderna.* Madrid: Editoria Tecnos, 1970.

MacLachlan, Colin. *Spain's Empire in the New World: The Role of Ideas in Institutional and Social Change*. Berkeley and Los Angeles: University of California Press 1988.

⸻, and Jaime E. Rodriguez. *The Forging of the Cosmic Race: A Reinterpretation of Colonial Mexico*. Berkeley: University of California Press, 1988.

MacLeod, Murdo J. "Las Casas, Guatemala and the Sad but Inevitable Case of Antonio de Remesal." *Topic* 2 (Fall 1970): 53–64.

MacNutt, F. *Bartholome de Las Casas: His Life, His Apostolate, and His Writings*. New York and London: Putman's Sons, 1909.

Mahn-Lot, Marianne. *Bartolomé de las Casas et le droit des indiens*. Paris: Payot, 1982.

Marcus, R. "El primer decenio de Las Casas en el nuevo munco." Ibero-Amerikanisches Archiv 3, no. 2 (1977): 87–122.

Martínez, Manuel M. *Fray Bartolomé de las Casas: "Padre de America": Estudio biográfico crítico*. Madrid: Private Printing, 1958.

⸻. "Las Casas on the Conquest of America." In *Bartolomé de las Casas in History: Toward an Understanding of the Man and His Work*, edited by Juan Friede and Benjamin Keen, 309–51. DeKalb: Northern Illinois University Press, 1971.

⸻. "Las Casas–Vitoria y la bula 'sublimus deus.'" In *Estudios sobre las Casas*, Universidad de Sevilla, No. 24 (1974): 25–51. Series: Filosofía y Letras.

⸻. "El padre Las Casas, Promotor de la evangelización de América." In *Estudios Lascasianos: IV centenario de la muerte de Fray Bartolomé de Las Casas, (1566–1966)*. Seville: Facultad de Filosofía y Letras de la Universidad de Sevilla, 1966.

Mattasoglio, Carlos Castillo. "El problema de los indios: Bartolomé de Las Casas." *Páginas* 14, no. 99 (October 1989): 51–67.

Menéndez Pidal, Ramón. *El Padre Las Casas: Su Doble Personalidad*. Madrid: Espasa-Calpe S.A., 1963.

Metzger, Bruce, ed. *The Apocrypha*. New York: Oxford University Press, 1965.

Milhou, Alain. "Las Casas profeta de su tiempo. Profeta para nuestro tiempo." In *Las Casas entre dos mundos*. Lima, Perú: Instituto

Bartolomé de Las Casas-Rimac-Centro de Estudios y Publicaciones, 1993. 177–205.

————. *Colón y su mentalidad mesiánica en el ambiente francesano español.* Valladolid: Universidad de Valladolid, 1983.

Morison, Samuel Eliot. *Admiral of the Ocean Sea: A Life of Christopher Columbus.* Boston, Toronto, London: Little, Brown & Co., 1970. First published 1942.

————. *Christopher Columbus, Mariner.* New York: Meridian, 1983. First published Little, Brown & Co., 1942.

————. *The European Discovery of America: The Southern Voyages, 1492–1616.* New York: Oxford University Press, 1974.

Morner, M. *Race Mixture in the History of Latin America.* Boston: Little, Brown & Co., 1967.

Motolinía, T. *Historia de los indios e la Nueva España.* Madrid: Castadia, 1985.

Moya Pons, Frank. "The Politics of Forced Indian Labour in La Española, 1493–1520." *Antiquity* 66 (March1992): 130–39.

O'Gormon, E. *La invención de América.* Mexico City: FCE, 1958; Mexico City: UNAM, 1977.

Pagden, Anthony. *European Encounters with the New World: From Renaissance to Romanticism.* New Haven and London: Yale University Press, 1993.

————. *The Fall of Natural Man: The American Indian and the Origins of Comparative Ethnology.* London and New York: Cambridge University Press, 1988. First published 1981.

————. Introduction to *A Short Account of the Destruction of the Indies.* Translated and edited by Nigel Griffin. London: Penguin Books, 1992. XIII–XLI.

————. "*Ius et Factum:* Text and Experience in the Writings of Bartolomé de Las Casas." In *New World Encounters,* edited by Stephen Greenblatt, 85–100. Berkeley, Los Angeles, Oxford: University of California Press, 1993.

Palacios Rubios, J. *De mas islas del mar océano.* Edited by A. Millares and S. Zavala. Mexico City: FCE, 1954.

Parish, Helen Rand. "Introduction: Las Casas's Spirituality—the Three Crises." In *Bartolomé de las Casas: The Only Way,* edited by Helen Rand Parish. New York: Paulist Press, 1991.

————, ed. *Bartolomé de las Casas: The Only Way.* New York: Paulist Press, 1992.

————. "Bartolomé de Las Casas: A Saga for Today." In *Bartolomé de Las Casas: Liberation for the Oppressed,* ed. Sister Michael Marie Zobelein, OP. Visalia, CA: Sister Michael Marie Zobelein, OP, Dominican Sisters, 1984.

————. *Las Casas as a Bishop: A New Interpretation Based on His Holograph Petition in the Hans P. Kraus Collection of Hispanic American Manuscripts / Las Casas, Obispo: Una nueva interpretación a base de su Hispanoamericanos.* Washington: Library of Congress, 1980.

————. *Las Casas en México: Historia y obras desconocidas.* Mexico City: FCE, 1992.

————. "Las Casas: una vida redescubierta." In *Las Casas entre dos mundos.* Lima, Peru: Insituto Bartolomé de Las Casas-Rimac-Centro de Estudios y Publicaciones, 1993.

————, and Harold E. Weidman, SJ. *Las Casas en Mexico: Historia y obra desconocidas.* México, D.F.: Fondo de Cultura Económica, 1992.

————, and Harold E. Weidman, SJ. "The Correct Birthdate of Bartolomé de Las Casas." *Hispanic American Historical Review* 56, no. 4 (1976): 385–403.

————, and Henry Raup Wagner. *The Life and Writings of Bartolomé de Las Casas in Mexico.* Albuquerque: University of New Mexico Press, 1967.

Parry, J. H. *The Spanish Theory of Empire in the Sixteenth Century.* Cambridge: Cambridge University Press, 1940.

————, and Robert G. Keith. *New Iberian World: A Documentary History of the Discovery and Settlement of Latin America to the Early 17th Century: The Conquerors and the Conquered.* Vol. 1. New York: Times Books, 1984.

Pennington, K. J., Jr. "Bartolomé Las Casas and the Tradition of Medieval Law." *Church History* 39, no. 2 (1970): 149–61.

Pereña, Luciano. "Fray Bartolomé de Las Casas, profeta de la liberación." *Arbor* 89, no. 347 (1974): 21–34.

Pereña Vicente, L. "Estudio preliminar." In Bartolomé de Las Casas, *De Regia Potestate.* Madrid: CSIC, 1969. XXI–CLV.

Pérez Fernandez, Isacio. *Bartolomé de Las Casas contra los negros?* Madrid: Editorial Mundo Negro, 1991.

―――. "Cronología comprada de las intervenciones de las Casas y Vitoria en los asuntos de América." In Carolos Soria, OP, ed. *I Diritti dell'Uomo el la Pace nel Pensiero di Franscisco de Vitoria e Bartolomé de Las Casas.* Roma, Marzo, 1985, 539–68.

―――. *Cronología documentada de los viajes, estancias y actuaciones de Fray Bartolomé de las Casas.* Bayamón, Puerto Rico: Centro de Estudios de las Dominicos de Caribe, 1984.

―――. "El perfil profético del Padre Las Casas." *Studium*, 15 (1975): 281–359.

―――. "El protector de los americanos y profeta de los Americanos y profeta de los españoles." *Studium* 16 (1976): 543–65.

―――. "La fidelidad de Padre Las Casas a su crisma profétio." *Studium* 16 (1976): 65–109.

―――. *Inventario Documentado de los escritos de Fray Bartolomé de Las Casas.* Bayamón, Puerto Rico: Centro de Estudios de los Domínicos de Caribe (CEDOC), 1981.

Peter, Anton. "Bartolomé de Las Casas y el tema de la conversión en la teología de la liberación." *Paginas* 17, no. 116 (July 1992), 49–63.

Prescott, William H. *History of the Reign of Ferdinand and Isabella the Catholic.* Vol. III. Philadelphia: J. B. Lippincott & Co., 1869.

Price, Robert M. "The Centrality and Scope of Conversion." *Journal of Psychology and Theology* (Spring 1981): 26–36.

Queraltó Moreno, R. J. *El pensamiento filosófico-político de Bartolomé de Las Casas.* Seville: Escuela de Estudios Hispanoamericanos, 1976.

Ramos Pérez, D. "La 'conversión' de Las Casas en Cuba: El clérigo y Diego Velázquez." In *Estudios sobre Las Casas,* Universidad de Sevilla, No. 24 (1974): 247–57. Series: Filosofía y Letras.

Ricard, Robert. *The Spiritual Conquest of Mexico: An Essay on the Apostolate and the Evangelizing Methods of the Mendicant Orders, 1523–1572.* Translated by Lesley Byrd Simpson. Berkeley: University of California Press, 1966. First printed in French 1933.

Richards, Lawrence O., ed. *Expository Dictionary of Bible Words.* Grand Rapids, MI: Zondervan, 1991.

Rubio, V. "Una carta inédita de Fray Pedro de Córdoba, O.P." *Communio* 13, no. 1 (1980): 411–25.

Saint Lu, André. "Bartolomé de Las Casas, teórico y promotor de la conquista evangélica." *Communio* 7, no. 1 (1974): 57–68.

———. "Vigencia histórica de la obra de las Casas." In *En el quinto centenario de Bartolomé de Las Casas (1484–1566).* Madrid: Ediciones Cultura Hispánica, Instituto de Cooperación Iberoamericana, 1986.

Salzman, Leon, MD. "Types of Religious Conversion." *Pastoral Psychology* (September 1963): 8–20.

Sánchez Albornoz, N. "The Population of Colonial Spanish America." In *The Cambridge History of Latin America,* edited by L. Bethell. New York: Cambridge University Press, 1984, 3–35.

Sánchez, Joseph P. "The Spanish Black Legend: Origins of Anti-Hispanic Stereotypes." *Encounters: A Quincentenary Review* (Winter 1989): 16–21.

Sauer, C. O. *The Early Spanish Main.* Berkeley: University of California Press, 1969.

Schäfer, Ernesto. *El Consejo Real y Supremo de las Indias: Su historia, organización y labor administrativa hasta la terminacion de la Casa de Austria.* 2 vols. Sevilla: Universidad de Sevilla. Vol. 1, 1935; Vol. 2, 1947.

Schneider, Reinhold. *Imperial Mission.* Translated by Walter Oden. New York: The Gresham Press, 1948.

Sepúlveda, Juan Ginés de. *Apología de Juan Ginés de Sepulveda. in Angel Losada Ed. and Trans. Apología de Juan Ginés de Sepúlveda contra Fray Bartolomé de las Casas y de Fray Bartolomé de Las Casas contra Juan Ginés de Sepúlveda.* Madrid: Editora Nacional, 1975.

———. *Demócrates segundo o De las justas causas de la guerra contra los indios.* Edited and translated by Angel Losada. 2nd ed. Madrid: CSIC, 1984.

Serrano y Sanz, Manuel. *Orígenes de la dominación española en América.* Madrid: Nueva Biblioteca de Autores Españoles, XXV, Vol. 1 (1918).

Bibliography

Simpson, Lesley Byrd. *The Encomienda in New Spain: Forced Native Labor in the Spanish Colonies, 1492–1550.* Berkeley: University of California Press, 1929.

———. *The Encomienda in New Spain: The Beginning of Spanish Mexico.* Berkeley and Los Angeles: University of California Press, 1982.

Soria, Carlos. "Fray Bartolomé de Las Casas, historiador, humanista, or profeta?" *Ciencia tomista* 101 (1974): 411–26.

Spilka, Bernard, et al. *The Psychology of Religion:* Englewood Cliffs, NJ: Prentice Hall, 1985.

Todorov, Tzvetan. *The Conquest of America: The Question of the Other.* Translated by Richard Howard. New York: Harper & Row Publishers, 1985. First published in French 1982.

Uffenheimer, Benjamin. "Prophecy, Ecstacy, and Sympathy." *Supplement to Vetus Testamentum* 40 (1988): 257–69.

Wagner, Henry Raup. "Three Studies on the Same Subject." *Hispanic American Historical Review* (May 1945): 155–211.

———, and Helen Rand Parish. *The Life and Writings of Bartolomé de Las Casas.* Albuquerque: University of New Mexico Press, 1967.

Zavala, Silvio. *Ensayos sobre la colonización española en América.* 3rd ed. México: Editorial Porrúa, 1978. First printed 1944.

———. *La encomienda indiana.* 2nd ed. México: Editorial Porrúa, 1973. First published in Madrid 1935.

———. *La filosofía política en lo conquista de América.* 3rd ed, corr. and aug. Mexico: Fondo de Cultura Econozómica, 1977. First published 1947.

———. "Las Casas ante la encomienda." *Cuadernos Americanos* 5, no. 17 (February 1974): 143–55.

Index